LEGENDARY LOCALS

OF

# JACKSONVILLE

## FLORIDA

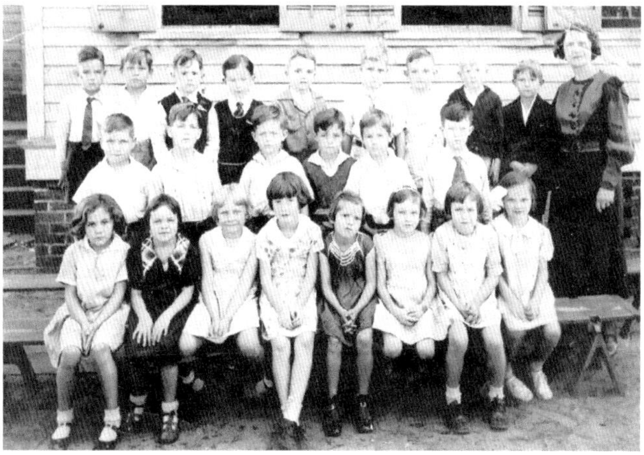

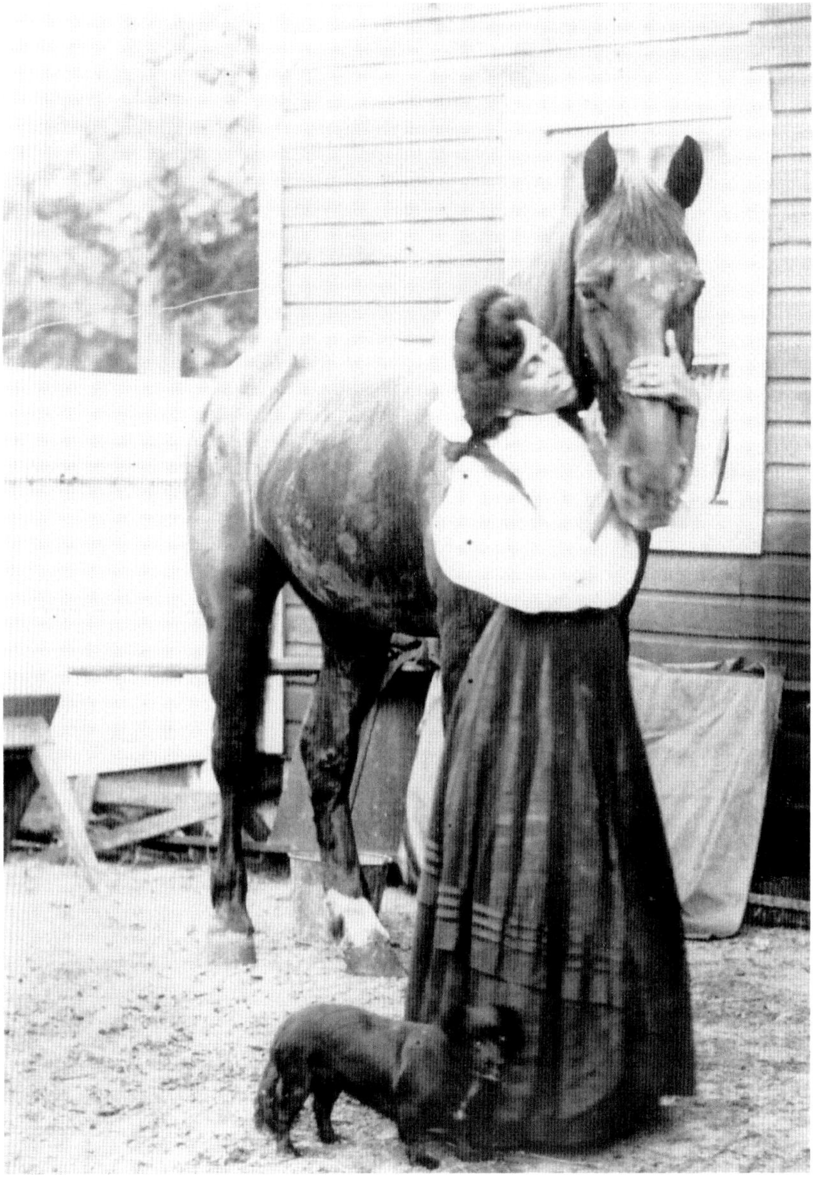

Eartha M.M. White

Eartha White helped her widowed mother, a former slave, collect surplus food to serve meals out of their two-room home to hungry neighbors and homeless people. Together, they created a legacy of caring that has spanned a century. For more information, see page 103. (Courtesy of the Eartha M.M. White Collection, Thomas G. Carpenter Library, University of North Florida, Jacksonville, Florida.)

**Page 1:** A Learning Process

Learning about Jacksonville is an educational process. As these first-grade students from Southside Grammar School in 1933 discovered, a city experiences growing pains and victories just as people do. Edward Booth Sr. (back row, fifth from the left), whose story appears on page 42, was instrumental in desegregating the city as it faced a new era of equal rights. (Courtesy of Edward Booth Jr.)

LEGENDARY LOCALS

OF

# JACKSONVILLE

## FLORIDA

LAURA JO BRUNSON AND KENDALL BRUNSON

LEGENDARY LOCALS

ISBN 978-1-4671-0174-5

Legendary Locals is an imprint of Arcadia Publishing
Charleston, South Carolina

Printed in the United States of America

Library of Congress Control Number: 2014935267

For all general information, please contact Arcadia Publishing:
Telephone 843-853-2070
Fax 843-853-0044
E-mail sales@arcadiapublishing.com
For customer service and orders:
Toll-Free 1-888-313-2665

Visit us on the Internet at www.arcadiapublishing.com

**Dedication**

*We dedicate this book to the people of Jacksonville, past, present, and future, whose lives have made and continue to make the story of this city worth telling.*

**On the Front Cover:** Clockwise from top left:
Leonard Skinner (Courtesy of Rosemary Skinner; see page 87), Henry J. Klutho (Courtesy of State Archives of Florida, *Florida Memory*; see page 26), Nat Glover (Courtesy of Nat Glover; see page 59), Stetson Kennedy (Courtesy of the Stetson Kennedy Foundation, www.StetsonKennedy.com; see page 54), Judge Marion Gooding (Courtesy of Mack Gooding; see page 94), Evelyn Nehl (Courtesy of Robin Patton; see page 110), Harriet Beecher Stowe (Courtesy of the Library of Congress; see page 68), Bonnie Upright (Photograph by Kendall Brunson; see page 109), and Doug Milne (Courtesy of Doug Milne; see page 69).

**On the Back Cover:** From left to right:
(Seated) Peter Bragan Sr. and Peter "Pedro" Bragan Jr; (standing) Mayor Jake Godbold, Mayor Ed Austin, Mayor John Delaney, Mayor Tommy Hazouri, and Mayor John Peyton (Courtesy of the Jacksonville Suns; see page 38), contestants from the Miss American Beach pageant (Courtesy of the Eartha M.M. White Collection, Thomas G. Carpenter Library, University of North Florida, Jacksonville, Florida; see page 114).

# CONTENTS

# ACKNOWLEDGMENTS

Where to begin? That is the challenge.

No project like this becomes real from the labor of one or two people. This book represents a synthesis of the efforts of many friends and acquaintances, old and new, who shared their memories, stories, and photographs about Jacksonville's Legendary Locals. Casual conversations with friends turned into discoveries of new stories that begged to be included. Friends introduced us to their friends and hunted down photographs. The spirit of generosity and encouragement is alive and well in this great city of ours.

We owe a debt of gratitude to the historians, both living and deceased, who have devoted their time to capturing Jacksonville's story. Some of their own stories are included within, and their help and direction cannot be more greatly appreciated. Both they and our local historical societies, such as the Jacksonville Historical Society, protect true treasures of Jacksonville, for without knowing our past, we cannot possibly plan a relevant future.

Many thanks to the Mandarin Museum and Historical Society for its dedication to keeping the memories of abolitionist and author Harriet Beecher Stowe and potter Charlie Brown alive. Likewise to the Norman Studios, who are committed to protecting Jacksonville's contribution to the silent film industry, the Stetson Kennedy Foundation, for preserving the multifaceted work of a great man, and www.MetroJacksonville.com, for its influence and insight into history and the value of public conversation.

It can be inspiring to interview legends of our time and find them warm, generous, and humble. More than once we had to explain that we were not looking for people who were famous; rather, we wanted to feature people who shaped the city where one million people now work and play. And, more than once, we found our subjects speechless. Every time, we left with grateful hearts that so many locals, past and present, followed their passions and lived legendary lives.

Our thanks to Erin Vosgien at Arcadia Publishing for her patience and support throughout this process, and to Eileen Moon, author of *Legendary Locals of Red Bank*, for suggesting this project.

Finally, we thank our families, who supported our efforts, patiently endured our moments of "thinking out loud," provided valuable feedback, and held our hands gently but firmly. You are legendary!

# INTRODUCTION

Jacksonville is a city of surprises. A striking statue of its namesake, Andrew Jackson, stands prominently Downtown; yet Andrew Jackson never lived here. Metropolitan areas aside, Jacksonville is Florida's largest city, but that fact escapes those who perceive the city limits of Miami, Orlando, and Tampa as having more people. Our beaches do not feature the waves that surfers seek worldwide, but many of our female surfers are champions.

Centuries before Europeans discovered the natural beauty, abundant fauna and wildlife, and strategically navigable waters of Jacksonville, Timucuans lived out their lives here. The Timucuans, who numbered in the tens of thousands in the 1500s and whose character French explorer Jean Ribault described as gentle, shared their food and aided the Europeans trying to acclimate to a new life that was raw and threatening by European standards. But as idyllic as life was for the Timucuans, contact with the Europeans in what is now Jacksonville brought disease and war with other native tribes. By 1765, the Timucuans were extinct.

Still, the city's strategic location and desirable clime never ceased to draw new residents. The St. Johns River, a black-water, north-flowing stream 310 miles long, ends its journey in Jacksonville, emptying into the Atlantic Ocean. The river runs up through the city, shaping its landscape, providing recreation, and attracting writers, traders, shrimpers, and the military.

As the Europeans settled in, the town became known as Cowford because of a narrow point in the river where cattle crossed. It was not until 1822 that the city was platted and its name was changed to Jacksonville. Although no battles occurred here during the Civil War, both the South and the North gained control of the town and its strategic port at different times. By the late 1800s, a growing Jacksonville boasted railroad lines, as well as the last port for steamboats, a boon for its tourist attraction, the Subtropical Exposition. Industry was bustling, and the city was growing.

But, on May 3, 1901, things changed when sparks from a lunchtime kitchen fire landed on dry moss at a nearby mattress company at the corner of Beaver and Davis Streets. The resulting fire raged until 8:30 p.m. By the time firefighters brought it under control, Downtown Jacksonville was a wasteland, with nothing but chimneys standing from Springfield to the St. Johns River. Seven people died, 10,000 people lost their homes, and more than 2,300 buildings were destroyed.

People saw smoke as far away as Savannah, Georgia, according to the *Florida Memory* website. And people across the river, miles southeast of the city limits, recalled fire debris raining down on their property.

The rebuilding effort resulted in some of Jacksonville's most admired buildings, designed by Prairie School architect Henry Klutho and his female contemporary Henrietta Dozier. One building that rose from the ashes was the St. James Hotel, said to be where journalist and author Stephen Crane met his future wife, journalist and brothel owner Cora Taylor. The St. James, one of the country's largest buildings when it opened in 1911, was later a department store and is now Jacksonville's city hall.

By the start of World War II, the city was a strategic military location for land, sea, and air operations. Thousands of men and women have passed through Jacksonville because of military orders, bringing the city some of its most beloved families. They have influenced the city, which has, in turn, embraced them, and, in many cases, provided opportunities for second careers.

While the "Great Fire of 1901" is considered the city's most devastating event, the second most important event was the vote to consolidate Jacksonville in 1967. Despite the postwar boom that brought a new city hall, civic auditorium, public library, and other structures, Jacksonville suffered from the great white flight to the suburbs. The city itself had a much poorer population, and the inadequate tax base impaired city services, such as schools, sanitation, and traffic. By 1958, the city began eyeing annexation of outlying areas, but distrustful voters outside the city limits rejected such efforts six times.

The black residents in the city wanted more involvement in their government, and the whites in the suburbs wanted more services and control over the central city. The loss of accreditation of public high schools in 1964 added momentum to the cries for government reform. People and government officials wanted lower taxes, better economic development, a unified community, better spending, and effective administration by a central authority.

On January 10, 1967, a commission issued a blueprint for improvement after 15 months of study.

The commission recommended an efficient form of government. "Based on the traditional separation of powers between the legislative, executive, and judicial branches of government, a strong emphasis is placed on checks and balances," it wrote. "The new structure is designed to return the local government to the people, and to build into it a climate for the ethical conduct of good government."

Voters passed consolidation on August 8, 1967, by a vote of nearly two to one. On October 1, 1968, county and city governments consolidated into the City of Jacksonville. The new city incorporated 841 square miles, some 20 times its former size of 38.9 square miles. Overnight, Jacksonville became, for a time, the largest city in land area in the world. Roughly the size of the state of Rhode Island, it remains the largest city in the contiguous United States.

Today, Jacksonville is sometimes called "the River City," "the Bold New City of the South," or "Florida's First Coast." Regardless, the city is home to major military bases, more than a dozen universities and colleges, including a law school and an historical black college, public and private corporations, four seaport facilities, three major railroads, several outstanding medical facilities, nationally and internationally renowned musicians and artists, and the people who bring the community to life.

This book looks at people who have been and are responsible for what Jacksonville is today. But it is a limited look, with surprise entries and omissions. The stories herein present a snapshot of some people who have shaped and are shaping Jacksonville. Many of them never sought to be "legendary." Rather, they simply did "the right thing" or followed their passion. Others found themselves in impossible situations and kept taking the next step. Still others did "the wrong thing" and stood in the shadows.

Regardless of fame, these Legendary Locals bear a fair share of the honors and responsibility for the rich tapestry that makes up the fabric of our community.

# CHAPTER ONE

# City Builders

No one knows the name of Jacksonville's first resident. Long before the Huguenot Jean Ribault erected a stone marker claiming the land for France's King Charles IX at Fort Caroline in May 1562, the Native Americans called Timucuans hunted, fished, and farmed the land here. Some estimate the Timucuan population was as high as 200,000 throughout North Florida. They lived in round villages filled with little round huts topped with thatched domes. The French presence here lasted only two years, after which Spain took possession. By the time the Timucuans died out in 1765, Jacksonville was under British rule and was called Cowford because ranchers could get their cattle across the St. Johns River at a narrow point.

Less than 100 years later, Spain and England had again traded possession of Florida before it was deeded to the US government, and citizens petitioned to name the city after Pres. Andrew Jackson, Florida's former military governor. The growth of the 1800s positioned Jacksonville for a strong future. It bustled with commerce and tourism. Plantations shipped commodities north, and steamboats brought tourists south.

Most contemporary residents do not know the names of influential citizens who nurtured the city prior to the 21st century. And yet, they use those names every day when crossing bridges, traveling the city's streets, and playing in a 46,000-acre preserve. Today's residents live off the fruit of those who went before and left a legacy that continues to influence the way people live, work, and play in Jacksonville.

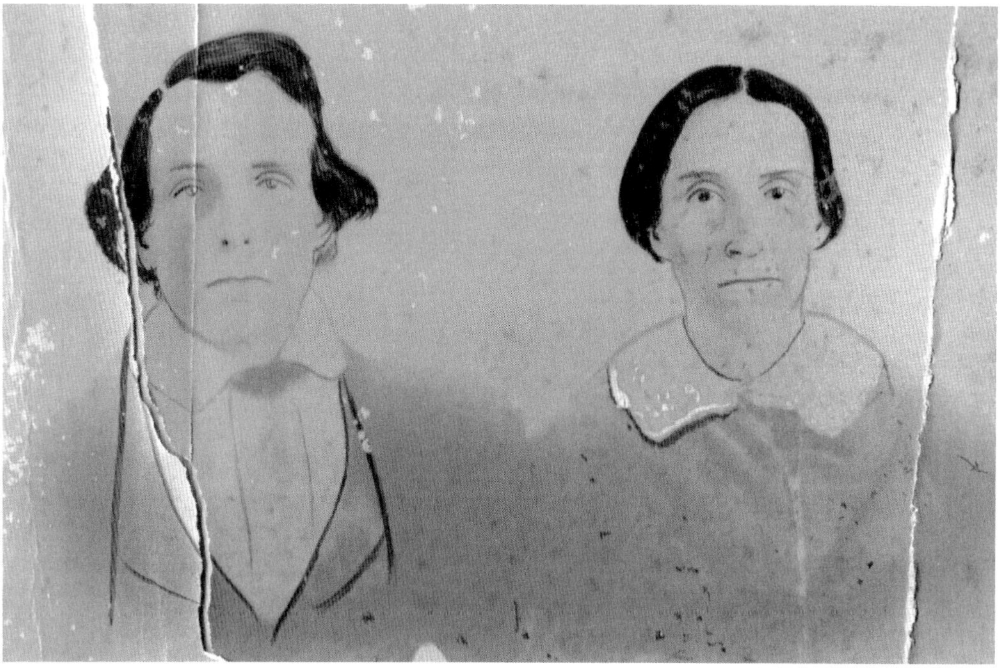

**Deep Roots**

Exactly when the Jacks family came to the First Coast is unclear, but family names first appeared on the 1850 census. Emigrating from Ireland, Robert Jack is thought to have met his wife, Jane Ann, in Jacksonville. Robert had a carpentry shop in downtown Jacksonville. Although the original surname was Jack, it is believed that the "s" was added as a plural and, over time, became part of the name. They had three children: John Henry, Letitia Jane, and Francis Elizabeth.

This is a picture of Robert and Jane Ann, possibly on their wedding day, in May 1846. (Courtesy of William Morrow.)

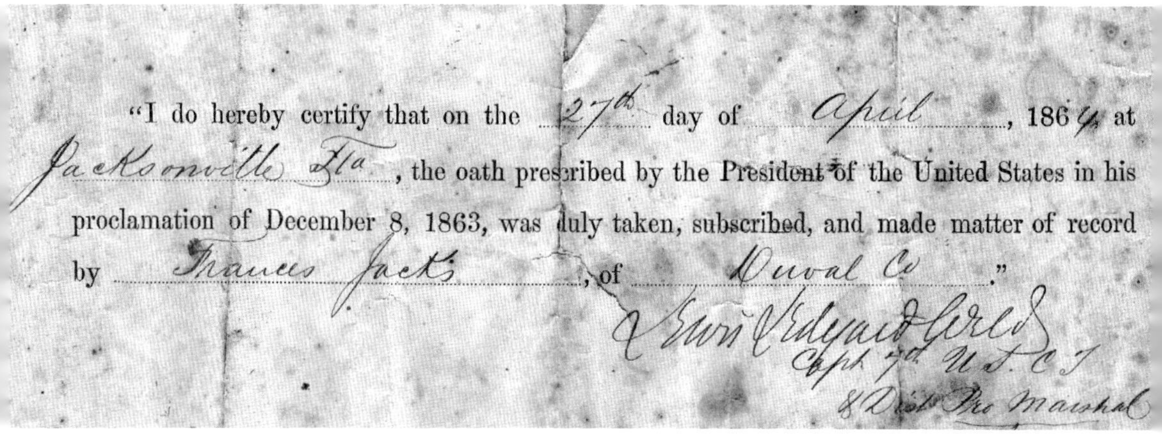

"I do hereby certify that on the 27th day of April, 1864 at Jacksonville Fla, the oath prescribed by the President of the United States in his proclamation of December 8, 1863, was duly taken, subscribed, and made matter of record by Frances Jacks, of Duval Co."

Capt 7th U.S.C.T.
8 Dist Pro Marshal

**Oath of Allegiance**

To help support the family, Francis Elizabeth Jacks lived in LaVilla, where she worked as a house servant. She had to cross through Union army lines during the occupation of Jacksonville in the Civil War to get to work. In order to do this, she had to sign and carry this oath to the Union. She is believed to have died at a young age and last appeared on an 1870 census. (Courtesy of William Morrow.)

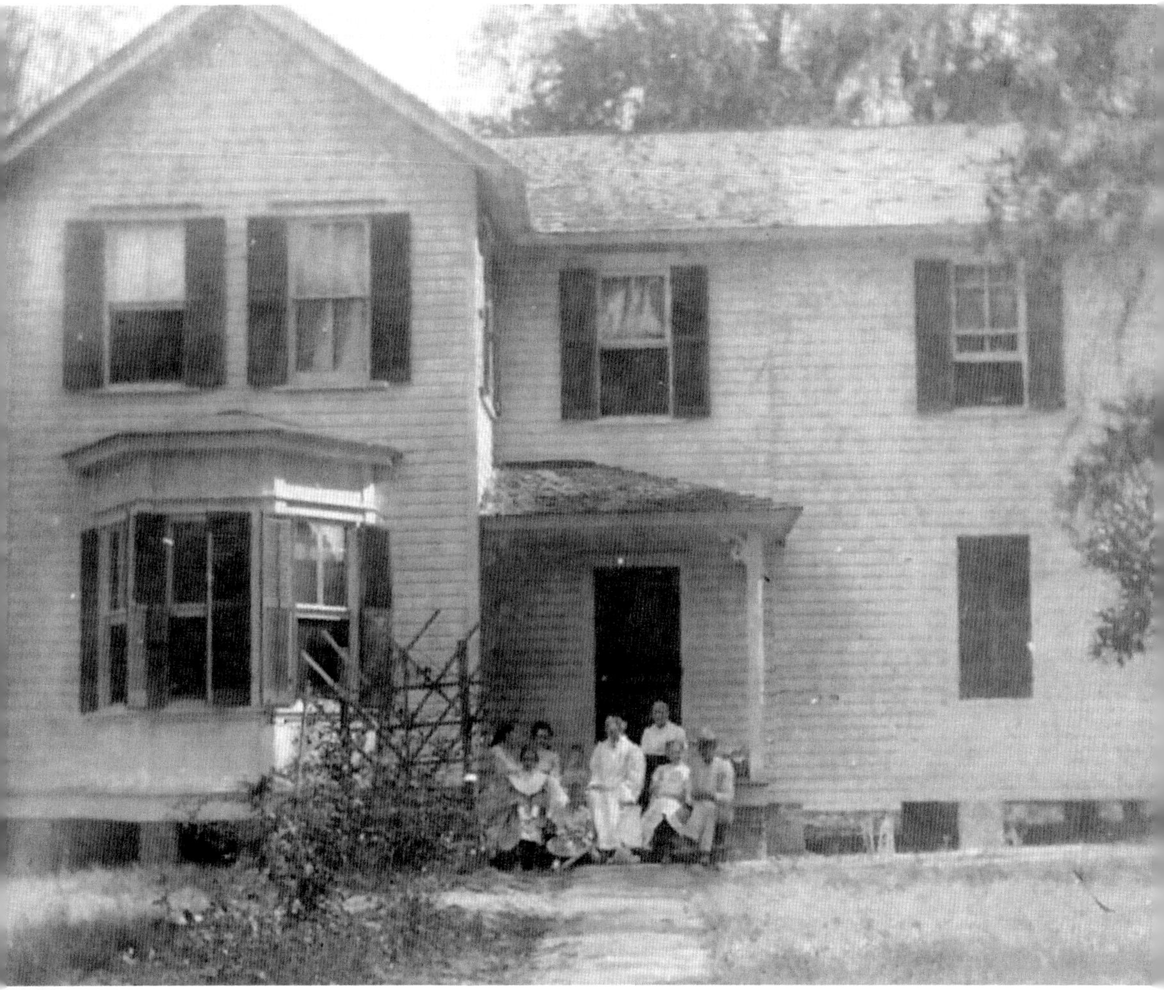

**Jacks House**

When Letitia Jane Jacks married architect William F. Monson, who also designed and built St. Joseph's Catholic Church, he built a beautiful house on Mandarin Road for her brother John Henry Jacks. The house stands to this day.

This photograph was taken in front of the John Henry Jacks house in early 1908. Pictured from left to right are Letitia Jane; Helen Kearsing Jacks, daughter of John Henry; Jenny Monson, daughter of Letitia Jane; Robert Henry Jacks (seated), only son of John Henry; Frances Elizabeth, youngest daughter of John Henry; Ella Evelyn Jacks, wife of John Henry; Mary Jane Eaton, Ella's mother; Mary Eaton Jacks, second child of John Henry; William Monson, only son of Letitia Jane; and William F. Monson. (Courtesy of William Morrow.)

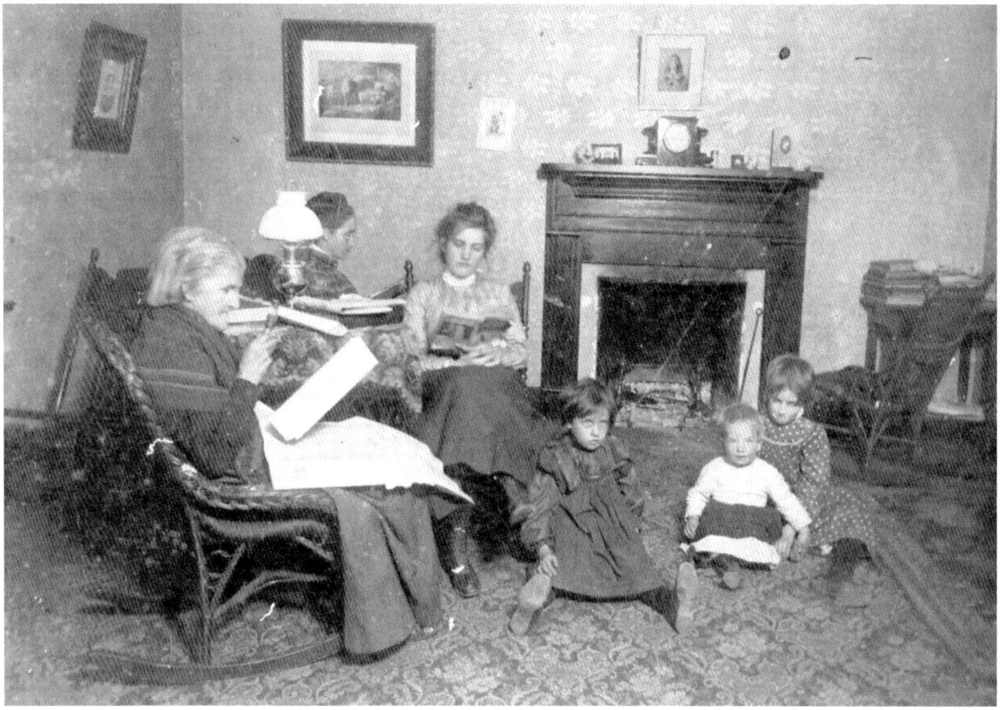

**Parlor Time**
This photograph of the parlor in John Henry Jacks's house is believed to have been taken around 1901. Ella Evelyn Jacks is partially hidden in the background because she was pregnant with her fifth child at the time of the photograph, and it was considered unseemly for a woman to be photographed, or even seen, during pregnancy. (Courtesy of William Morrow.)

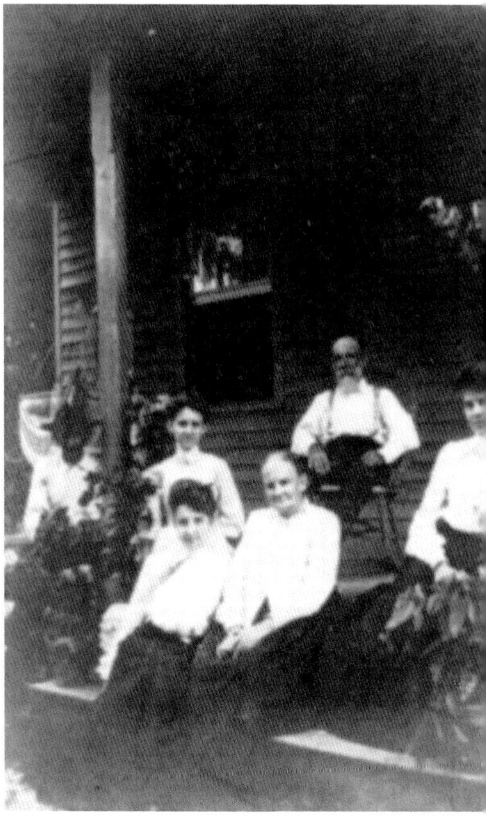

**Monson House**
Here is the Monson family in front of the home that William F. Monson built for his wife, Letitia Jane Monson, and children in Mandarin. Unfortunately, the house has since been torn down.

From left to right are William "Willy" Monson, son of William F. Monson; daughter Katherine Monson; daughter Jenny Monson; Letitia Jane Monson; William F. Monson; and daughter Adele Monson. (Courtesy of William Morrow.)

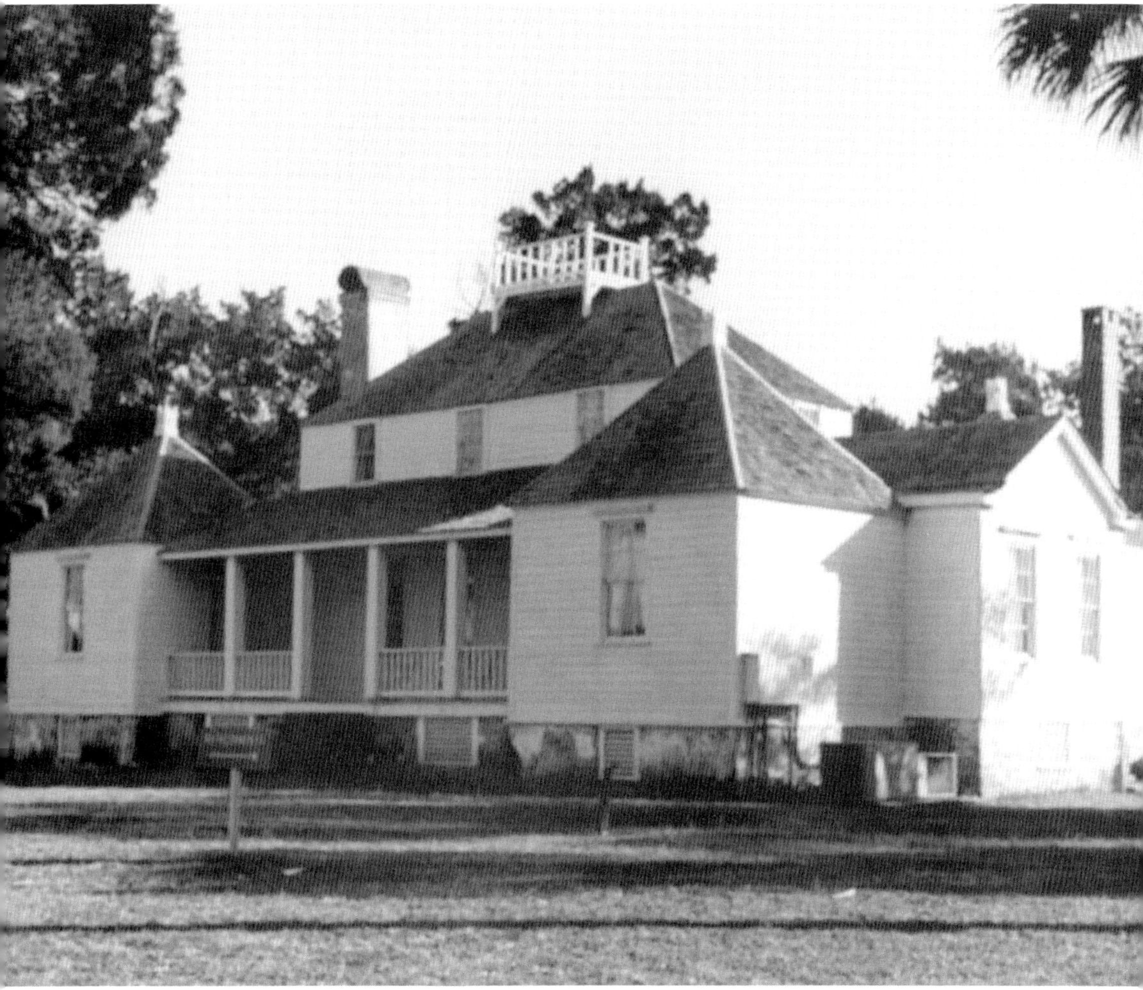

**Anna and Zephaniah Kingsley**
In 1806, Anna Kingsley was kidnapped from Senegal and shipped to Havana, where she was sold as a slave. By the time she arrived in Jacksonville, the 13-year-old was pregnant by her owner, Zephaniah Kingsley, who claimed her as his wife and freed her.

A Spanish territory at the time, Florida recognized slavery as a temporary situation, not a condition of race. Anna proved to be smart, managing and expanding Kingsley holdings while Zephaniah traveled for business.

In 1814, they established Kingsley Plantation at Fort George Island. When Florida became a US territory, prejudice against them became intolerable. The Kingsleys moved to Haiti in 1837. Anna returned as a widow in 1860 but waited out the Civil War in the North. After the war, she returned again. She died in 1870. Today, the plantation is owned by the National Park Service. This photograph depicts the home at Kingsley Plantation. (Courtesy of State Archives of Florida, *Florida Memory*, www.floridamemory.com/items/show/41428.)

### Alfred I. duPont

Industrialist, banker, world traveler, musician, composer, individualist; all of these describe Alfred I. duPont, one of Jacksonville's greatest philanthropists.

He was the oldest of five children in a happy family of the duPont gunpowder dynasty in Delaware. In 1877, at the age of 13, he lost what money could not replace when both of his parents died. He attended the Massachusetts Institute of Technology, which he left early to work in the family business, where his mechanical aptitude led to improved safety and more efficient machines. He held more than 200 patents, most related to the powder-making process. When his uncles died, the board wanted to sell the mill, but Alfred and two cousins bought the business. Just 15 years later, he left the company he had saved and transformed. A year after his second wife died, Alfred married Jessie Ball and set out for Florida. By then, he was almost completely deaf from a swimming accident in his youth.

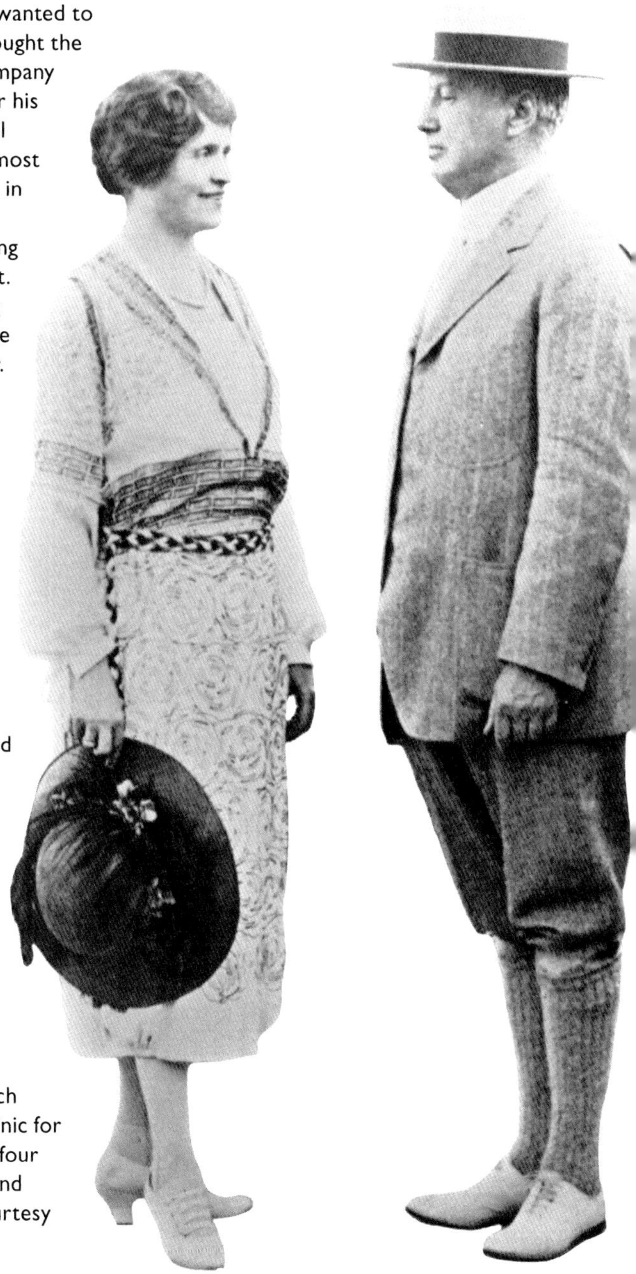

The couple settled in Jacksonville, building a mansion with formal gardens along the St. Johns River. They named the estate Epping Forest after the home of Mary Ball, George Washington's mother and Jessie's ancestor. Alfred and his brother-in-law Ed Ball invested in Florida real estate and banks and helped develop the Florida panhandle.

The duPonts were committed to their new community. In 1927, Alfred wrote, "We expect to spend the balance of our days here. We have all the money necessary for any reasonable effort to help Florida grow and prosper. Our business undertakings should be sound, but our primary object should not be the making of money. Through helpful works, let us build up good in this state and make it a better place in which to live. In my last years, I would much rather have the people of Florida say that I helped them and their state than to double the money I now have."

Alfred I. duPont died in Jacksonville in 1935 at the age of 71. He left his vast fortune to care for crippled children.

Since its inception shortly after Alfred's death, the Alfred I. duPont Testamentary Trust has provided more than $1.9 billion to support the Nemours Foundation, which includes a children's hospital and health clinic for the elderly in Wilmington, Delaware, and four Nemours Children's Clinics in Delaware and Florida, including one in Jacksonville. (Courtesy of Nemours Children's Health System.)

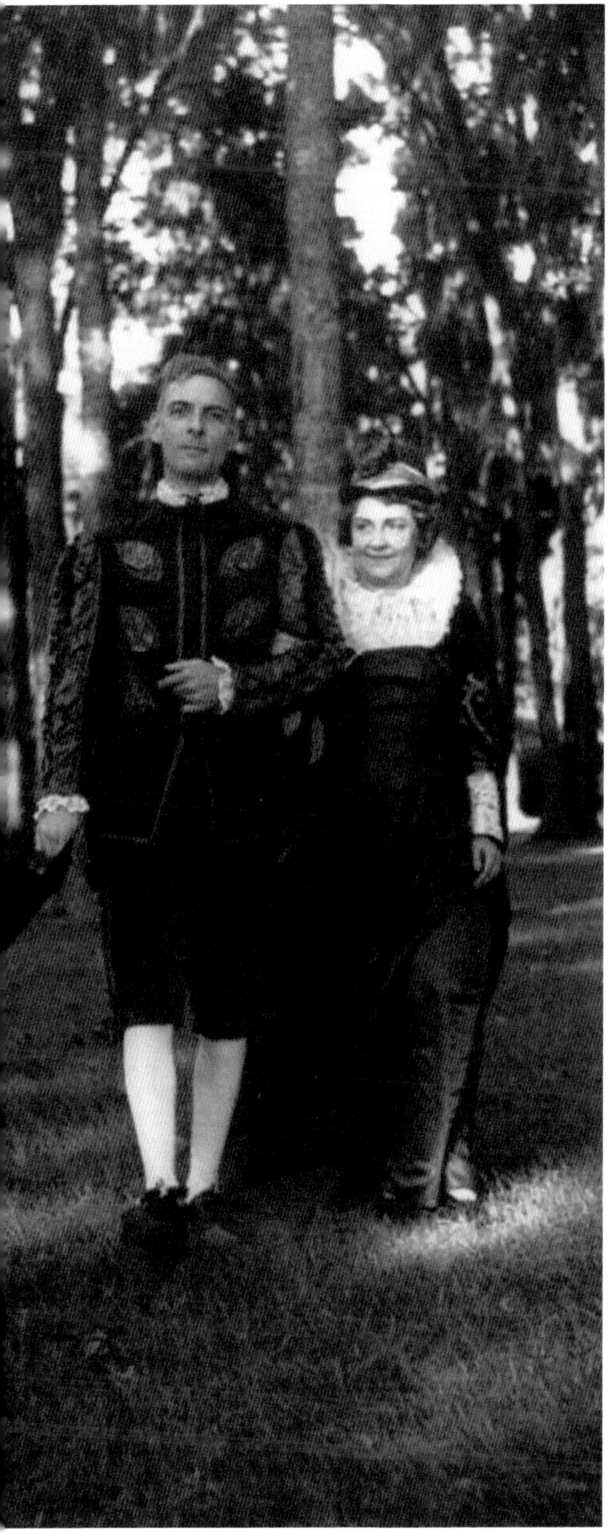

### Jessie Ball duPont

Jessie Ball began her philanthropic efforts at an early age. When she moved to San Diego with her parents in 1908, the young woman, who had attended a one-room school before going to college, became a teacher and then the assistant principal of the city's largest elementary school. In addition to helping support her elderly parents, she began awarding scholarships to needy students from her personal income, managing more than 100 scholarships in all.

Jessie had met industrialist Alfred I. duPont in the late 1800s when he made hunting trips to her Virginia home. Shortly after they married in 1921, Jessie became a business confidante and protector of Alfred, who was almost completely deaf from a childhood accident. They settled in Jacksonville, where they built a lavish Mediterranean-style mansion along the St. Johns River, which they named Epping Forest for her ancestral home. Her brother, Ed Ball, joined them in Jacksonville to help keep an eye on their property.

After Alfred died, Jessie became the first chair of his trust and the Nemours Foundation. She not only chaired the trust but also made significant contributions to it from her personal income. When she died in 1970 at the age of 86, Jessie left her own separate trust, the Jessie Ball duPont Fund, worth about $42 million. According to the fund's website, it limits grants to a defined universe of organizations. An organization is eligible if it received a contribution from Mrs. duPont between January 1, 1960, and December 31, 1964. The first year, the fund made about $4 million in grants. Today, the fund's grants total $12–$18 million a year.

In this photograph, Jessie Ball duPont is being escorted at a costume party at her Epping Forest home in 1940. (Courtesy of State Archives of Florida, *Florida Memory*, www.floridamemory.com/items/show/4664.)

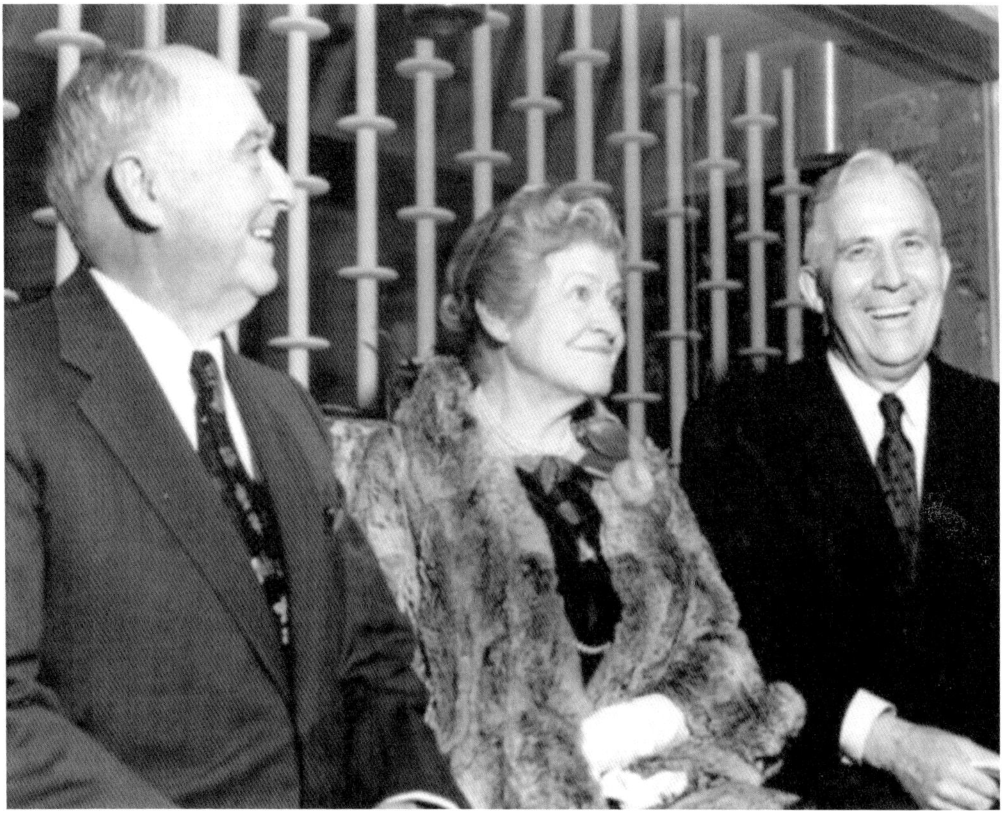

### Ed Ball

Ed Ball, the son of a country lawyer in Virginia, dropped out of school as a teenager to sell cash registers and legal books. By the time he died in 1981 at the age of 93, Ball had amassed a fortune worth $2 billion.

Ball moved to Jacksonville at the age of 35, two years after his sister Jessie married the wealthy industrialist Alfred I. duPont. The duPonts wanted Ball to help manage some of their property. During the Depression, Ball began buying bankrupt companies, including a railroad and a telephone company. Throughout his career, he built banks and bought acreage and companies, but he was known to be thrifty.

A story on *The Ledger* website says Ball insisted on marble floors and Oriental rugs for the new Florida National Bank building because they would appreciate in value. However, the nine-story building had neither hot water taps nor executive washrooms.

He was known to raise a glass of bourbon every evening to the toast: "Confusion to the enemy!" Two biographies, one official and one not, include that toast in their titles. He earned an undesirable reputation as a robber baron and a bigot toward African Americans, liberals, and labor unions. Ball was a driving force of the "Porkchop Gang," a powerful group of rural politicians and segregationists in Florida's legislature. He was married briefly but sought an annulment when he realized his wife was barren.

Ball grew his brother-in-law's estate from about $30 million to $2 billion. For his own estate, Ball followed his brother-in-law's lead, but he stipulated that his estate be used to care for children exclusively in Florida.

This photograph shows Ed Ball with his sister Jessie Ball duPont and businessman Roger Main. (Courtesy of State Archives of Florida, *Florida Memory*, www.floridamemory.com/items/show/30599.)

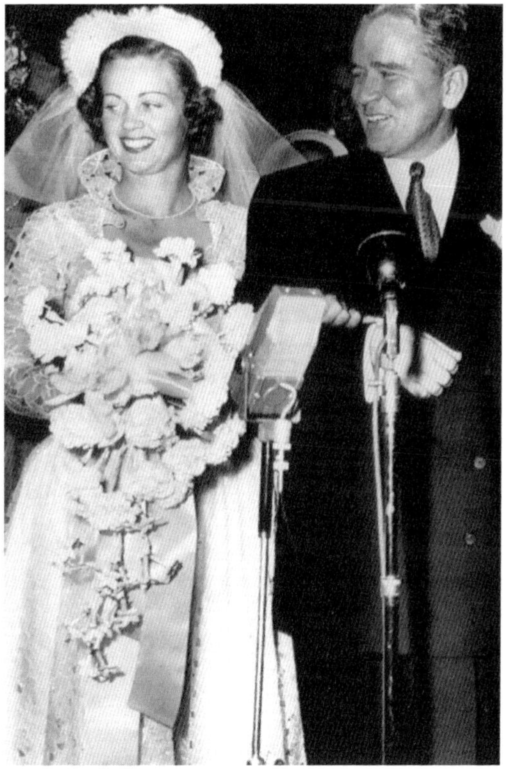

**Fuller Warren**
Fuller Warren was in college when he was elected to the Florida House of Representatives in 1927. He moved to Jacksonville in 1929 to practice law, and served three terms on the city council before returning to the legislature. He fought in World War II and then became governor in 1949. After serving one term, he moved to Miami. Jacksonville's Fuller Warren Bridge opened in 1954. Governor Warren married his wife, Barbara, in 1949. He died in 1973, days before his 68th birthday. (Courtesy of State Archives of Florida, *Florida Memory*, www.floridamemory.com/items/show/128820.)

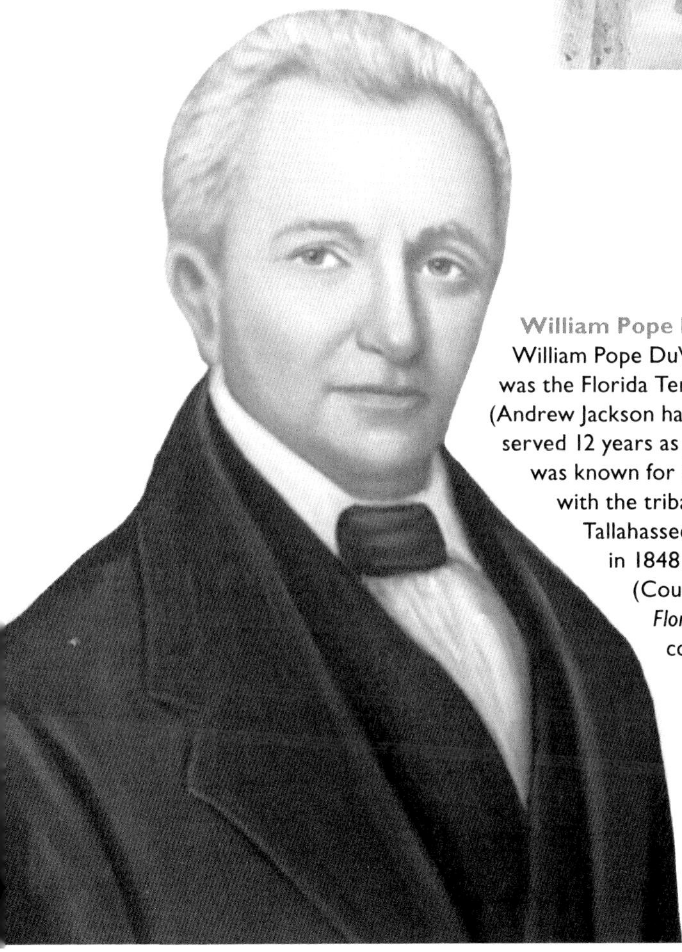

**William Pope DuVal**
William Pope DuVal, the namesake of Duval County, was the Florida Territory's first civilian governor (Andrew Jackson had been a military governor). DuVal served 12 years as governor, from 1822 to 1834, and was known for maintaining peaceful relationships with the tribal nations as well as establishing Tallahassee as Florida's capital. He left Florida in 1848 for Texas, where he died in 1854. (Courtesy of State Archives of Florida, *Florida Memory*, www.floridamemory.com/items/show/136859.)

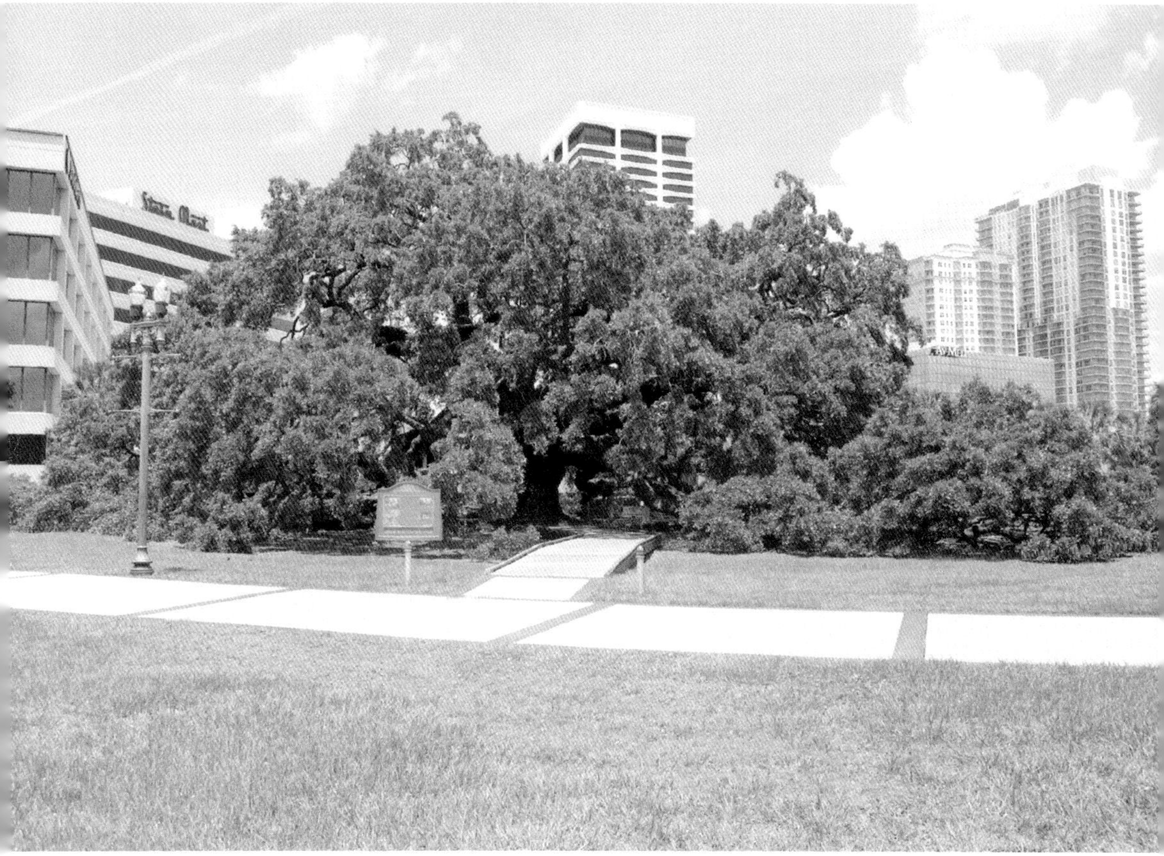

**Treaty Oak**

With a 25-foot circumference and a height of more than 60 feet, the grand oak tree growing on the south side of the St. Johns River is a majestic sight. Although its exact age is in dispute, Treaty Oak, with its heavy branches resting on the ground below, is thought to be one of the oldest living things in Jacksonville.

The name Treaty Oak was supposedly coined by *Times-Union* reporter Pat Moran, who spread a rumor that a peace treaty was signed under the massive tree between Indians and white settlers. Beneath the legendary canopy, the community comes together to celebrate weddings, watch movies in the park, and attend parties. (Photograph by Kendall Brunson.)

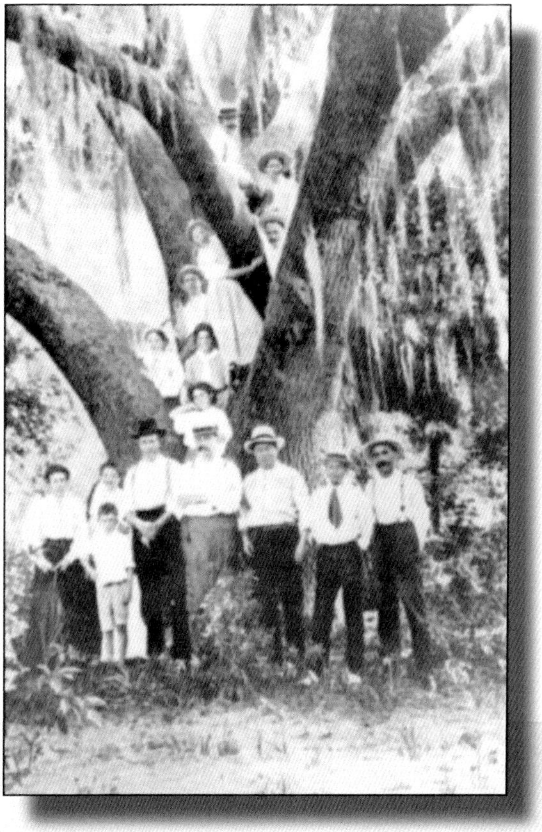

**Main Attraction**

The majestic old oak was the main attraction for Dixieland Amusement Park. After the park closed, Treaty Oak's existence was threatened by budding businesses along the river.

Treaty Oak and the surrounding land were purchased by the Alfred I. duPont Foundation in 1934 at the request of local philanthropist Jessie Ball duPont and donated to the city in 1964. (Right, courtesy of State Archives of Florida, *Florida Memory*, www.floridamemory.com/items/show/159099; below, courtesy of State Archives of Florida, *Florida Memory*, www.floridamemory.com/items/show/118364.)

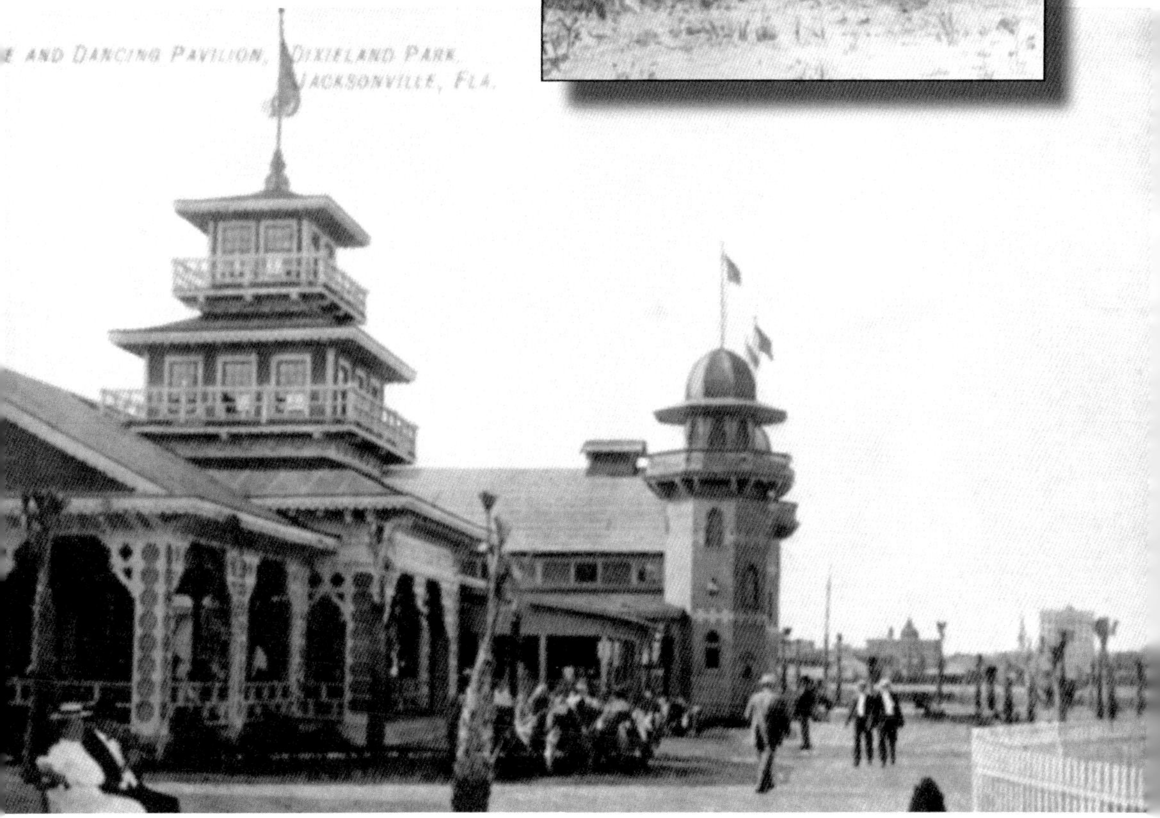

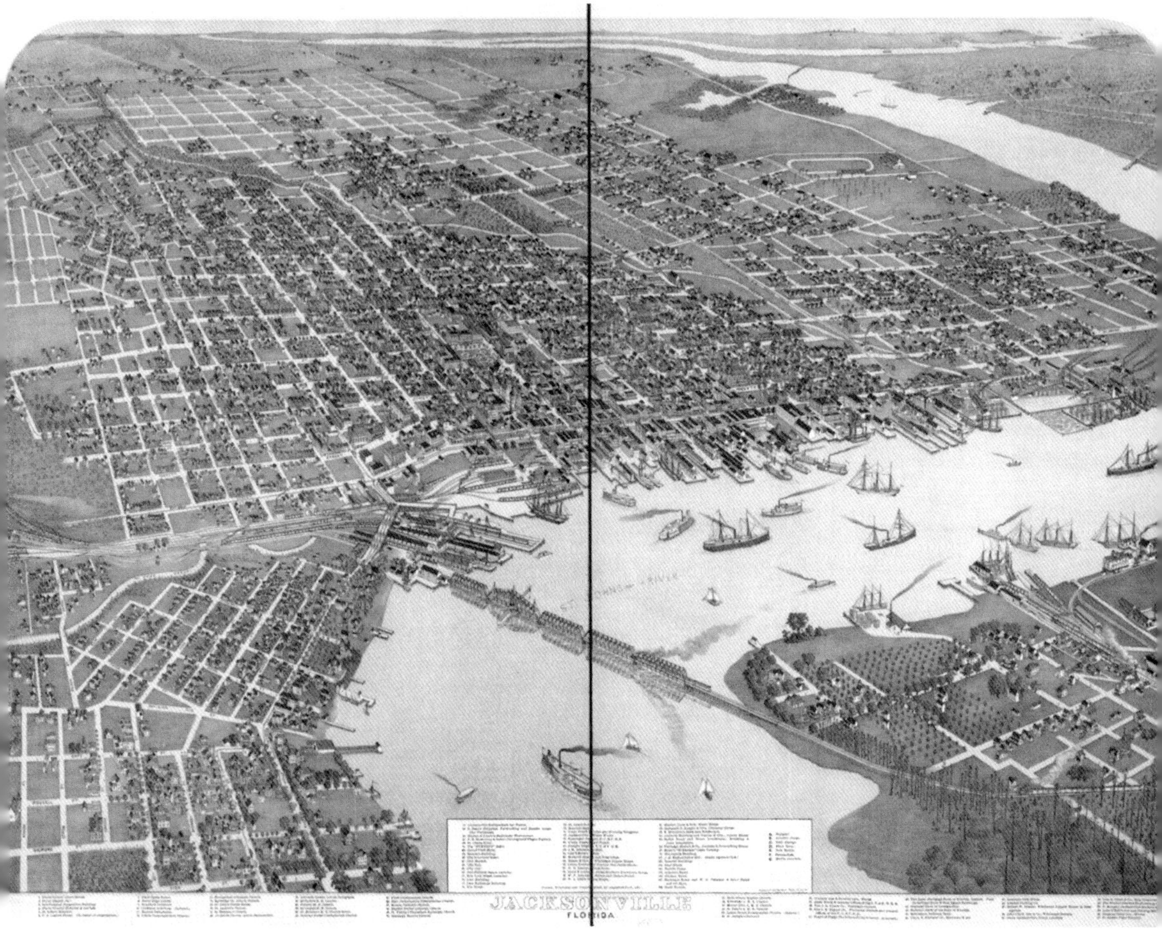


### Isaiah D. Hart

The southwest corner of Market and Bay Streets in downtown Jacksonville marks an important spot in Jacksonville's history. It is the very point where Isaiah D. Hart and some neighbors began laying the grid for the streets that would become Jacksonville. Because of that work, which lay the foundation for the map above, he is referred to historically as Jacksonville's founder.

Hart was a wealthy plantation owner who moved from Georgia to what was then Cowford in 1822. He was thought to hold many positions in town, including postmaster and court clerk. Jacksonville's founder is the namesake of a truss bridge over the St. Johns River connecting the downtown he planned and mapped out to the south side of the river. The bridge opened in 1967. (Courtesy of William Morrow.)

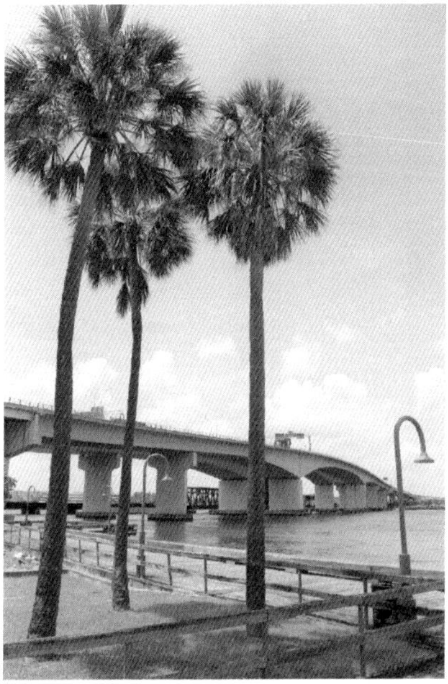

### St. Elmo "Chic" Acosta

Jacksonville's first bridge was the St. Elmo W. Acosta Bridge. It opened in 1921 and was named after the former city council member who fought for the $950,000 bond issue. "Chic" was elected to the city council in 1910, served in the Florida legislature, and concluded his political career as a city official from 1919 to 1935. In the Federal Writers' Project's *American Life Histories*, he lamented the state of politics in Florida and Jacksonville and said he had no desire to serve. Acosta died in 1947 at age 72. (Photograph by Kendall Brunson.)

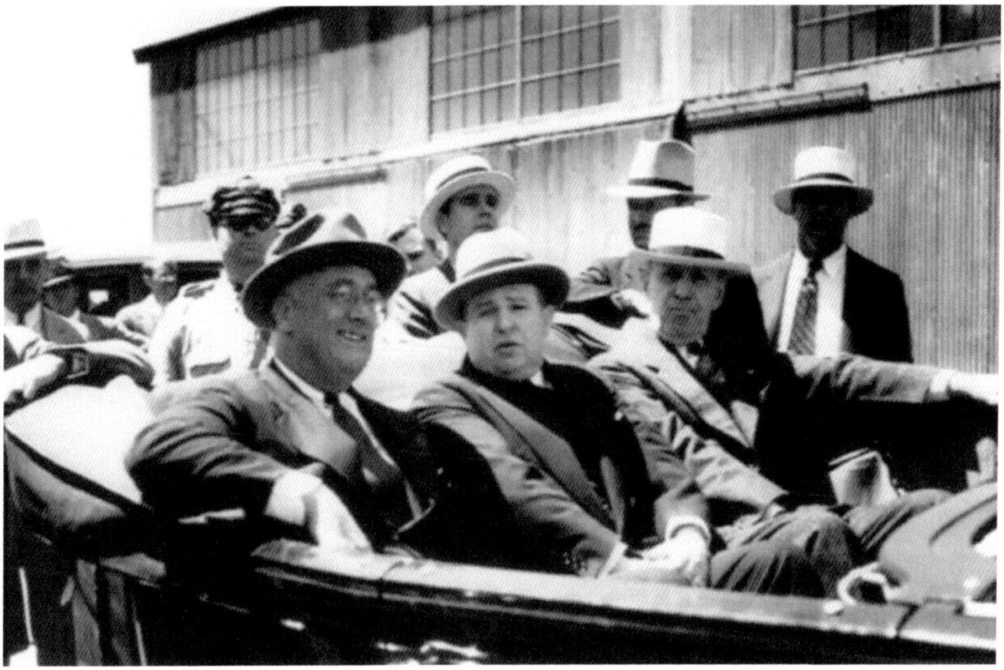

### John T. Alsop Jr.

John T. Alsop Jr. served 18 years as mayor, more than any other mayor. A former member of Pres. Theodore Roosevelt's "Rough Riders," he first served from 1923 until 1937. A *St. Petersburg Times* article announcing Alsop's reelection in 1941 called him Jacksonville's "super salesman." However, in *Keeping the Faith*, Abel Bartley says Alsop's political career later fell to black voters. In 1957, the city renamed the Main Street Bridge after Alsop, who died in 1958. This photograph shows Pres. Franklin D. Roosevelt, Gov. David Sholtz, and Alsop. (Courtesy of State Archives of Florida, *Florida Memory*, www.floridamemory.com/items/show/128490.)

### John E. Mathews Sr.

Born in 1892, John E. Mathews Sr. was one of Jacksonville's most formidable politicians. He served two terms in both the Florida House of Representatives and the Senate. His efforts in the 1940s raised the necessary $11 million to finance Jacksonville's bridge from Downtown to Arlington, officially named the John E. Mathews Sr. Bridge. In *Keeping the Faith*, Abel Bartley says Mathews's efforts to replace Jacksonville's ward-based voting with an at-large system weakened the black vote, which defeated his political career. However, his friend Gov. Fuller Warren appointed Mathews to the Florida Supreme Court in 1951. Justice Mathews died in 1955 at the age of 63. Justice and Mrs. Mathews were both present for the dedication of the Mathews Bridge in 1953. (Photograph by Robert E. Fisher; courtesy of State Archives of Florida, *Florida Memory*, www.floridamemory.com/items/show/167037.)

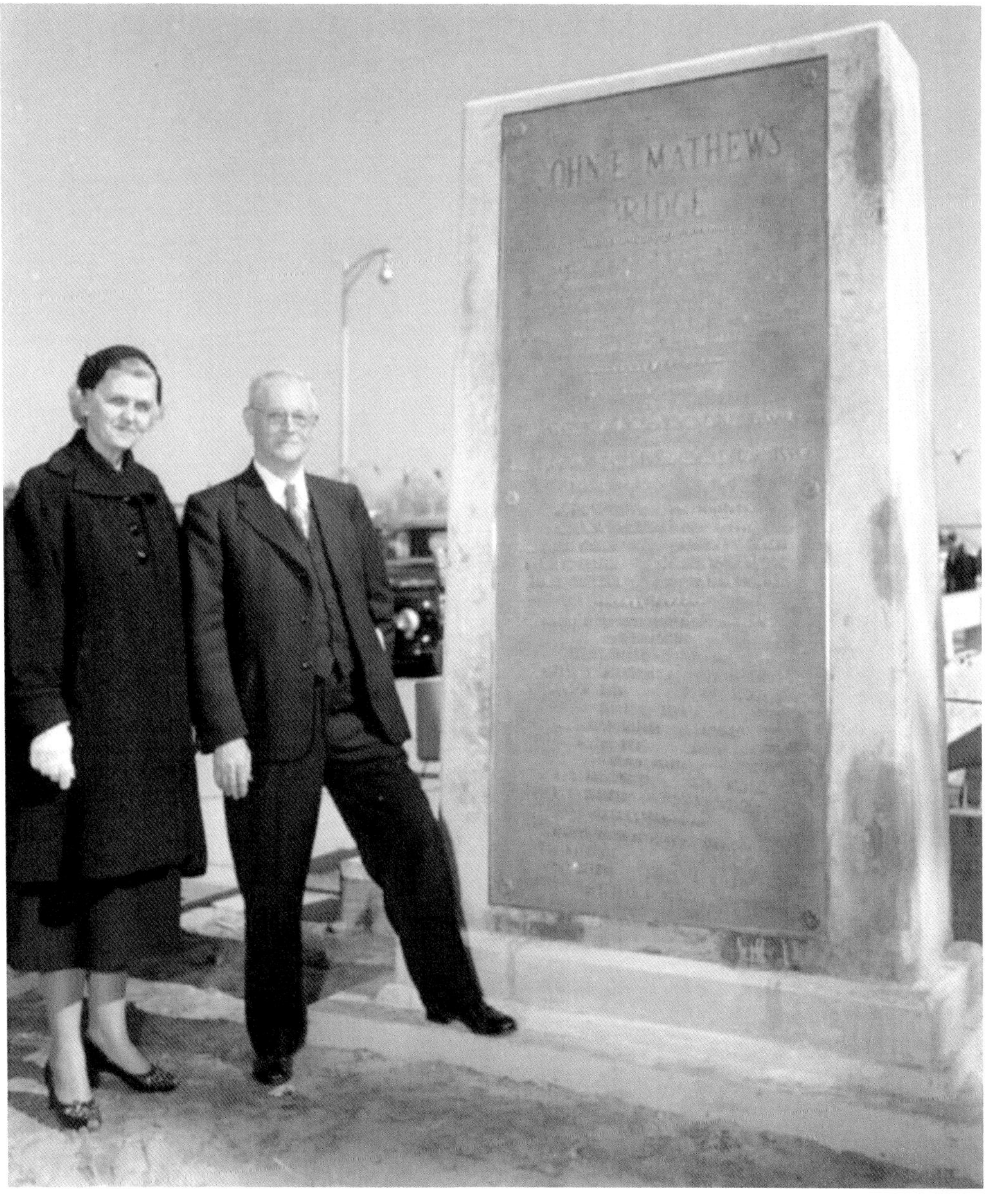

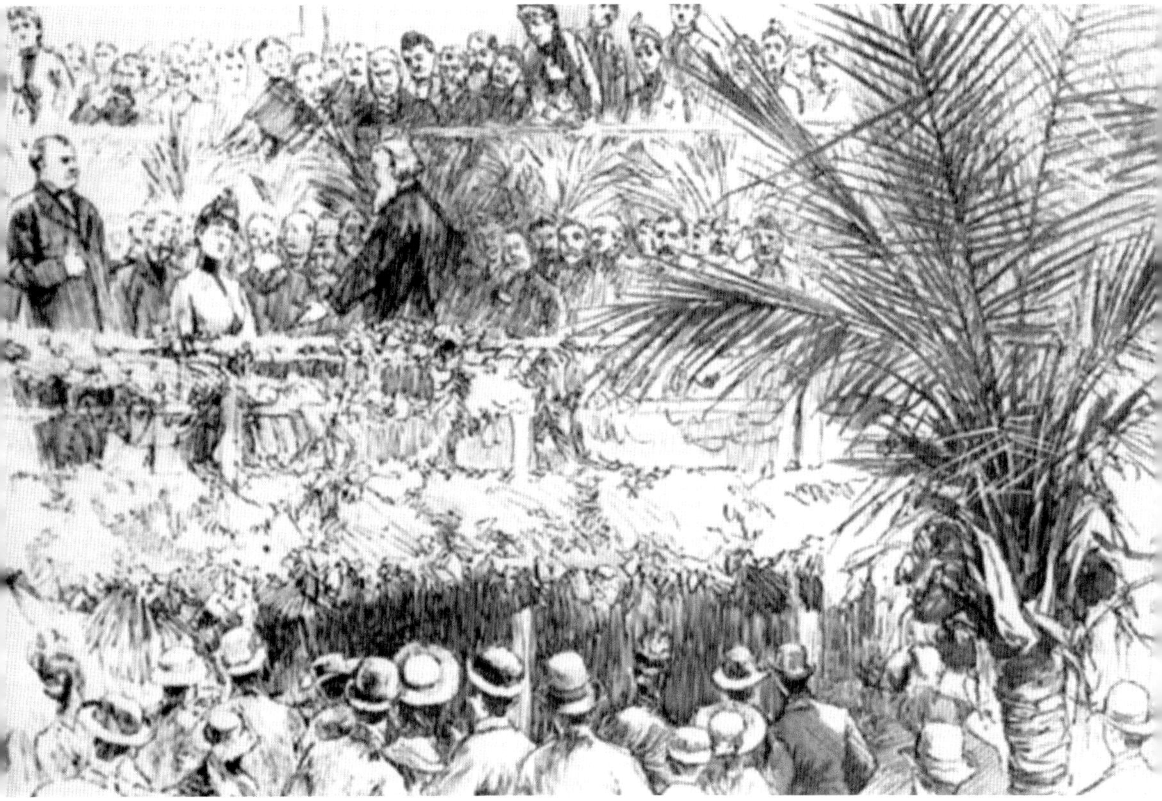

**J.J. Daniel**

Col. J.J. Daniel commanded the 1st Florida Infantry Reserves after most of the regular Confederate forces withdrew from the state. Daniel was wounded by Union troops. He was one of Jacksonville's most influential citizens after the war. He was also a principal in the Jacksonville law firm Fleming & Daniel and a philanthropist. He reorganized the chamber of commerce and worked tirelessly to help yellow fever victims before dying in the epidemic of 1888. He was also the first president of Florida Publishing Co. A century later, his grandson, also named J.J. Daniel, served as the publisher of the same company. This sketch illustrates Colonel Daniel's address welcoming Pres. Grover Cleveland to Jacksonville's Florida Exposition in 1888. (Courtesy of State Archives of Florida, *Florida Memory*, www.floridamemory.com/items/show/7400.)

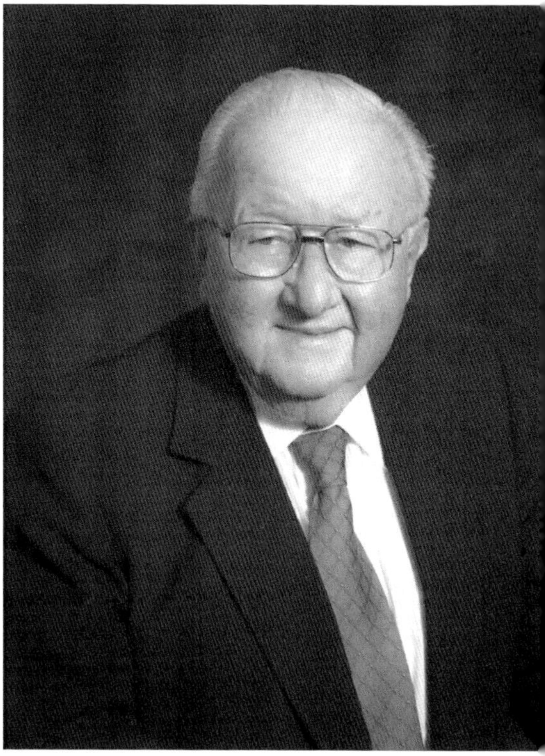

## An Escape to Freedom

When Nazis invaded Austria in 1938, Harry Frisch escaped to the shores of British Palestine. In 1953, Harry, his wife, Lilo, and their sons Ben and Karl left Israel to join Harry's brother, mother, and stepfather in Jacksonville in operating a fresh seafood store, Beaver Street Fisheries. Since then, four generations of his family have built the business into a $500-million food distributorship with hundreds of employees. (Both courtesy of Harry Frisch.)

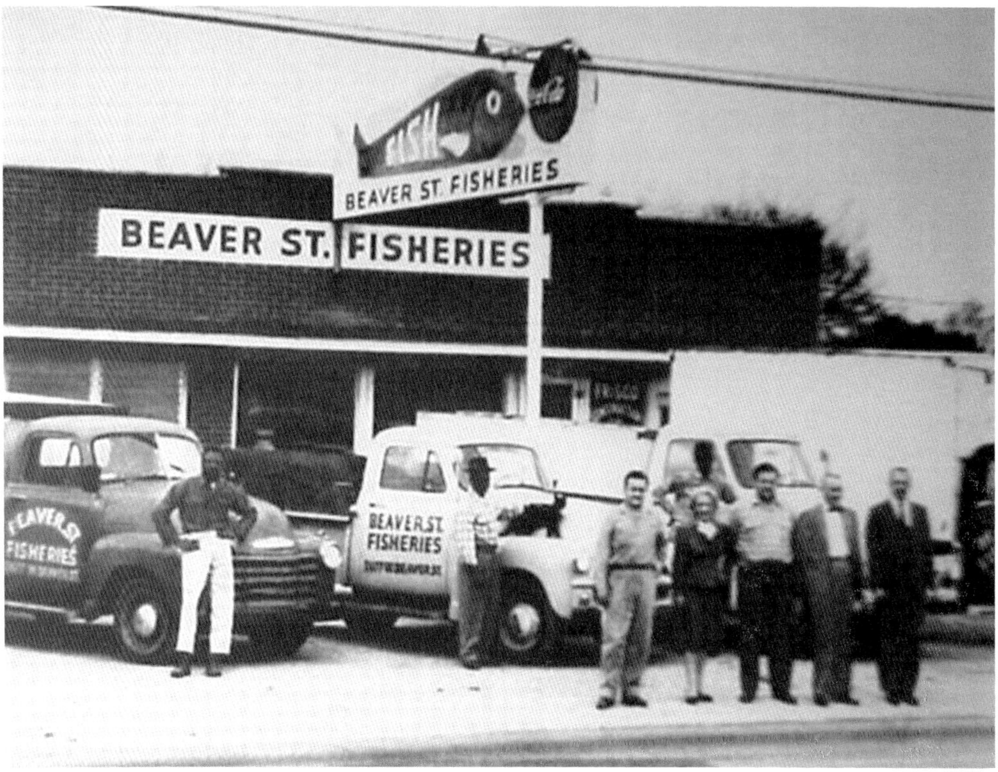

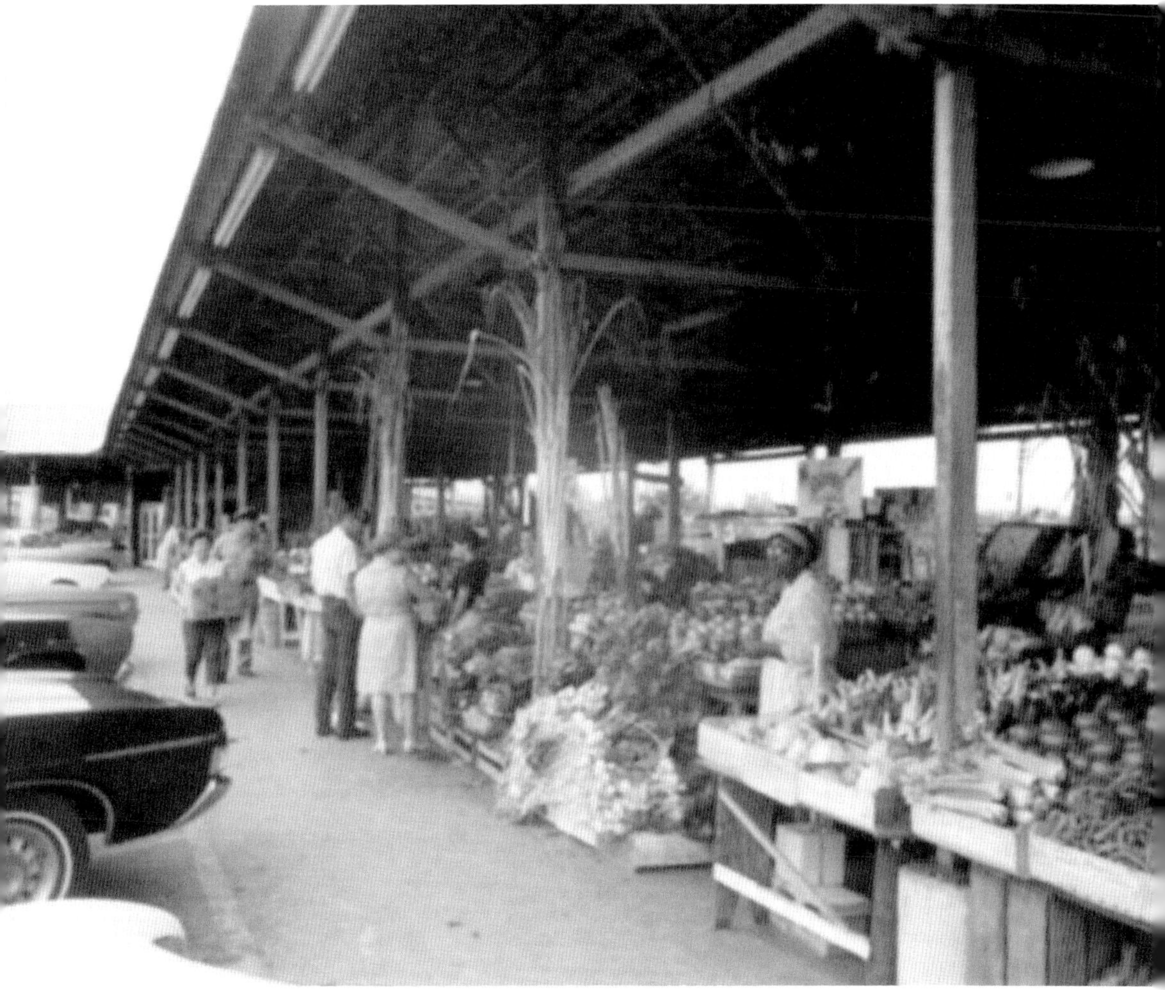

**Florida's Oldest Farmers Market**

More than 20,000 people visit the Jacksonville Farmers Market every week of the year, with more than half of those on weekends. Established in 1938, it is Florida's oldest farmers market and operates from dawn to dusk every day. Often called the Beaver Street Farmers Market because of its location, the operation features produce and goods from more than 200 farmers and vendors. The market is owned by Beaver Street Fisheries. (Photograph by Karl E. Holland; courtesy of State Archives of Florida, *Florida Memory*, www.floridamemory.com/items/show/85866.)

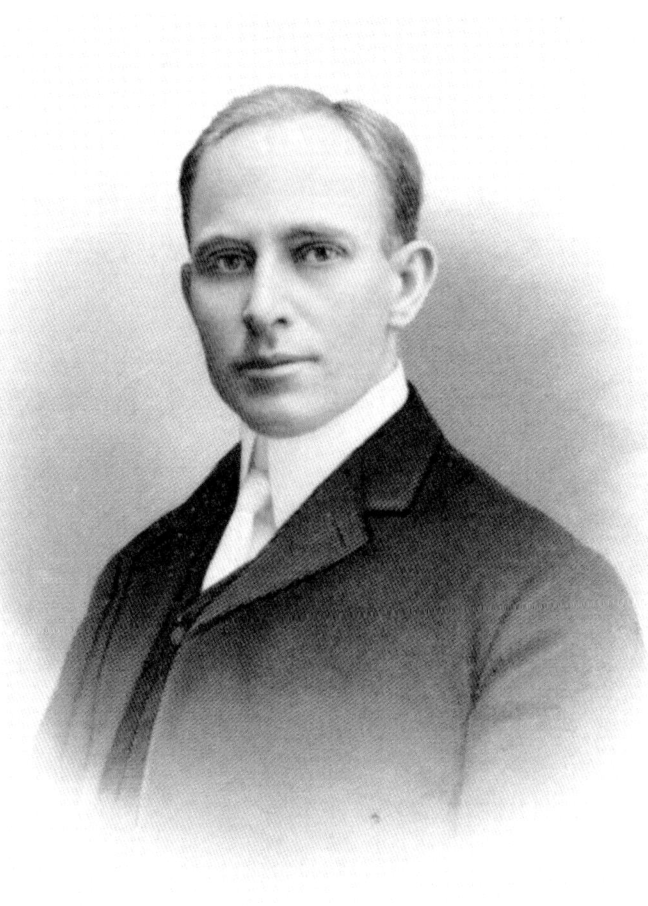

**Henry J. Klutho**

Henry John Klutho was a budding architect in New York City when he saw the opportunity of a lifetime. The "Great Fire of 1901" had destroyed much of Jacksonville, leaving a blank slate.

He quickly closed his projects in New York and headed south. Klutho's style of architecture, now known as part of the Prairie School, punctuates the River City to this day, including the neighborhoods of Downtown, Springfield, Riverside, and Avondale.

Klutho had an opportunity that very few architects, if any, experience: having so much singular influence on rebuilding a city. His first project was the six-story Dyal-Upchurch Building, at Main and Bay Streets. He worked on some of Jacksonville's most iconic buildings, including the Morocco Temple, the YMCA Building, and the St. James Building. In 1908, Klutho also designed Jacksonville's first skyscraper, the Bisbee Building, on Forsyth Street, which stood 10 stories high.

Architecture was not Klutho's only interest, however. He invested in the motion picture business on the First Coast, and, in 1917, he built the last major film studio in Jacksonville. The Klutho Studios were located in Springfield near Ninth and Main Streets, and he produced the *Sunbeam Comedies* there. However, his investment came too late to save the industry in Jacksonville, and Klutho lost $40,000 in the studio.

Nearly penniless when he died in 1964 at the age of 91, Klutho outlived his style. In the article "Henry John Klutho: An Architect for a New Century," Wayne Wood wrote, "In the years since Klutho's death, over a dozen of his finest buildings have been demolished or mutilated beyond recognition." However, his legacy lies with the buildings and homes still standing. (Courtesy of State Archives of Florida, *Florida Memory*, www.floridamemory.com/items/show/5904.)

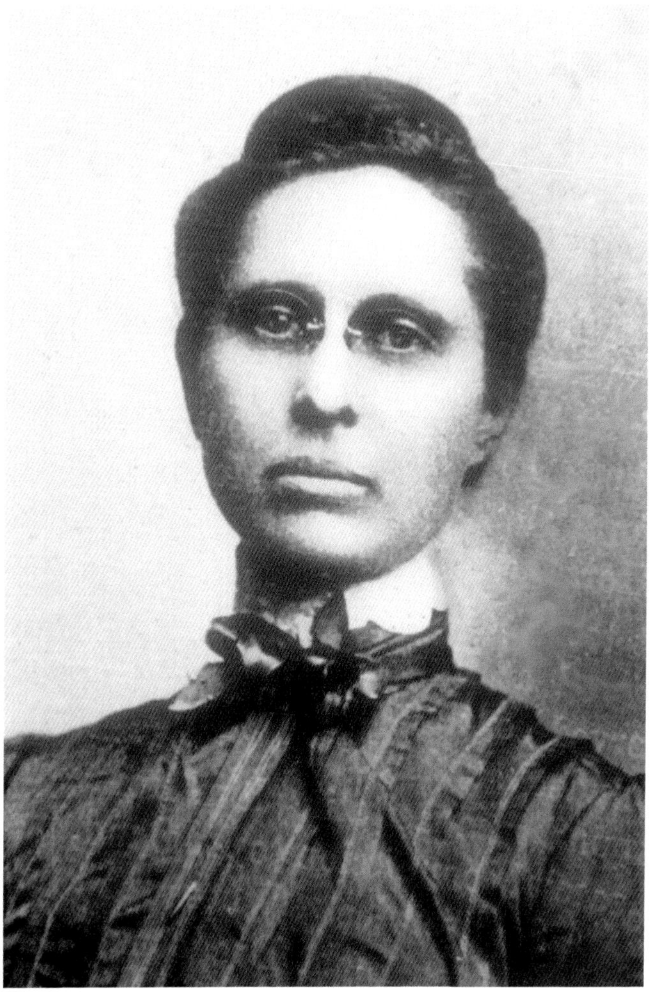

**Henrietta Dozier**

A contemporary of Henry J. Klutho, Henrietta Dozier was the first female architect in the South with a formal degree, and the third female member of the American Institute of Architects (AIA). Henrietta was known by a few aliases, including H.C. Dozier and "Cousin Harry."

Architecture was her singular career pursuit. In a Federal Writers' Project interview in 1939, Henrietta said, "Even in my childhood I wanted to study architecture, and have drawn plans since I was seven. In fact, when I was just a little tot I used to draft patterns for doll dresses for my own and the neighbor children's dolls. So it seemed the natural thing when I reached the age to decide what my life work was to be, to select architecture as a vocation."

Henrietta was born in Fernandina but grew up in Atlanta. She moved north to study at the Pratt Institute before earning a degree in architecture from the Massachusetts Institute of Technology in 1899.

Although Henrietta initially began practicing in Atlanta, she packed her bags for Jacksonville in 1914. Once settled, she opened her own firm and designed offices, banks, churches, and residences, including the Old Federal Reserve Building and St. Philip's Episcopal Church.

During the Depression, business slowed, and Henrietta lost her home. This setback inspired her to redirect her firm to provide residents with a combination of good design and low cost. She died in 1947. (Courtesy of Wayne Wood.)

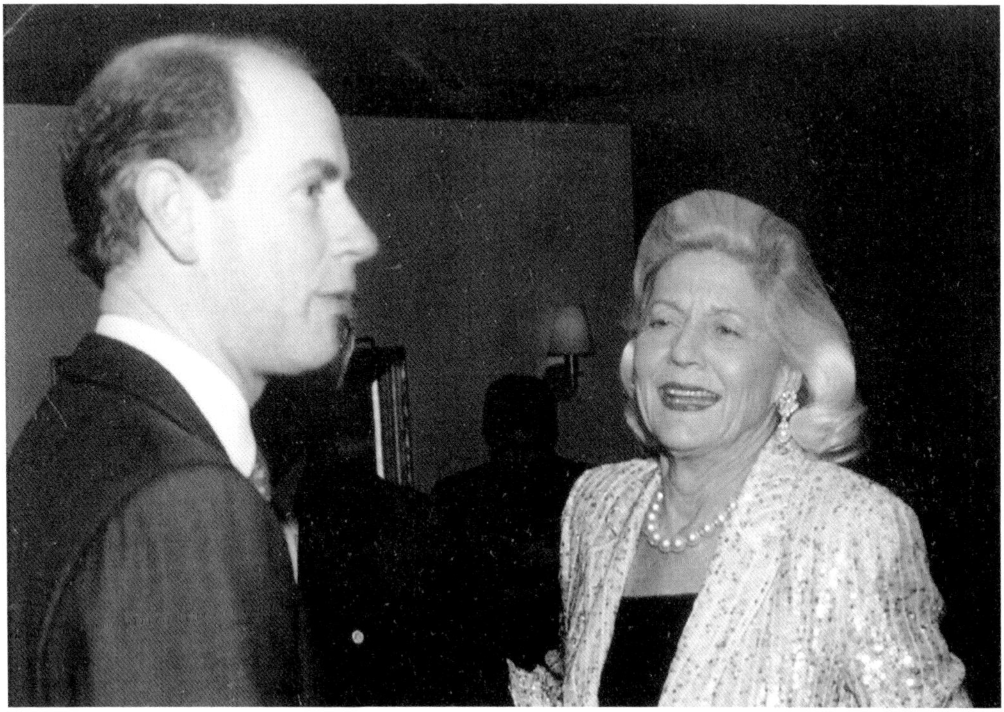

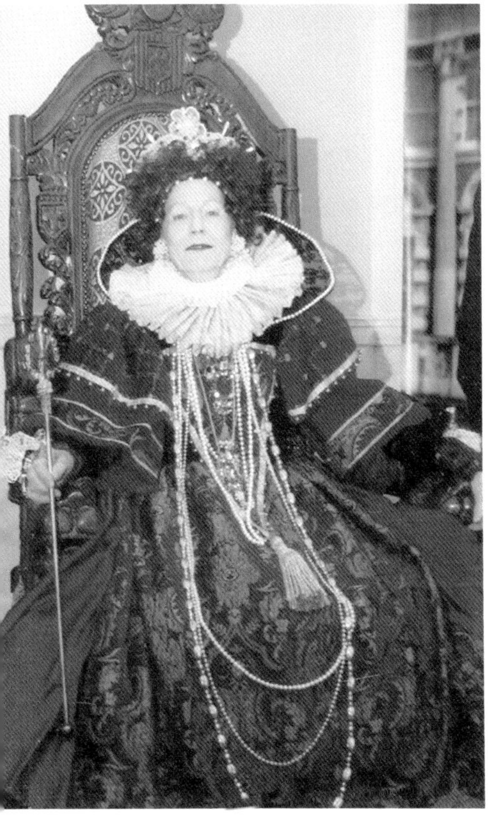

**Betsy Lovett Entertaining Royalty**
Jacksonville's own Betsy Ross (now Betsy Ross Lovett), can hunt and fish with the best of them and speaks easily of 12-gauge shotguns, 30-aught-6 rifles, and fly rods. But she is just as on-target when it comes to supporting important causes in the community, including health care, education, the environment, and the library. She is shown here with Prince Edward, Earl of Wessex, at a fundraiser she chaired for Wolfson Children's Hospital at the River Club. (Courtesy of Betsy Lovett.)

**Queen for an Evening**
Betsy's commitment to the city's public library runs the gamut, from reading story books to children to leading the library foundation and raising hundreds of thousands of dollars. A favorite local wedding and event space is the 10,000-square-foot Betsy Lovett Courtyard, complete with pergolas and fountains, at Jacksonville's Main Library. She has an affinity for costume events. At an English-themed gala for the library, Betsy dressed at Queen Elizabeth I. (Courtesy of Betsy Lovett.)

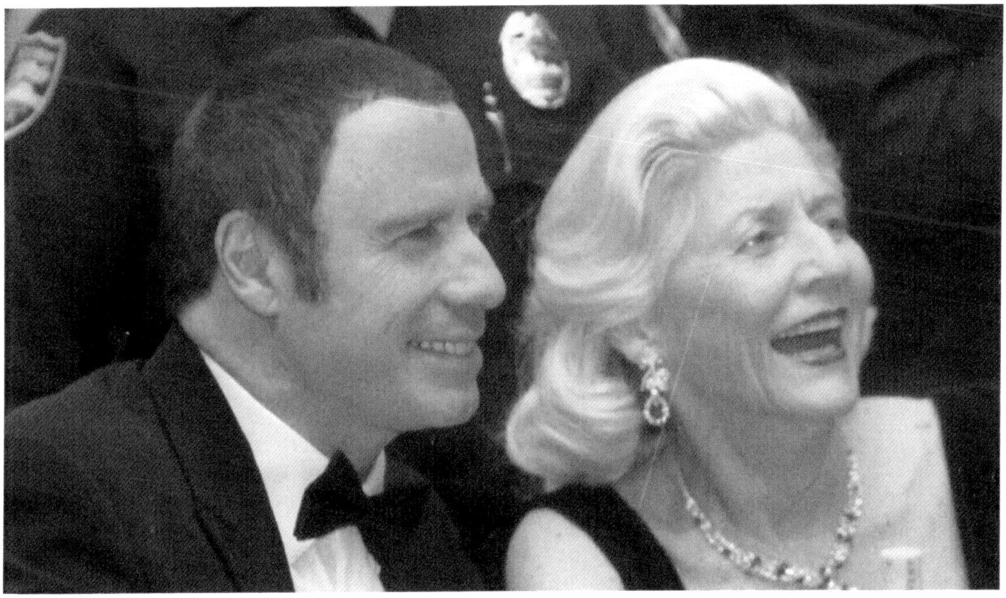

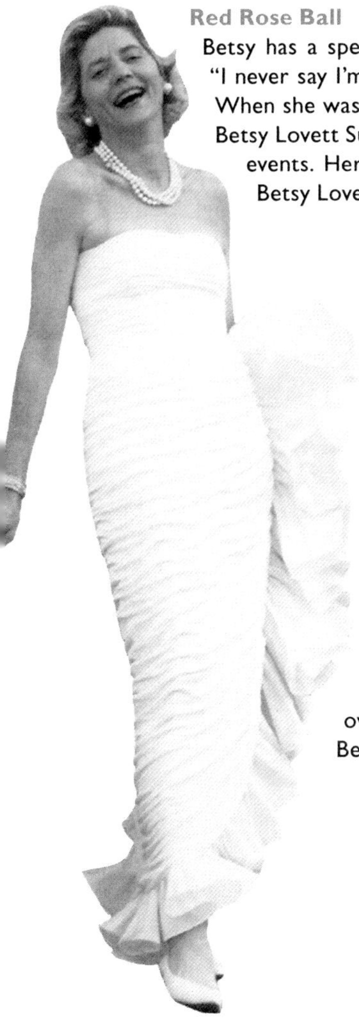

**Red Rose Ball**

Betsy has a special fondness for St. Vincent's Medical Center, where she was born. "I never say I'm old. I've just been younger a lot longer than most people," she says. When she was nine, doctors there saved her life. The medical center is home to the Betsy Lovett Surgery Center. St. Vincent's annual Red Rose Ball is one of her favorite events. Here, she and John Travolta enjoy a moment at the event. (Courtesy of Betsy Lovett.)

**A Prize Role**

In the 1989 made-for-TV movie *Roxanne: The Prize Pulitzer*, Betsy played the part of a Palm Beach socialite. The role was a far cry from the real Betsy, who is a formidable opponent. She fought Amoco subsidiary Waste-Tech over plans to build a hazardous waste incinerator near the farm she and her husband, Billy, owned in Madison County, and she won. (Courtesy of Betsy Lovett.)

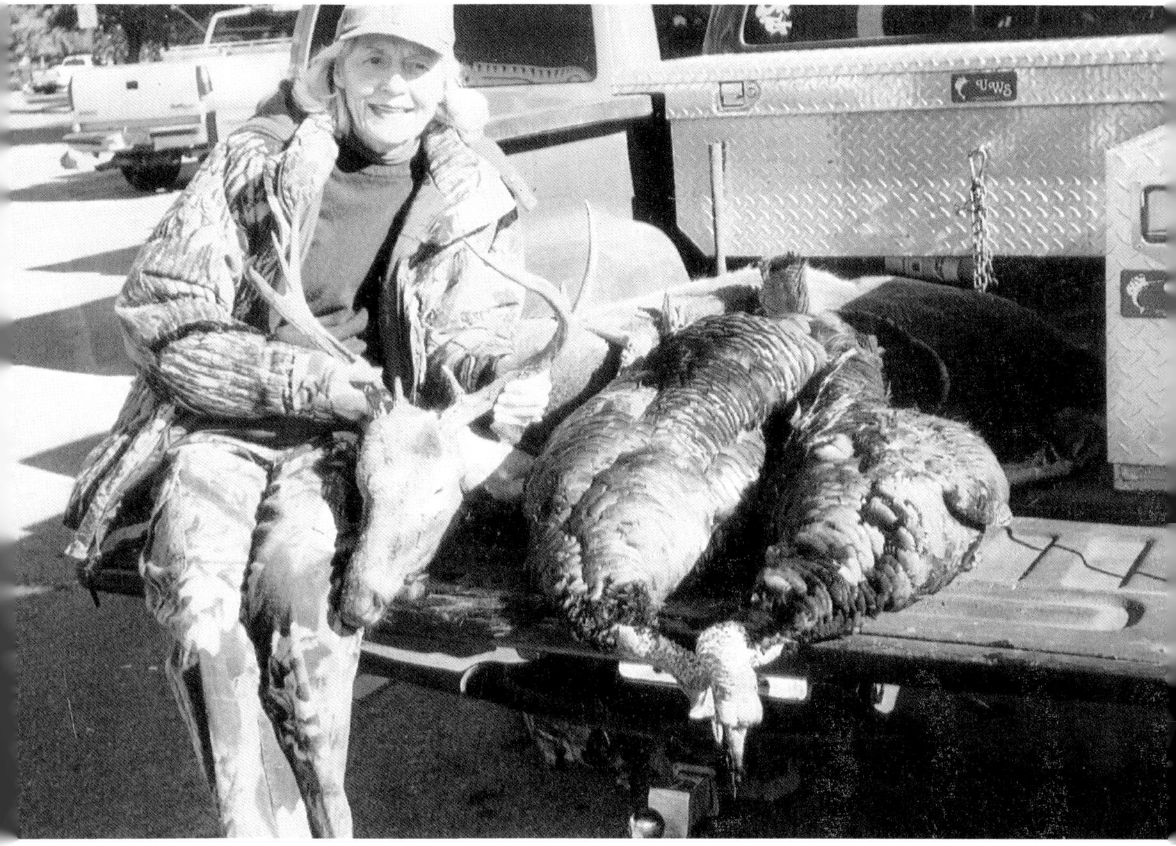

**Betsy on Safari**

In her childhood, during World War II, Betsy Ross Lovett cultivated victory gardens and knitted "bundles for Britain" (squares sewn into quilts for servicemen). She also learned to hunt and fish during that time, and she never lost interest in those skills. Betsy finds that time spent in nature "renews the soul" and is magical. She and her late husband, Billy, owned a large farm in Madison County where she hunted deer and wild turkeys. Sometimes, the hunt is not about shooting, she says, but rather a challenge of self to see how many turkeys she can draw near the blind. She is also a licensed alligator trapper. She is shown here with some of her kill from a hunt. (Courtesy of Betsy Lovett.)

# CHAPTER TWO

# All in the Family

Family is that wonderful, basic social unit that bonds a sometimes strange band of characters trying to make the most of this life. In centuries past, as well as the current one, families have shaped Jacksonville and marked it with the same fiber that distinguishes their members.

Southsiders in Jacksonville know Hendricks Avenue and Philips Highway, two of the thoroughfares that connect Southside to Downtown, going north, and Mandarin, going south. In 1800, Isaac Hendricks owned the largest tract of land south of the St. Johns River and operated a river ferry. His grandson Henry Bethune Philips was appointed a criminal court judge and was considered to be a master of the law.

After the four sons of a Miami businessman inherited the family's small chain of grocery stores, they moved the headquarters to Jacksonville and grew it into a major regional chain. The Davis brothers were champions of the city, supporting charitable organizations and the business community and donating land for the first satellite location of the Mayo Clinic.

Present-day families are taking the city in bold, new directions. As a father retired from a career in journalism, he and his son began roasting coffee beans to sell at weekend markets. Soon, they opened a coffee shop that inspires customers to drive past national chains and enjoy a genuinely handcrafted "cup of joe." Another family turned a son's passion for home-brewing beer into the city's first microbrewery. They are already making plans for the next generation.

The families in this chapter represent the thousands of families that have lived in and shaped Jacksonville over the centuries. One can only imagine the friction and camaraderie that surfaced among their members as they struggled to follow their dreams, and, at times, merely to survive. The accomplishments of these families are part of the common thread that binds the city together.

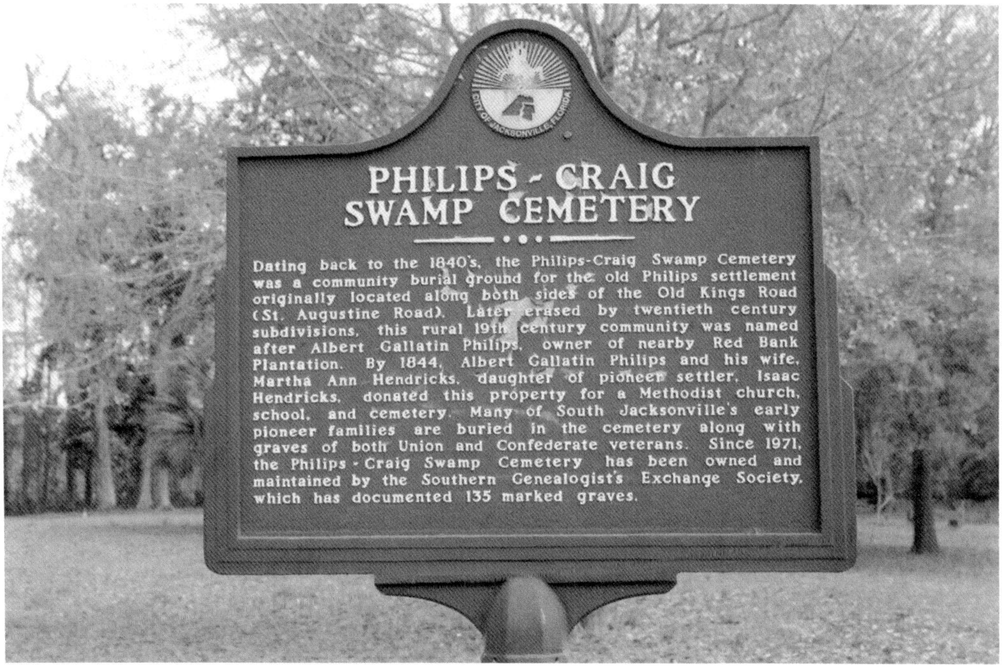


**Isaac Hendricks**

In the 1700s, Spain granted 216 acres on the south side of the St. Johns River to William Jones. In 1796, Jones rebelled against Spain, and the land went to William Hendricks, whose son Isaac cultivated the land. By 1800, Isaac ran the first ferry across the river, and, in 1824, he secured a ferry monopoly from the territorial legislature. The road from the ferry point south became Hendricks Avenue. (Photograph by Laura Jo Brunson.)

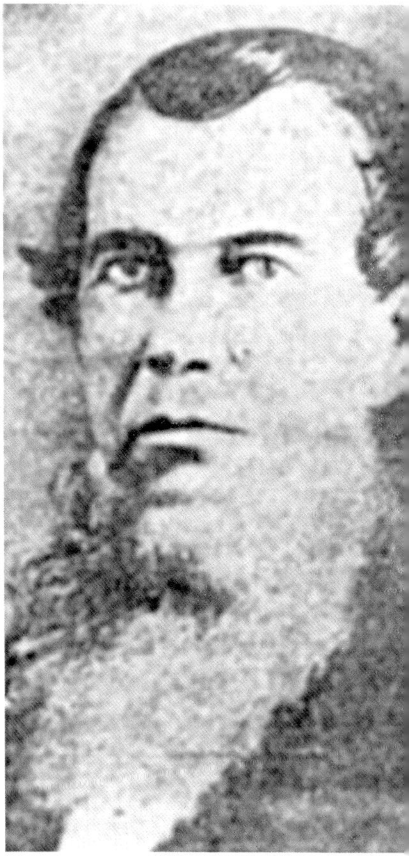

**A.G. Philips**

Albert Gallatin "A.G." Philips married Isaac Hendricks's daughter Margaret and built San Marco's Red Bank Plantation. According to Thomas Davis's *History of Early Jacksonville*, A.G. was the first Jacksonville–Tallahassee mail carrier. He befriended Native Americans along the route, giving them coffee and tobacco and receiving dried venison and honey in return. Gov. William DuVal appointed him Jacksonville's first sheriff in 1833. One of A.G. and Margaret's sons, Henry B. Philips, became a judge. (Courtesy of Stephen Dare, www.MetroJacksonville.com.)

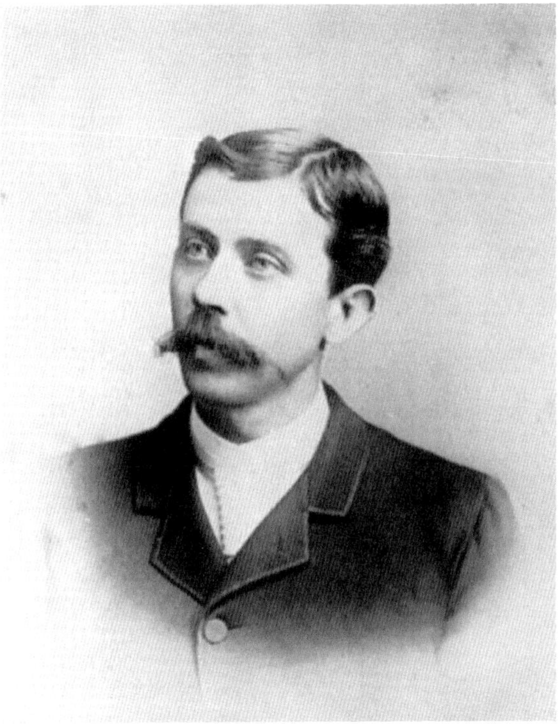

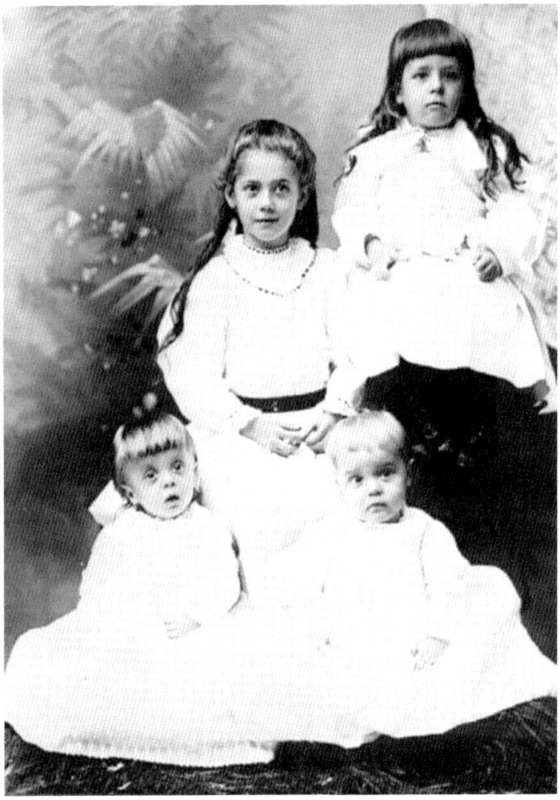

**Henry B. Philips**
In 1880, Jacksonville native Henry Bethune Philips entered law at Vanderbilt University, where he completed two years of study in one. He returned to Jacksonville to practice law. In 1891, Governor Fleming appointed him to Duval County's criminal court to finish the term of a deceased judge. Two years later, he was appointed to a four-year term. He became the first chairman of the Florida State Road Board (now the Florida Department of Transportation). Judge Philips is the namesake of Philips Highway (US 1). He and his wife, Stella, had four children: Henry and Harold are pictured in the front, and Charlotte and Matthew are in the back row (left to right). (Above, courtesy of the Library of Congress; below, courtesy of State Archives of Florida, Florida Memory, www.floridamemory.com/items/show/153042.)

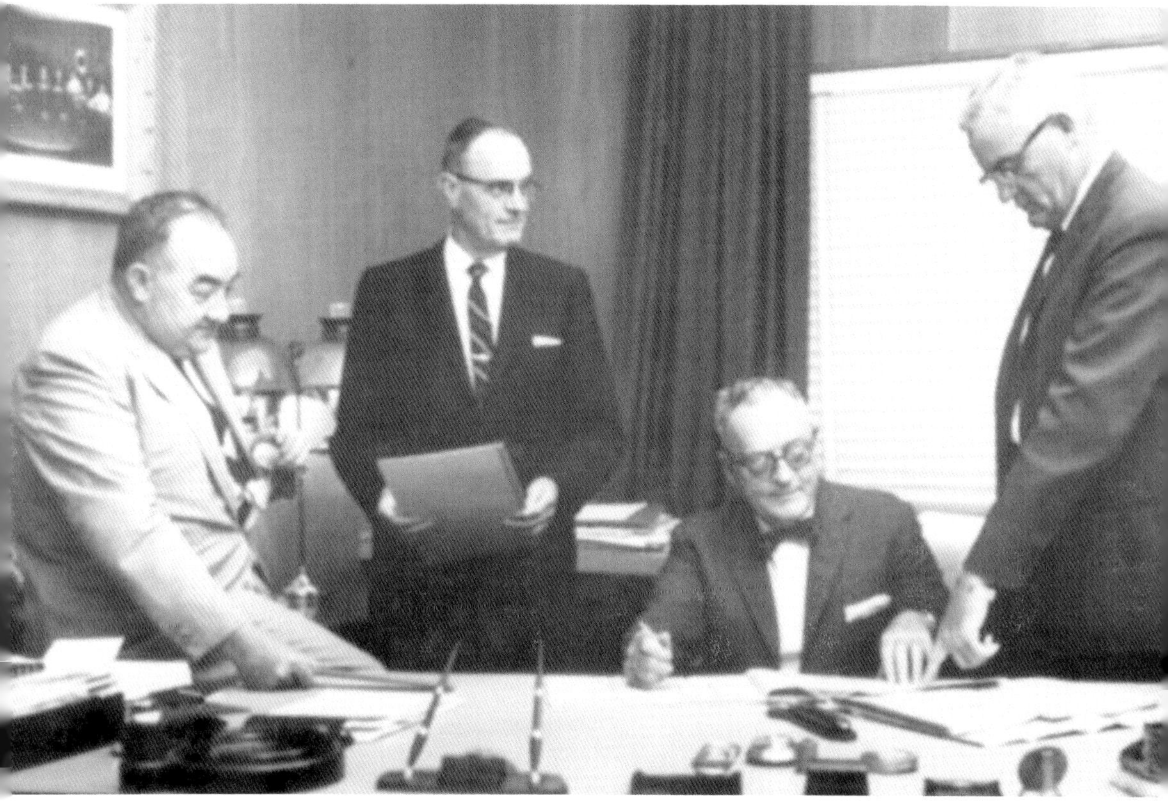

### The Davis Family

The death of Miami businessman William Milton Davis in 1934, in a roundabout way, brought great things to Jacksonville. Davis left control of his chain of grocery stores, Table Supply, to his four sons, Artemus Darius, James Elsworth, Milton Austin, and Tine Wayne, who not only grew the business but also relocated its headquarters to Jacksonville a decade later. By that time, Table Supply had become Winn & Lovett, which continued to grow, and, in 1952, became Florida's first industrial corporation to be traded on the New York Stock Exchange. With more growth and acquisitions throughout the Southeast and into the Midwest, the company adopted the name Winn-Dixie in 1955. Continued growth to 1,000 stores proved a burden. In 2005, the chain declared bankruptcy, from which it emerged in 2006 as a subsidiary of Bi-Lo Holdings, now headquartered in Jacksonville.

The Davis family's impact on Jacksonville extends far beyond the economic impact of a major employer. The city and its quality of life have benefited significantly from charitable contributions, chamber support, and political involvement by the Davis family, their foundations, and Winn-Dixie. According to the archived history on the company's website, the family believed Mr. Davis's death from pneumonia could have been prevented with better medical care. It was then that the family began its relationship with the Mayo Clinic. Because of that relationship, James Elsworth Davis and his wife, Flo, donated the 140-acre woodland site for the clinic's first satellite clinic, about 14 miles from Downtown Jacksonville, which opened in October 1986. The clinic's campus features the Davis Building, a four-story diagnostic center staffed by 37 physicians and about 150 support staff. Artemus Darius Davis, who outlived his three younger brothers, died in 1995 at the age of 89. Pictured from left to right are James Elsworth, Milton Austin, Tine Wayne, and Artemus Darius Davis. (Courtesy of State Archives of Florida, *Florida Memory*, www.floridamemory.com/items/show/39066.)

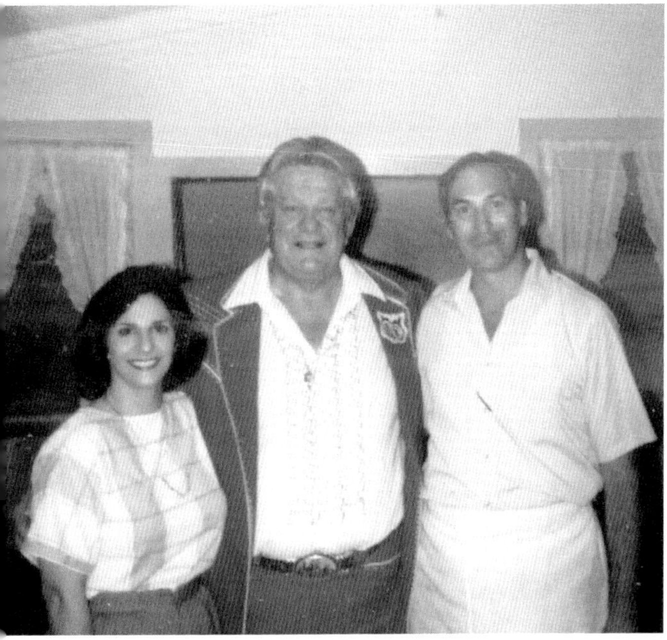

**Vincent and Mary DeSalvo**
After 40 years of running Beach Road Chicken Dinners, Earl Majors wanted to retire, but he preferred to close the restaurant than see it in the wrong hands. Then, Vincent and Mary DeSalvo asked to buy it. Mary's family owned Solomon's Bargain Center, two doors down from the restaurant, and Vincent's family ran a Westside chicken restaurant. On January 1, 1980, the DeSalvos bought the restaurant, and they owned it for 23 years before selling it to Vincent's sister. They served many celebrities, including country performer Jerry Clower (flanked by Mary and Vincent in this photograph). (Courtesy of Mary DeSalvo.)

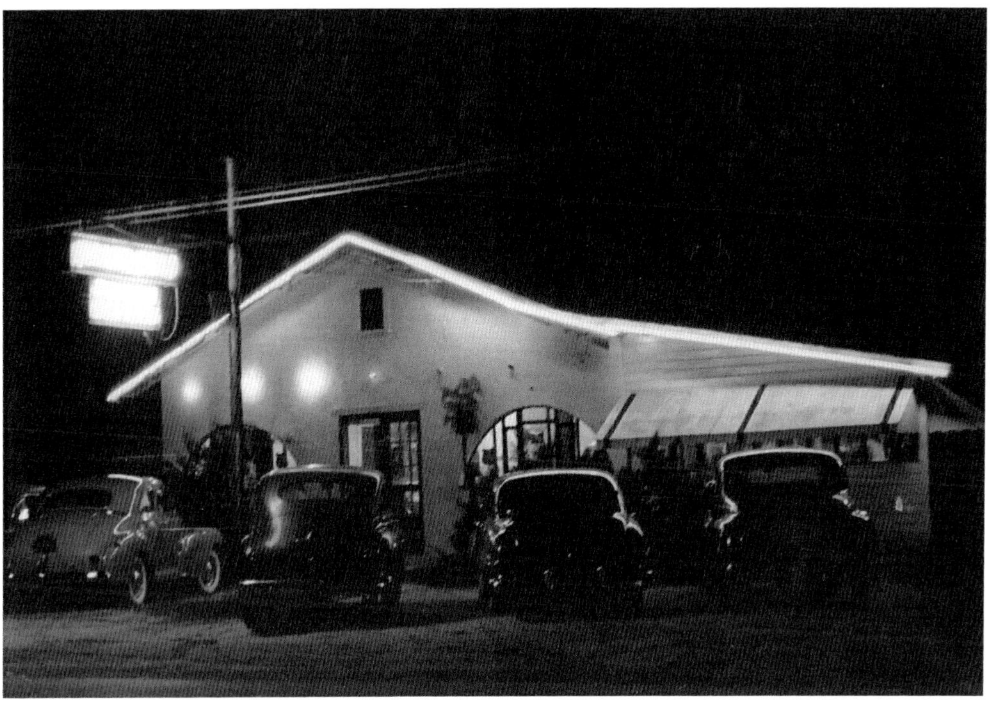

**Jacksonville's Oldest Restaurant**
In 1939, when Beach Road Chicken Dinners opened, Jacksonville had one road to the beach, Atlantic Boulevard, or "beach road." The restaurant's all-you-can-eat, family-style service was second in popularity only to its signature fried chicken and creamed peas, and lines still form outside the restaurant as people wait to be seated in the dining room. Diners still enjoy all-you-can-eat side dishes, but chicken is now limited to four pieces per customer. (Courtesy of Mary DeSalvo.)

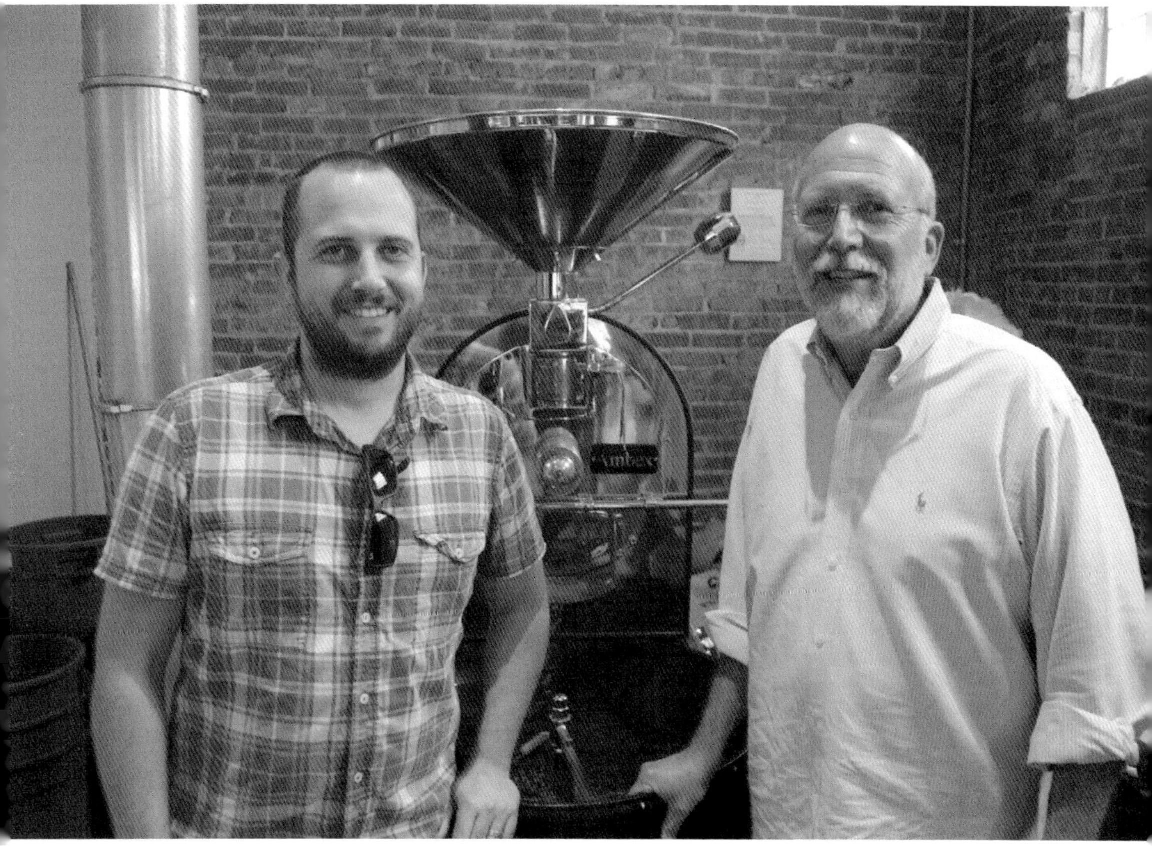

### A Bold Idea

Newspapers run on pot after pot of coffee, so it came as little surprise when Jay Burnett purchased a coffee roaster after he retired from his job as a journalist at the *Times-Union*. Having been a connoisseur of fine wine and food, he thought it would be fun to roast coffee beans to keep busy.

After his son Zachary graduated from college, the father-son duo teamed up to sell coffee beans at the Riverside Arts Market. Once they began brewing, they wanted to open a location where they could roast and prepare a handcrafted cup of coffee in person.

When Bold Bean Coffee Roasters opened on Stockton Street in Riverside, the community flocked to the shop. Zachary notes that people from the beach "cross the ditch" for a great cup of coffee, which is why they revamped an empty Starbucks on Third Street in Jacksonville Beach for their second location.

Zachary's brother Adam also joined the family business, making all of the baked goods sold at Bold Bean. As Zachary and Jay develop a coffee culture on the First Coast, they bring awareness to their customers of the coffee process, from where their beans are grown all the way to the person who serves it.

Both father and son prefer a black cup of handcrafted coffee, and when Jay is asked where he sees himself and the business in five years, he jokes, "Maybe I'll finally be retired." (Photograph by Kendall Brunson.)

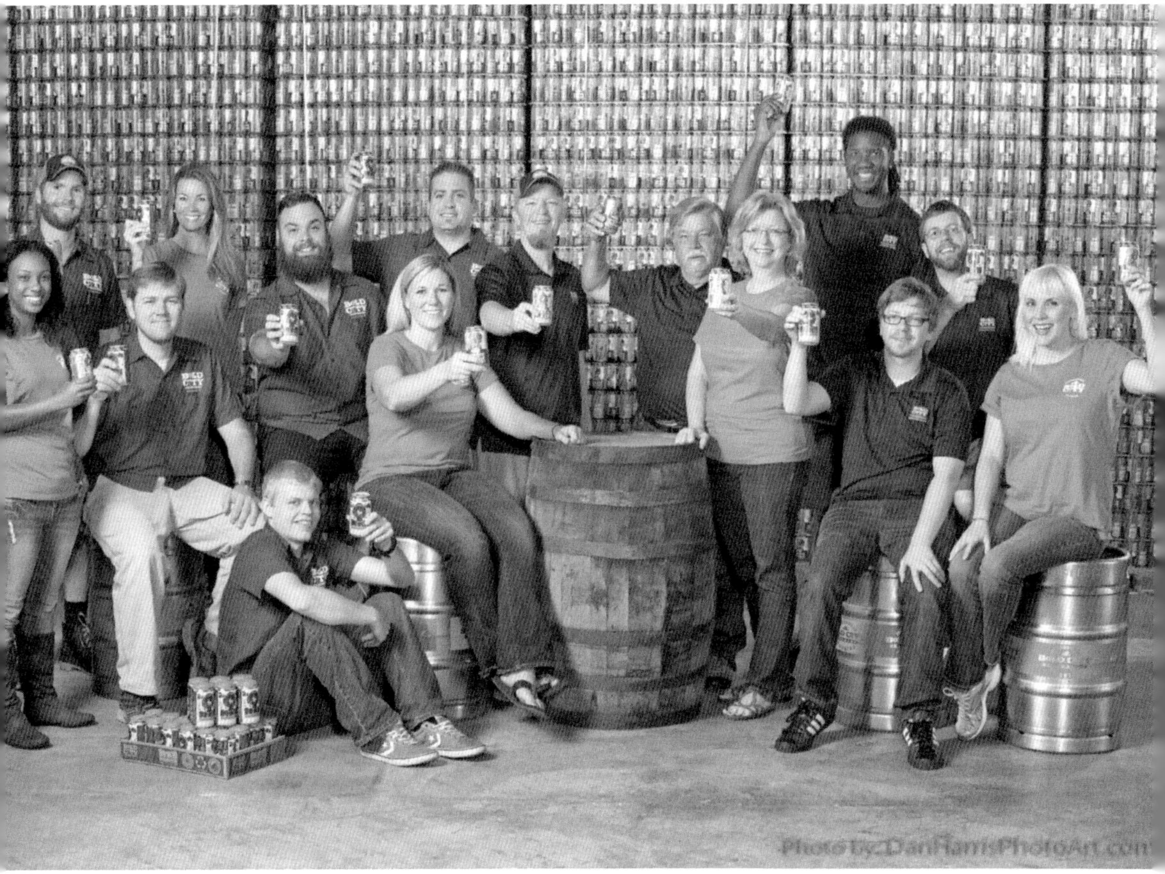

**Family Brew**

While sitting at his desk at work, Brian Miller sent his mom, Susan, an e-mail that said, "Let's start a brewery." The Millers, a close family, always talked about how nice it would be to have a family business and be able to work together. When Brian's passion for home-brewing began to expand beyond his backyard, he knew it was time to take the next step.

A trip to San Diego for a craft brewers' conference sold Susan on the idea. She quit her job of 23 years at Blue Cross and Blue Shield of Florida and took out equity against her house because she believed in her son and his vision.

Bold City Brewery opened in 2008. Out of its 11 employees, seven are family members, and that is not counting the four-legged family members, Barley and Beryl, who go to work most days at the brewery.

As owners of a community-grown business, Brian and Susan always make sure to take care of Jacksonville first. They help germinate a microbrewing community with other craft brewers coming to the River City, and they hope to leave Bold City to the next generation of Millers. (Photograph by Dan Harris Photo Art; courtesy of Bold City Brewery.)

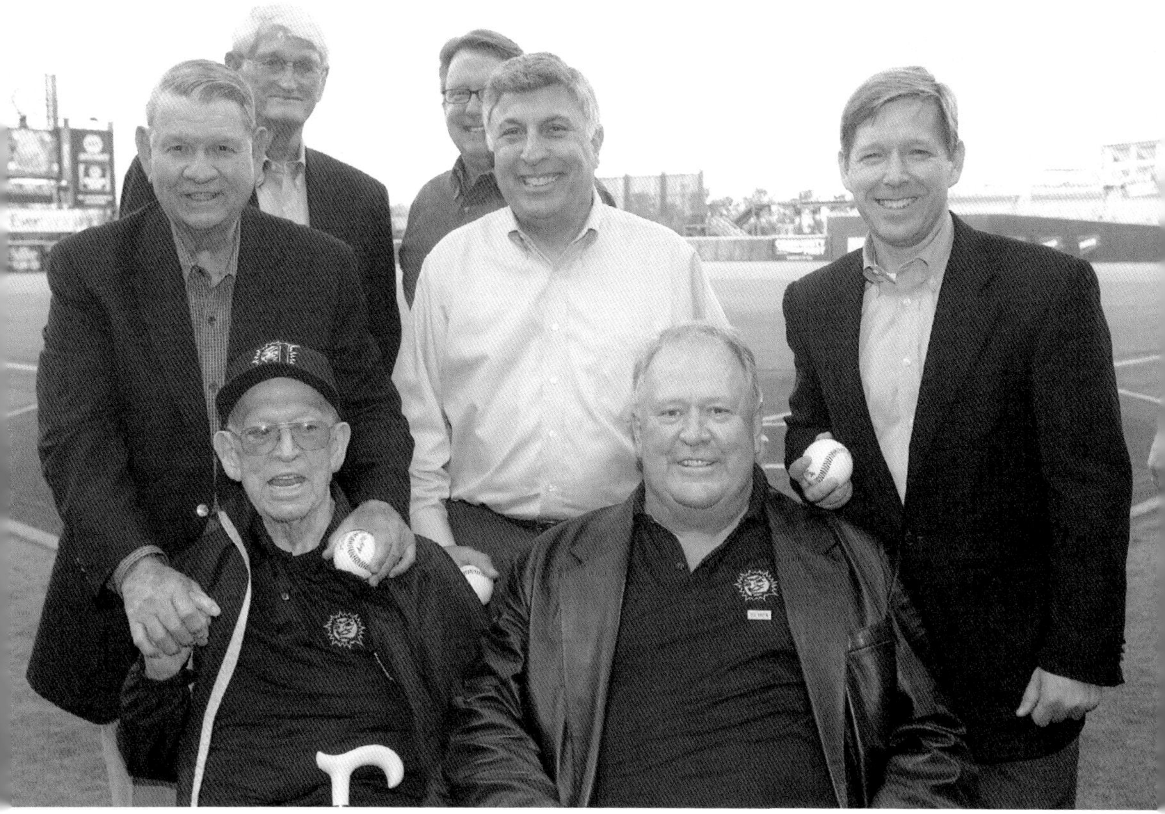

### Take Me Out to the Ball Game

In Jacksonville, the name Bragan has been synonymous with baseball since 1984, when an automobile dealer from Birmingham, Alabama, bought the Jacksonville Suns. Peter Bragan Sr. and his family renamed the Double-A team the Jacksonville Expos after an agreement with a new parent club, the Montreal Expos. In 1991, they changed the name back to the Jacksonville Suns, and the club became affiliated with the Florida Marlins in 2009.

Peter ran a winning club. The Suns won consecutive Southern League titles in 2009 and 2010. Peter and his son were also named Minor League Executives of the Year in 2004. Peter Sr. was known by mayors to be a tough negotiator, evidenced by the new Baseball Grounds of Jacksonville, a $34-million complex built as part of the Better Jacksonville Plan. But he understood baseball at a level much deeper than mere business.

Peter came from a professional baseball family, one of seven brothers who all thrived on the game. His son Peter Jr., known as "Pedro," and his daughter Bonita worked the club with him, and his wife, Mary Frances, was ever present at the games. He cultivated a family tone at the games with a clean atmosphere, fair prices, and activities for children. Families responded, helping the Suns set league attendance records. Fans looked forward to hearing his bell ring when a Suns batter hit a home run. Peter Sr. died in 2013 at age 89.

The photograph above features Peter Sr. (seated, left), Pedro, and the five Jacksonville mayors that have been in office since the time the Bragans bought Jacksonville's baseball team: (from left to right) Mayor Jake Godbold, Mayor Ed Austin, Mayor John Delaney, Mayor Tommy Hazouri, and Mayor John Peyton. (Courtesy of the Jacksonville Suns.)

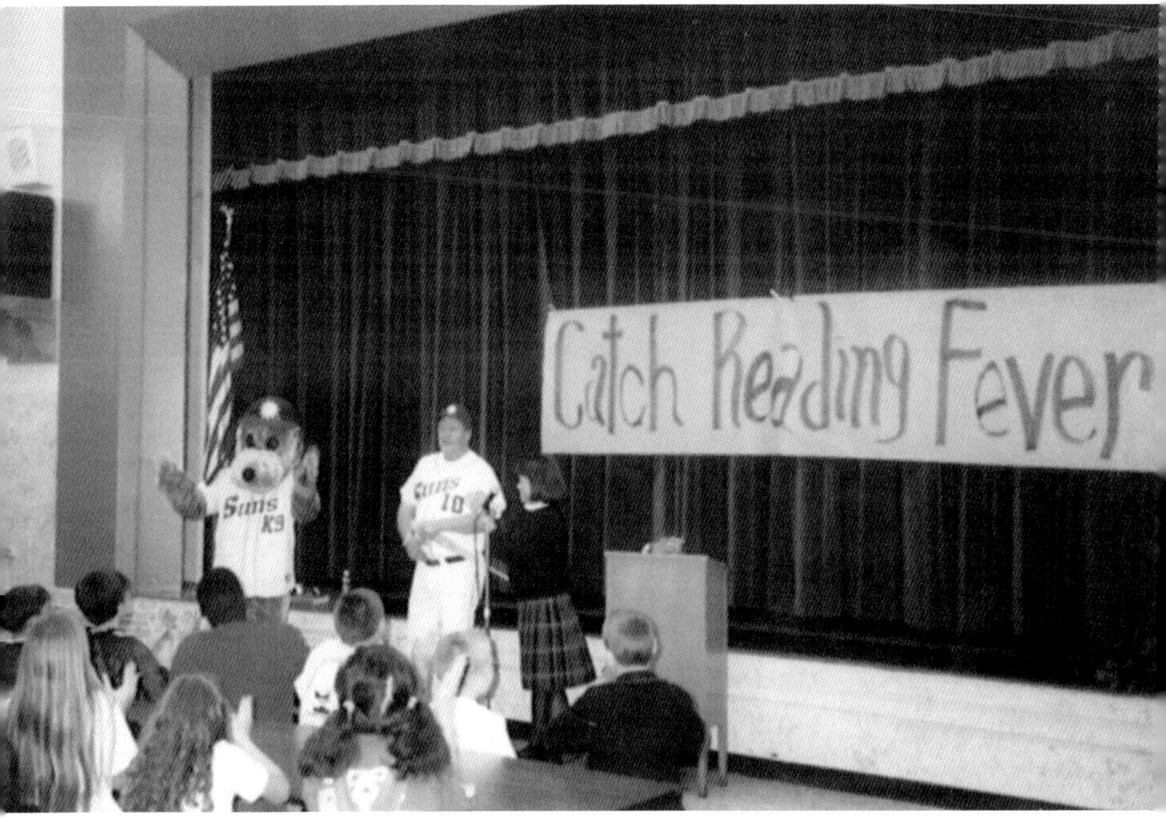


**Casey at the Bat**

Peter Bragan Jr., nicknamed Pedro by his sister, continues the Bragan family baseball legacy today. He and his father built Jacksonville's Double-A team into a winning franchise, one of the best in the Southern League. He has been known to say, "I don't work for a living. I'm in baseball."

Pedro led his college team to two straight appearances in the NJCAA World Series and played for the University of South Alabama. His peers in the Southern League twice voted him Executive of the Year.

Well known at the baseball complex and in the city, Pedro is also familiar to many schoolchildren through the Casey Challenge literacy program. For more than 20 years, Pedro, dressed in a classic baseball uniform, has recited "Casey at the Bat" at local schools and challenged students to memorize it themselves. He rewards those who do with a Suns bat or glove. It was through the challenge that Pedro met his wife, Nancy Miller, a retired elementary principal. (Courtesy of the Jacksonville Suns.)

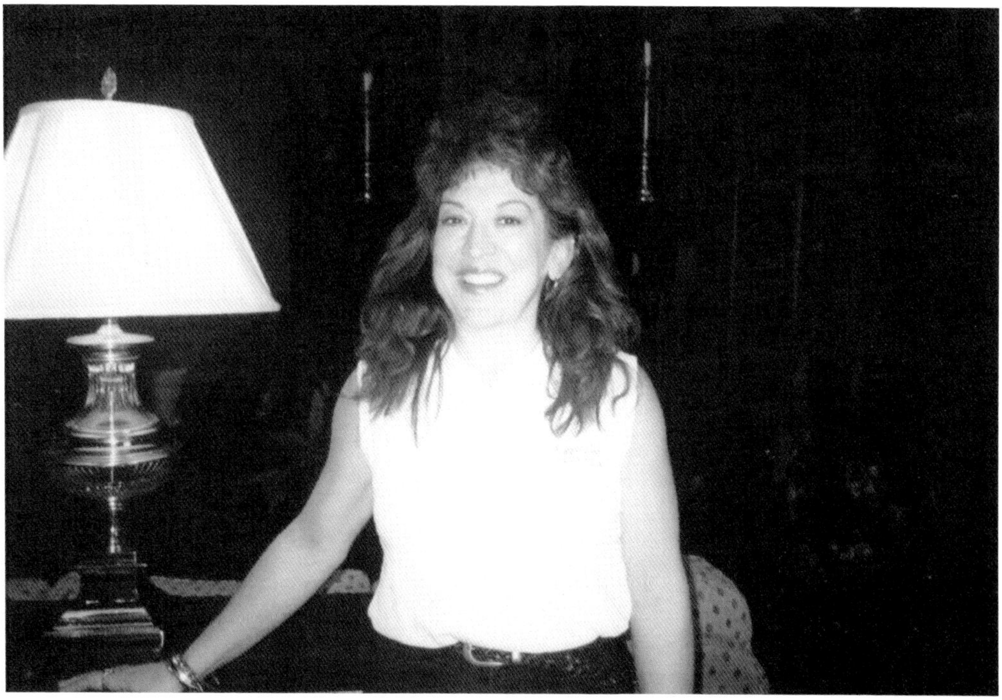

### The Lady Bragans

The first friendly face in the Suns business office is that of Bonita Bragan, daughter of Peter Sr. and Mary Frances. Bonita was a safety engineer with US Steel in Birmingham before her parents bought Jacksonville's minor league team in 1984. A jack-of-all-trades, she works as the receptionist part-time these days so she can care for her mother, Mary Frances (right), in the afternoons. Through the years, she worked in many areas of the organization, including in the old ballpark's press box, concessions, souvenirs, and with the cheerleaders (now called the Sunbeams), before moving to the front office. Bonita echoes her brother's sentiments about not feeling like her job is work. It is not that she "has to go to work," but, rather, that she "gets to work" with family. She adds, "Not many families get to do this." (Both courtesy of the Jacksonville Suns.)

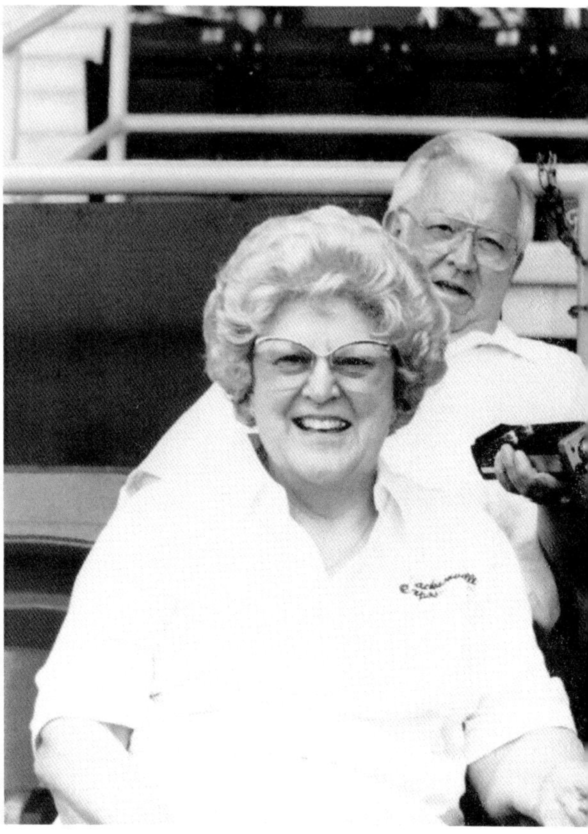

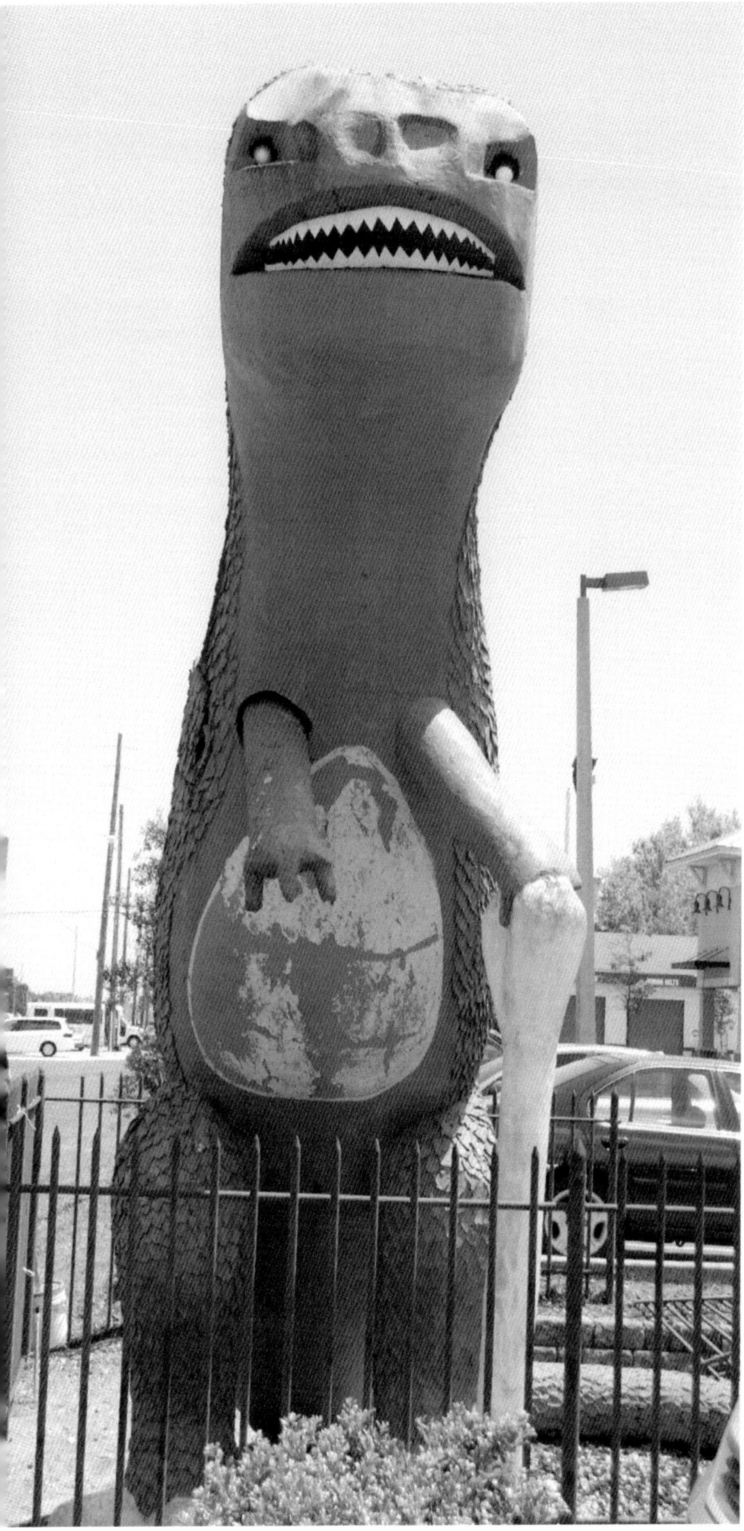

**City's Adopt-A-Rex**
Jacksonville is a city full of Southern hospitality, which it extends in odd ways at times. One such time involved the community-adopted dinosaur. It is rather difficult to miss the 20-foot, green-eyed, orange Tyrannosaurus Rex, affectionately named Rex by the locals, that has punctuated the long drive down Beach Boulevard for more than 40 years. Originally standing guard over Goony Golf, Rex faced a dim fate after the funny little golf course closed in 1999. Once the land was purchased by a developer, members of the community worried about what would happen to it. Telephone calls poured in to the new owner by the hundreds.

After more than 1,000 people voiced their concerns, the developer understood that Rex had been adopted into Jacksonville's community family and had to stay. The developer partnered with students at the University of North Florida to design the shopping center using Rex as the centerpiece.

Rex is one dinosaur that will not go extinct, as long as Jacksonville has anything to say about it. (Photograph by Kendall Brunson.)

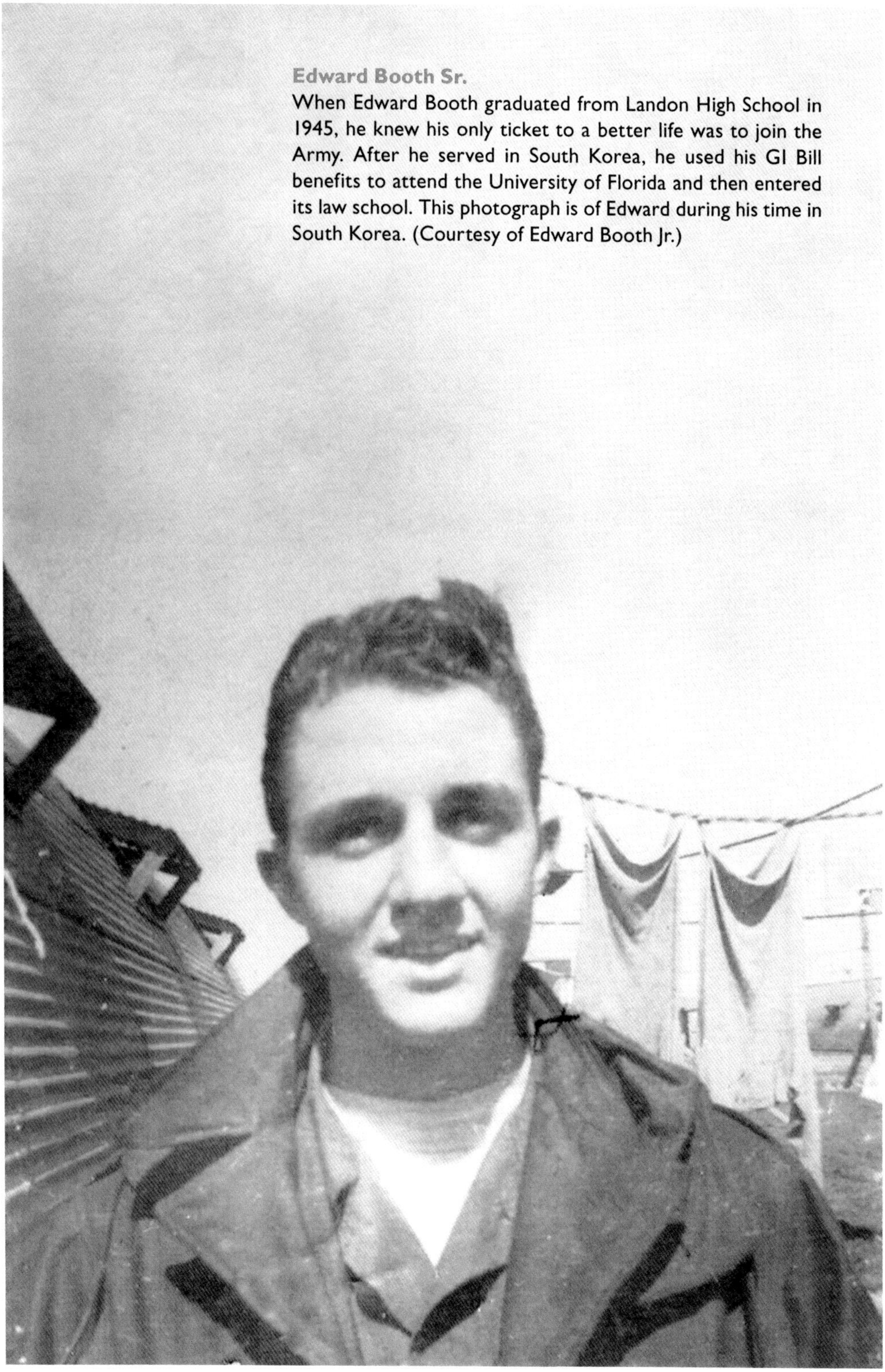

**Edward Booth Sr.**
When Edward Booth graduated from Landon High School in 1945, he knew his only ticket to a better life was to join the Army. After he served in South Korea, he used his GI Bill benefits to attend the University of Florida and then entered its law school. This photograph is of Edward during his time in South Korea. (Courtesy of Edward Booth Jr.)

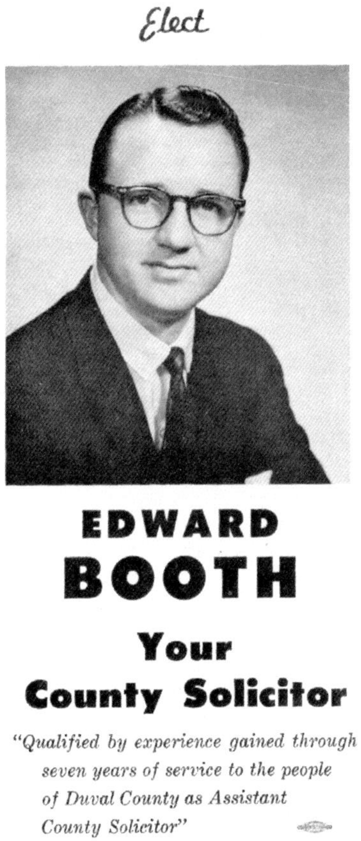


**Public Servant**
In 1959, Edward Booth ran a successful bid for county solicitor. He gave then-up-and-comer Ed Austin his first job as assistant county prosecutor.

As county solicitor, Edward worked to end segregation in Jacksonville. He hired the first African American attorney, Alfred R. Taylor, to work for city government on November 15, 1963, in conjunction with Ed Austin, who hired Leander J. Shaw, also an African American attorney who later served as chief justice of the Florida Supreme Court.

His son Edward Booth Jr. remembers when racial tensions heightened in the late 1960s, and his father successfully prosecuted four Ku Klux Klan members for a vicious attack on a black minister. The family house was protected by the police, young Ed rode to and from school in a police car, and slurs were spray-painted on the family car. (Courtesy of Edward Booth Jr.)

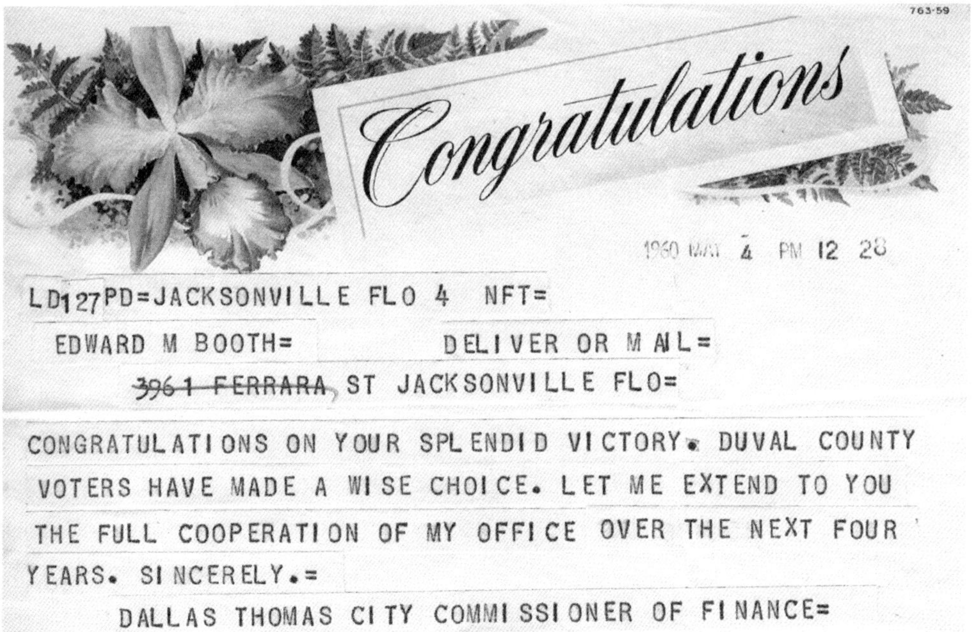
763-59

Congratulations

1960 MAY 4 PM 12 28

LD127PD=JACKSONVILLE FLO 4 NFT=
EDWARD M BOOTH= DELIVER OR MAIL=
~~3961 FERRARA~~ ST JACKSONVILLE FLO=

CONGRATULATIONS ON YOUR SPLENDID VICTORY. DUVAL COUNTY VOTERS HAVE MADE A WISE CHOICE. LET ME EXTEND TO YOU THE FULL COOPERATION OF MY OFFICE OVER THE NEXT FOUR YEARS. SINCERELY.=
DALLAS THOMAS CITY COMMISSIONER OF FINANCE=

**Note of Irony**
This 1960 congratulatory telegram to Edward Booth from the county commissioner of finance, Dallas Thomas, became ironic in 1966 when Edward sent Thomas to prison for public corruption. (Courtesy of Edward Booth Jr.)

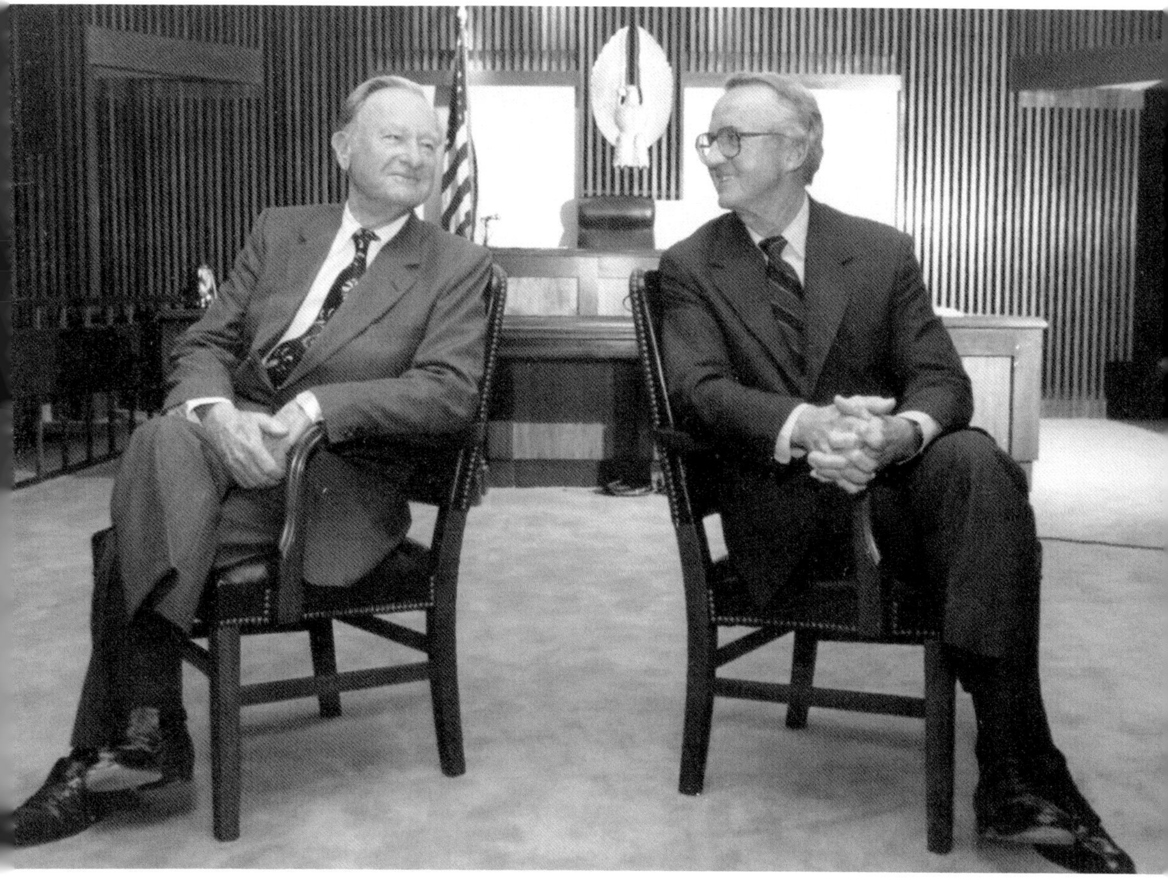

**Private Practice**

After he left his job as county commissioner, Edward went into private practice with his brother-in-law Walter Arnold. As a private attorney, Edward tried many notable cases, including the first fatal air piracy case.

He also successfully defended Alan Griffin Stanford Jr., who was charged with the murder of his next-door neighbor Athalia Ponsell Lindsley, a former model and actress. The two neighbors feuded, and after Athalia was found beheaded on her front porch in St. Augustine one morning, Alan was suspect number one. The case garnered national attention, including a fictional book based on the case, *Bloody Sunset*, and an A&E television special.

This photograph is of Walter Arnold and Edward Booth in 1992. (Courtesy of Edward Booth Jr.)

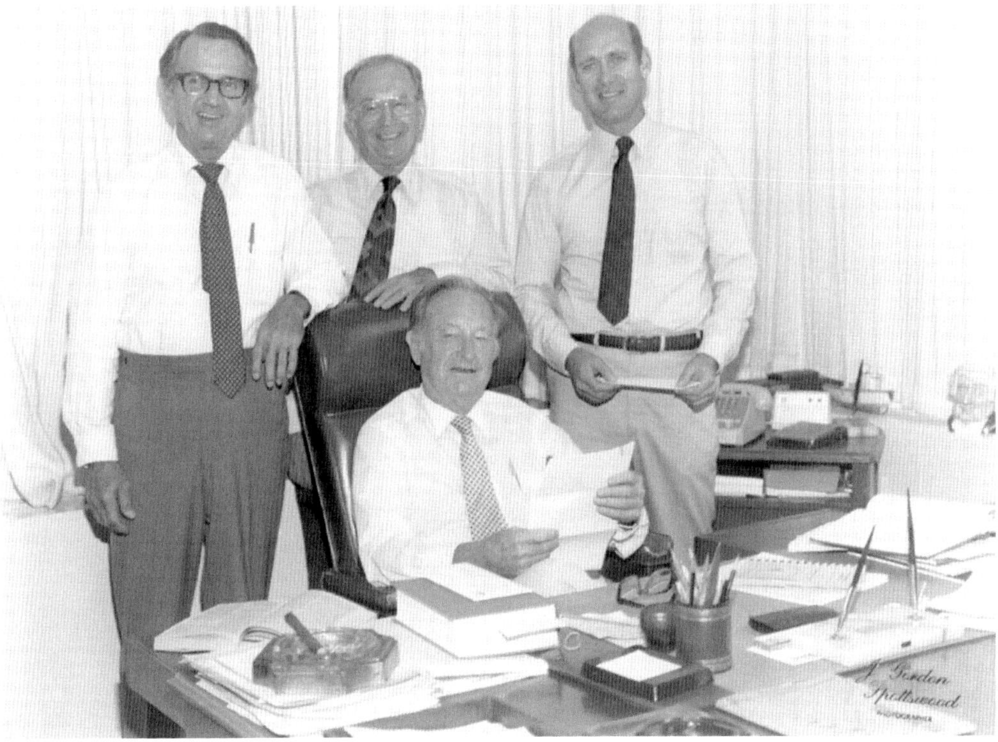

### Walter Arnold

Walter Arnold was considered one of the preeminent trial attorneys on the First Coast. Upon his death in 2009, Walter had been a member of the Florida Bar for 72 years. Although he was already a lawyer and assistant county solicitor, he joined the Naval Reserves after the bombing of Pearl Harbor. He began in Naval Intelligence but requested a combat position. Walter then participated in the invasions of Bataan, Mindanao, and Borneo, among others.

After he left active duty, Walter resumed his position as assistant county solicitor. He had several private practice firms, including one with his brother-in-law Edward Booth.

This photograph was taken at their private practice. Seated is Walter Arnold, and standing behind him from left to right are Edward Booth, Walter's nephew Chuck Arnold, and Steve Stratford. (Courtesy of Edward Booth Jr.)

### Carrying the Torch

Edward Booth Jr. always wanted to be a lawyer, like his father and uncle. Inspired that his father tried the first aviation piracy case, Edward Jr. earned his board certification in aviation law.

Edward Jr. began his career under the leadership of State Attorney Ed Austin as an assistant state attorney, along with fellow rising star John Delaney.

This photograph shows Edward Jr. and his father in 2006 standing in front of a 1982 Mercedes that has been driven by three generations of family members. It is still used daily today, with more than 360,000 miles on the odometer. (Courtesy of Edward Booth Jr.)

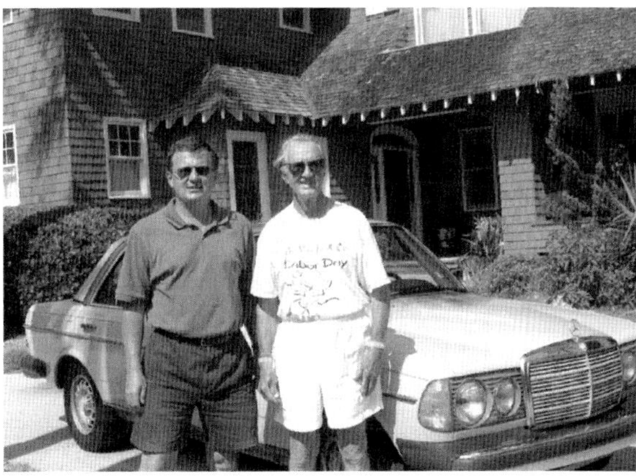

### A Sweet Idea

No name is sweeter than Peterbrooke. By the time Phyllis Lockwood Geiger moved to Jacksonville, she had spent years training in the art of European chocolate making.

Knowing her chocolate had to be the best, Phyllis traveled to the Nestle Fabrika in Switzerland, where she worked with chocolatiers on special blends for Peterbrooke. Named after her two children, Peter and Brooke, the first shop opened in 1983 in San Marco Square.

The most popular item, chocolate-covered popcorn, was invented a few years later. For a holiday party, Phyllis needed a tasty item she could share but that would not break the bank. She bought bags of popcorn from the San Marco Movie Theatre and covered them with melted chocolate. The item became so frequently requested that Phyllis knew she had a hit on her hands. (Courtesy of Phyllis Lockwood Geiger.)

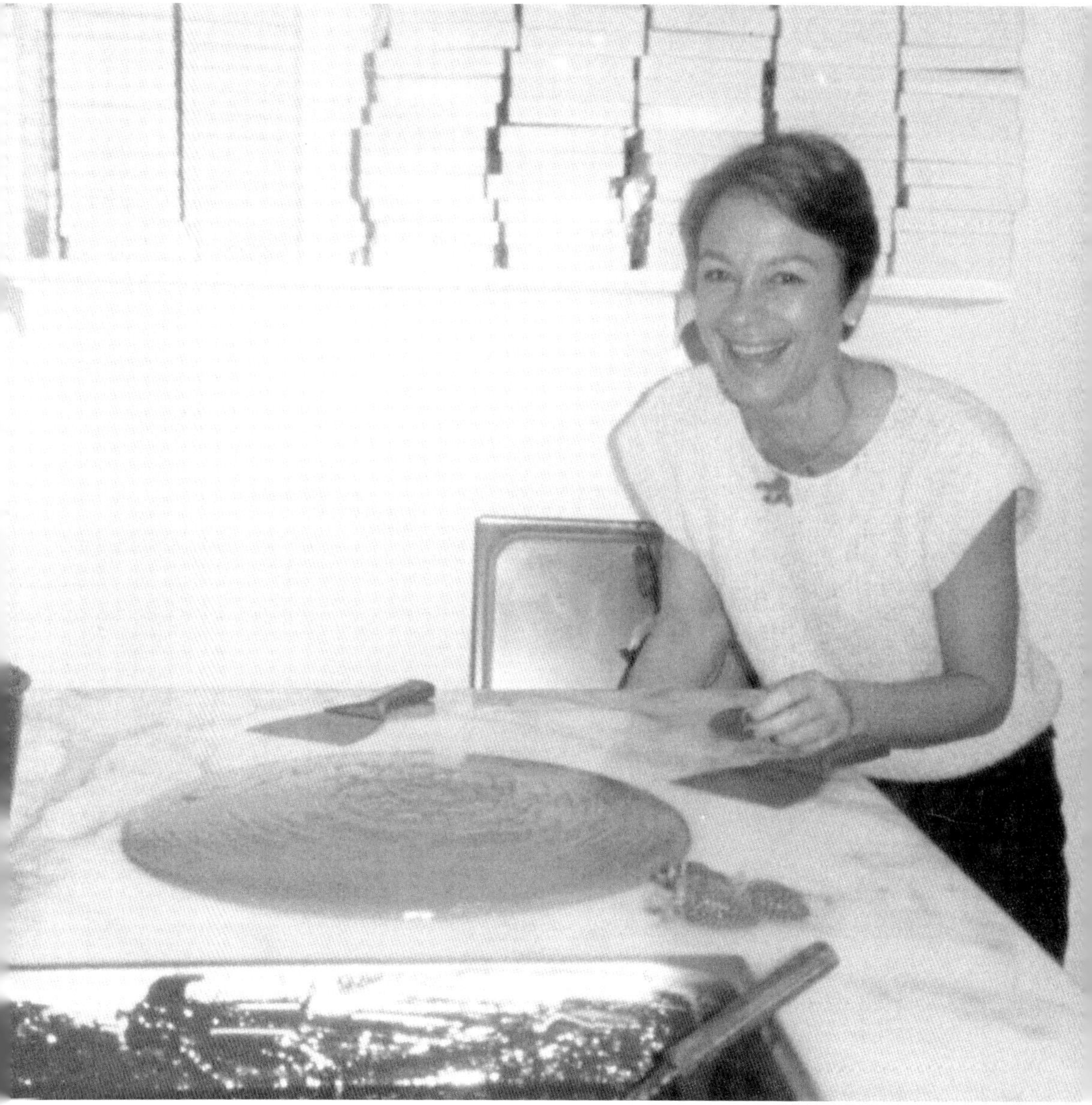

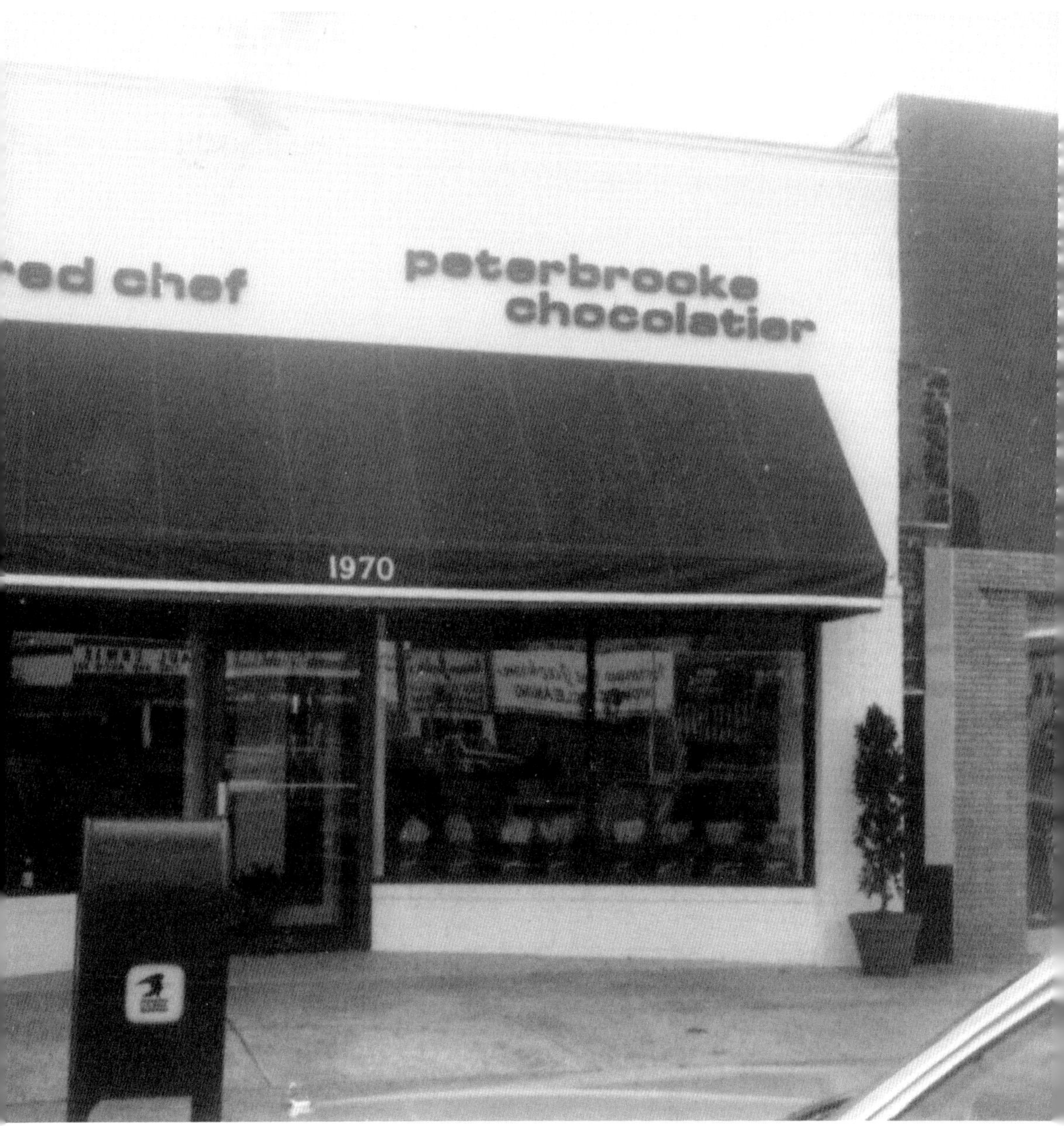


**A Sweet Beginning**

This is the first Peterbrooke location in San Marco Square. While there is still a location in the square, it is now a few doors down in the adjacent shopping center. There are more than a dozen Peterbrooke shops throughout the First Coast. (Courtesy of Phyllis Lockwood Geiger.)

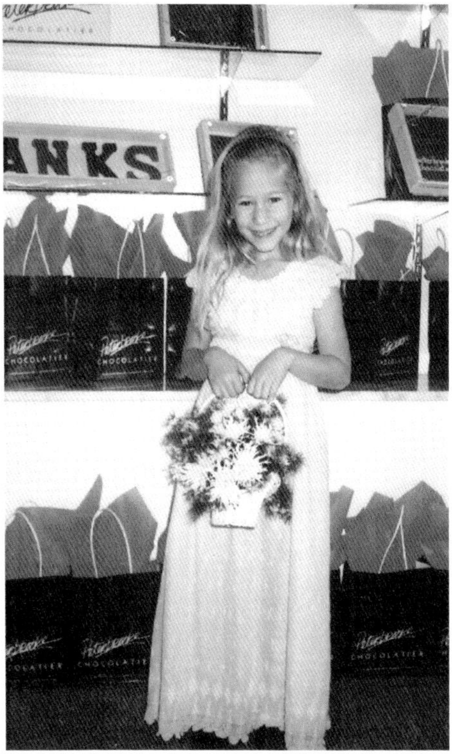

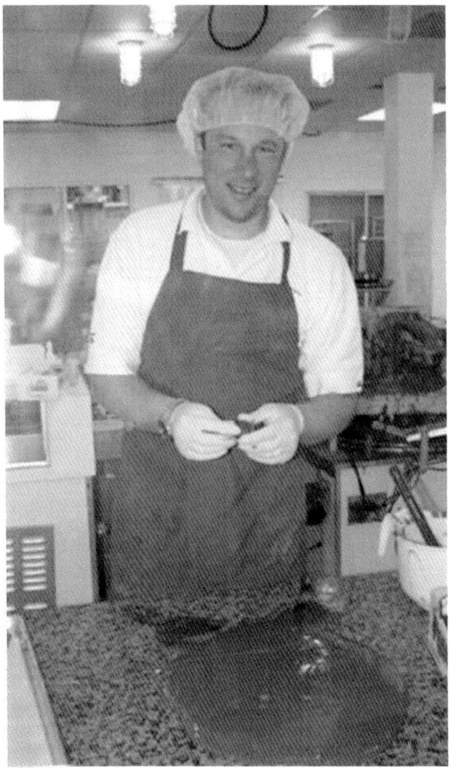

**A Sweet Tradition**

What Phyllis Lockwood Geiger loves most about the candy industry is that it tends be a family business. Not only did her children grow up behind the counter and help her run it, but families also buy and run Peterbrooke franchises together.

Brooke Joyner, pictured above on opening day of the original shop in San Marco Square, now owns and operates her own Peterbrooke location in Atlantic Beach. Her brother Peter Behringer (below) owns his own candy shop as well: Sweet Pete's.

Is there anything sweeter? (Both courtesy of Phyllis Lockwood Geiger.)

### A Big Roar

Curt LoGiudice has an extended family living in his backyard—about 50 big cats, to be exact—who find sanctuary at the Catty Shack Ranch in the Northside. Curt began breeding shar-peis and training police dogs, when he fell in love with exotic and endangered animals and knew he wanted to spend his life saving them.

In 2005, he purchased 10 acres in north Jacksonville for his big cats, many of which come from closing zoos. Unlike other sanctuaries or zoos, Curt feeds his cats at night, when they eat the most, because they are nocturnal. Visitors travel from all over the world to see these night feedings, and they have kept the Catty Shack Ranch the number-one attraction on Trip Advisor.

Curt has created a symbiotic relationship with the community. Local schoolchildren come to tour the sanctuary, and University of North Florida students helped build better habitats and food platforms for the lions, tigers, and leopards. Curt keeps the three miles of road fronting the sanctuary litter-free under the city's adopt-a-road program. He is also close with his neighbors, who often open their front yards for parking.

Besides the cats, Curt also keeps chickens and three horses, which help maintain the 244 acres of wetlands adjacent to the sanctuary. He does not allow hunters and rescues injured animals until they can be released back into their habitat.

The Catty Shack is a self-funded nonprofit. Despite his personal sacrifices for his animals, he says the commitment is more than worth the effort: "Every day is a day in paradise." It is not always easy to stock the three walk-in freezers and the cat's vitamin and mineral supplements, but Curt's children, who grew up with exotic animals, also work and volunteer at the Catty Shack.

Just do not ask which cat is Curt's favorite. He looks around with a worried glance and a twinkle in his eye and says, "Shhh. They're listening." (Courtesy of Curt LoGiudice.)

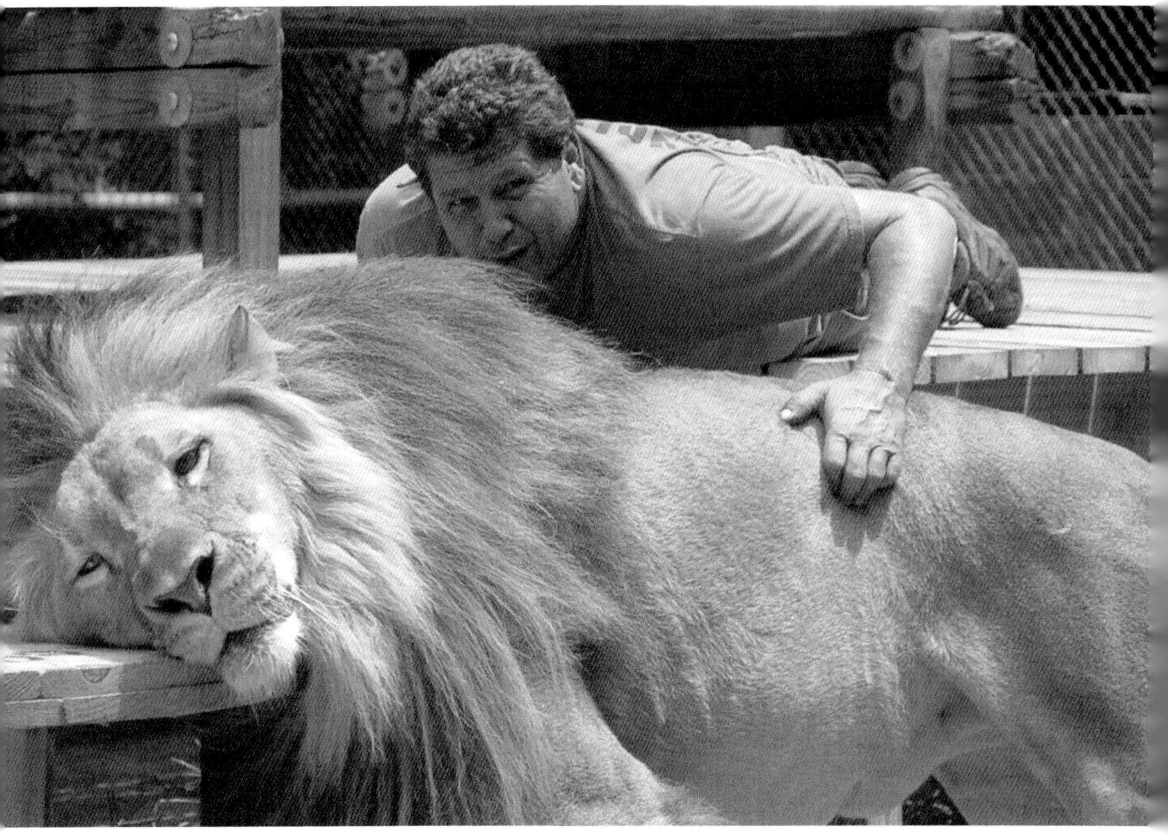

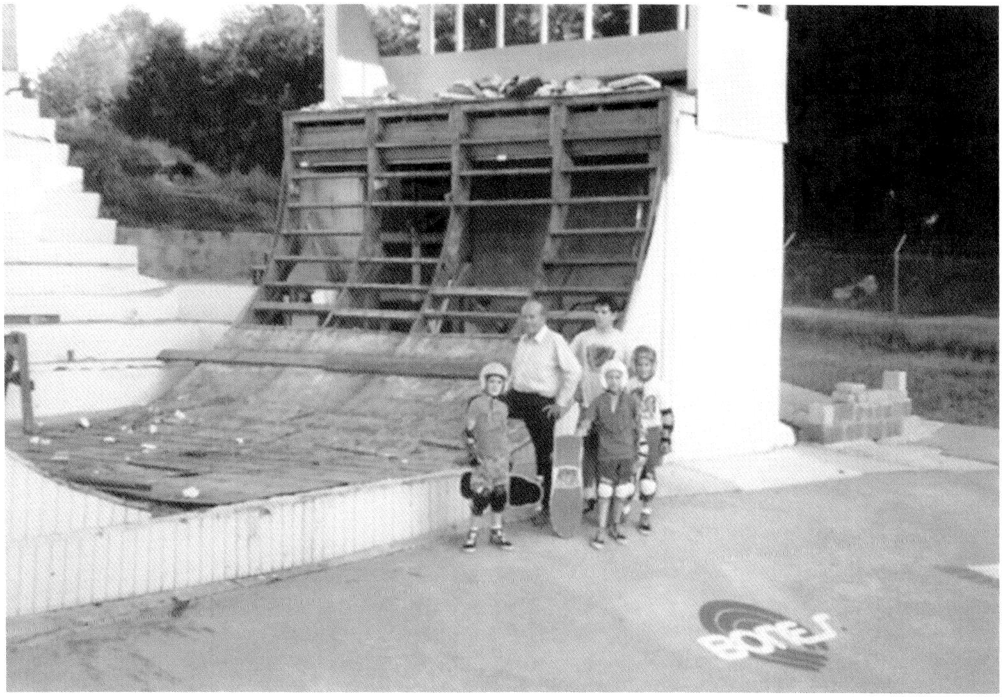


**Skater Life**

Martin Ramos always had an entrepreneurial spirit. When the local skate park, Kona, closed, and his son no longer had any place to skate, Martin purchased it. More than 35 years later, his skater son, Martin Ramos III, manages Kona.

Martin III's parents worked to develop a safe place for families and children with a welcoming atmosphere. Father and son are pictured here with skaters in front of a ramp being repaired. (Courtesy of Martin Ramos III.)

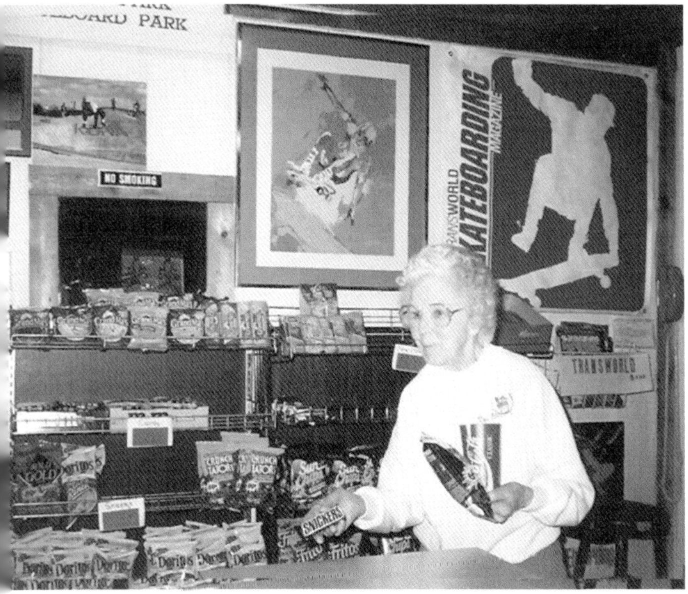


**Grandma Peabody**

Martin III credits Grandma Peabody with keeping Kona open. "It was her money and faith in our vision that made Kona possible for the Ramos Family." She passed away in 2001, two days after Martin III's wedding to his wife, Laurie. In this photograph, Grandma Peabody works the Kona counter. (Courtesy of Martin Ramos III.)

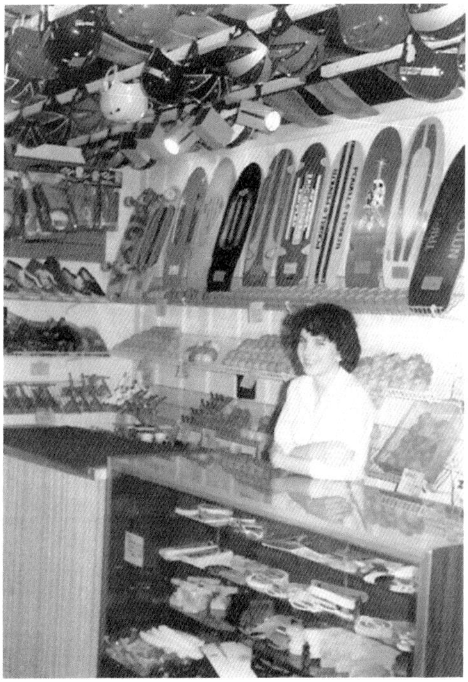

**Afterschool Job**

Martin III and his sisters Stacy and Michelle grew up working the shop, learning the family business early on. Martin III is now sharing the family traditions with his three daughters. This photograph shows Michelle working at Kona. (Courtesy of Martin Ramos III.)

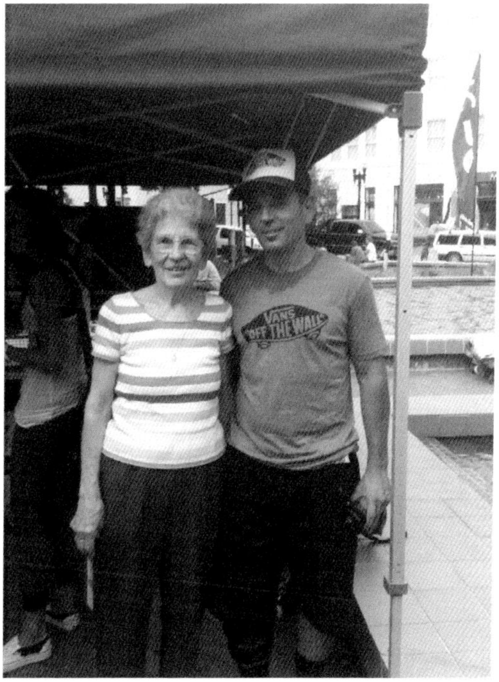


**Helen and Martin III**

After his father's passing in 1995, Martin III took over Kona operations. Tony Hawk, who first skated there at age 14, featured Martin III and his mother, Helen, in his video game *Tony Hawk Pro Skater 4*. It has brought such attention to the park and the family that they have had visitors travel all the way from Colombia just to skate there. Helen and Martin III are seen here at a Go Skate Day. (Photograph by Stefan Judge; courtesy of Martin Ramos III.)

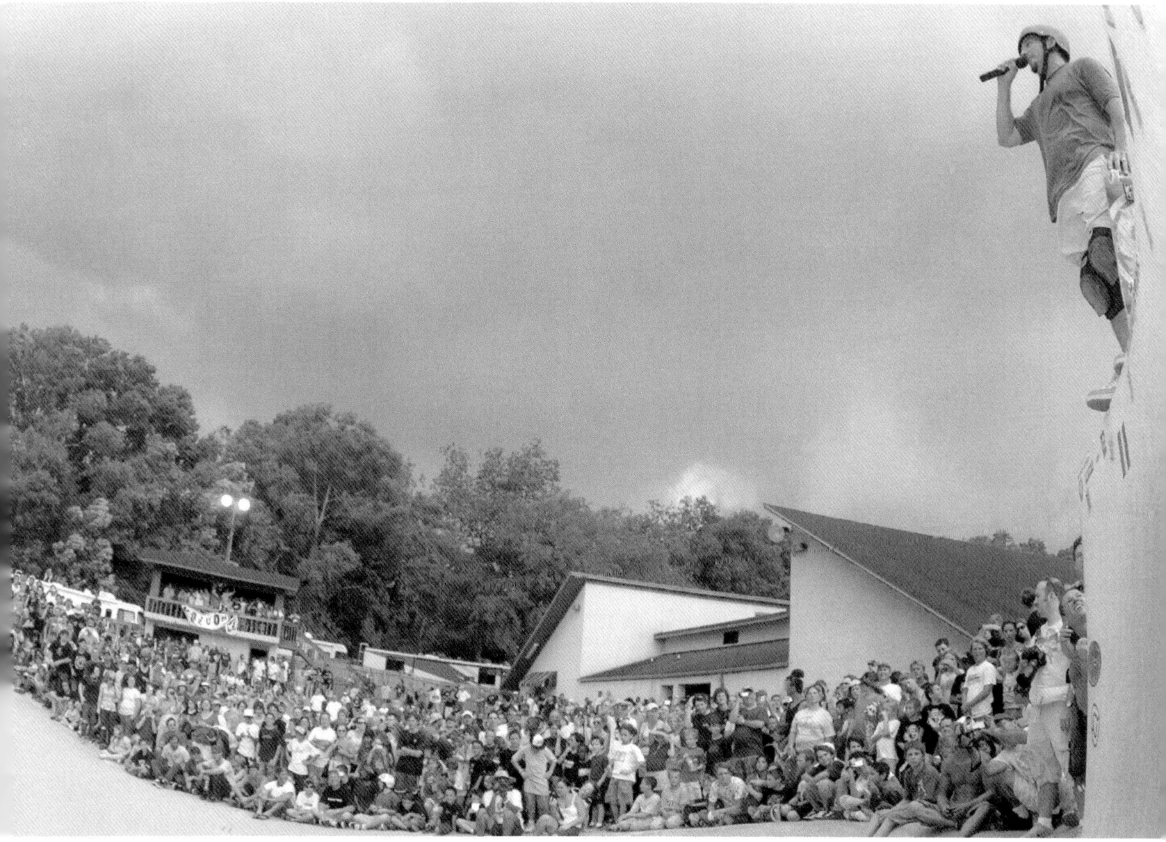

### Three Decades Later

Although Kona's impact on skating culture is without question, it remains a community park. Martin Ramos III says multiple generations have now experienced the park. "It's great to see adults who used to skate here bring their kids to experience it for the first time. They're sharing the heritage with the next generation." Here, Martin III hosts Kona's 30th-anniversary party. (Photograph by Stefan Judge; courtesy of Martin Ramos III.)

# CHAPTER THREE

# Heroes, Leaders, and Other Legends

With its diverse population, significant military presence, and a climate that invites activity year-round, Jacksonville provides the perfect setting for heroes, natural leaders, and other legends.

From war heroes to Olympic champions, Jacksonville is home to an eclectic cast of legendary characters.

Retired Navy captain Chet Smith earned the Navy Cross, the second-highest military decoration for valor, but he treasures the Silver Star more, because he received that "for saving lives."

Jacksonville is also home to writer Stetson Kennedy, who infiltrated the Ku Klux Klan, helped revoke the Klan's corporate charter in Georgia, and exposed secret code words and rituals.

In an obituary, the *Washington Post* called Tillie Fowler a "Steel Magnolia," often "described as a hybrid of a Southern belle and a Marine drill sergeant." Those were words the former congresswoman and top-ranking woman in the Republican Party heard often and considered compliments.

Charlie Bennett wrote nine books on North Florida's history and worked tirelessly to preserve Jacksonville's treasures, such as Fort Caroline and the Timucuan Preserve. He is best remembered as a beloved congressman who served from 1949 to 1993, whose constituency elected him to the office 23 times.

Nat Glover, who listened to crime-buster stories on Radio Theatre growing up in Jacksonville's projects, is now the president of his alma mater, Edward Waters College. It was the first black college and the first independent institution of higher learning in Florida. Before being named college president, Nat was elected Jacksonville's first black sheriff after a highly successful career with the sheriff's office.

America's boycott of the 1980 Olympics in Moscow forced swimmer Nancy Hogshead to set aside her hopes of a gold medal. However, she earned a team spot for the 1984 Olympics and brought home three gold medals and a silver.

The stories of these and other heroes, leaders, and legends serve as more than interesting tales. They also set the bar for those who want to live their lives to the fullest and pave the way for future generations.

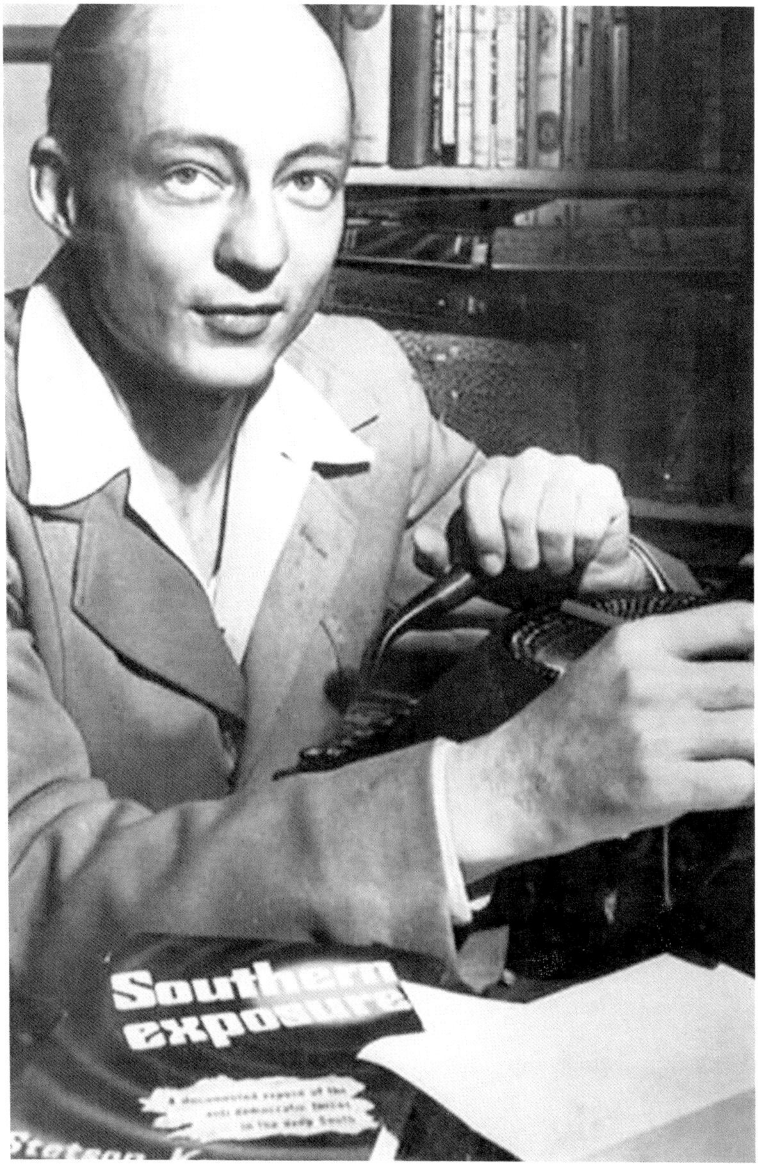

**Stetson Kennedy**

Jacksonville native Stetson Kennedy knew the pen was mightier than the sword. And no less than the Ku Klux Klan felt the sting of Kennedy's pen. Kennedy infiltrated the Klan and other white supremacist groups as early as the 1940s. His writings helped revoke the Klan's corporate charter in Georgia and exposed secret code words and rituals. According to the Stetson Kennedy website, he passed Klan secrets to the writers of the Superman radio program, culminating in a series in which Superman battled the KKK. In 1937, Kennedy dropped out of a creative writing course taught by Marjorie Keenan Rawlings to join the Florida Writers' Project. He led a statewide effort to collect Florida folklore and supervised the work of writer Zora Neale Hurston. Among the books he wrote are *Southern Exposure*, published in 1947, *The Klan Unmasked*, published in 1954, and a history of Florida folklore, *Palmetto Country*. Kennedy was an advocate for the environment and civil rights. He died in 2011, just weeks before his 95th birthday. (Courtesy of the Stetson Kennedy Foundation, www.StetsonKenney.com.)

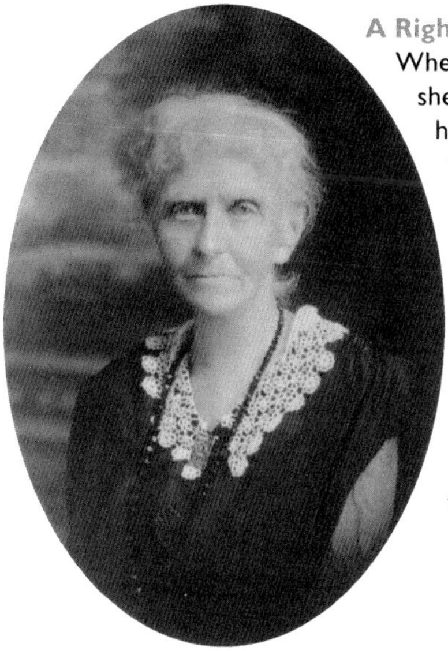

### A Right to Vote

When Mary A. Nolan joined the National Woman's Party in 1917, she was more than 70 years old, one of the oldest suffragettes. She had traveled from Jacksonville to Washington, DC, to protest the arrest of party leaders, when she herself was arrested for blocking traffic. Mary was in the Occoquan Workhouse in Virginia on the "Night of Terror," November 15, 1917, when guards violently abused the imprisoned suffragettes. Upon her release, she immediately resumed protesting. Mary was arrested many times for fighting for women's right to vote, and she was one of the first registered women voters in Jacksonville. Although she dedicated the later part of her life to the National Woman's Party, she did not have many opportunities to cast her vote. She died in 1925. (Courtesy of the Library of Congress.)

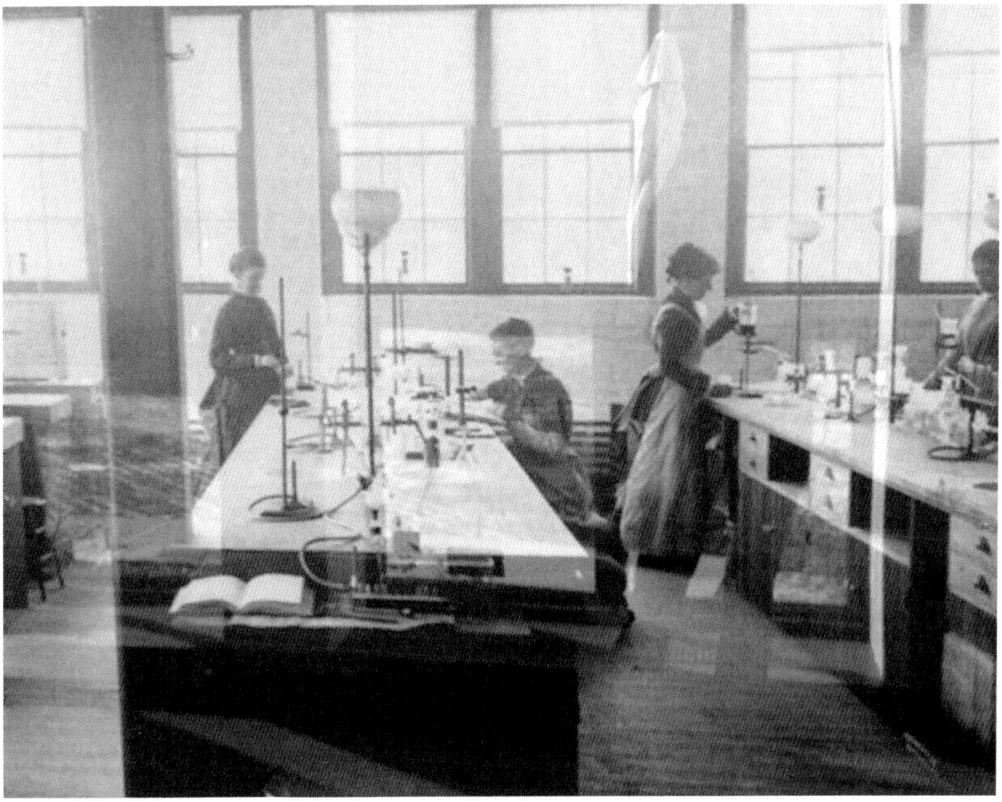

### Anita Tyng

While Anita E. Tyng was the first female doctor appointed to serve in a hospital in Boston, in 1865, she was turned down to study at Harvard because the school did not accept women. It is not known when she opened her practice in Jacksonville, but Dr. Tyng was the resident physician at St. Luke's Hospital. She lived in Arlington. (Courtesy of Stephen Dare, www.MetroJacksonville.com.)

### Ed Jackson

After learning to fly at the end of World War II, Navy aviator Edward D. Jackson fought in the sky over Korea in 1950. As he dove toward enemy troops, aerial cables strung by Koreans to capture enemy planes shattered the right wingtip of his F9F Panther. A cable whipped through the windshield, gashing Ed's face and head, leaving him momentarily unconscious. It also left him temporarily blind.

After regaining consciousness, he radioed his wingman, who talked him through the flight back to the USS *Philippine Sea*, where a lieutenant helped him perform a "normal" landing. Ed first saw the flight deck when the flight surgeon climbed up and wiped the blood from his eyes. Amazingly, Ed had no permanent damage to his eyes, but he was left with a scar on his cheek. He continued his Navy career, training the forces deploying to Vietnam, and then retired in Jacksonville in 1975 as a commander with 31 years of service.

His granddaughter Nikki says her grandfather was her hero. He was a larger-than-life man with a big heart. She says, "He would give you the shirt off his back if you needed it." After retiring, he opened a used car dealership on 103rd Street, halfway between two military bases, NAS Jacksonville and Cecil Field. But Ed was an atypical used car salesman; he never made any money at it because he basically gave the cars to the servicemen at cost. He died in 2010 at the age of 85 and is buried in the Jacksonville National Cemetery.

The photograph, taken after Ed landed his plane on the USS *Philippine Sea*, shows the gash and blood on his face from the cable that snapped his windshield. (Courtesy of Nikki Jackson Smith.)

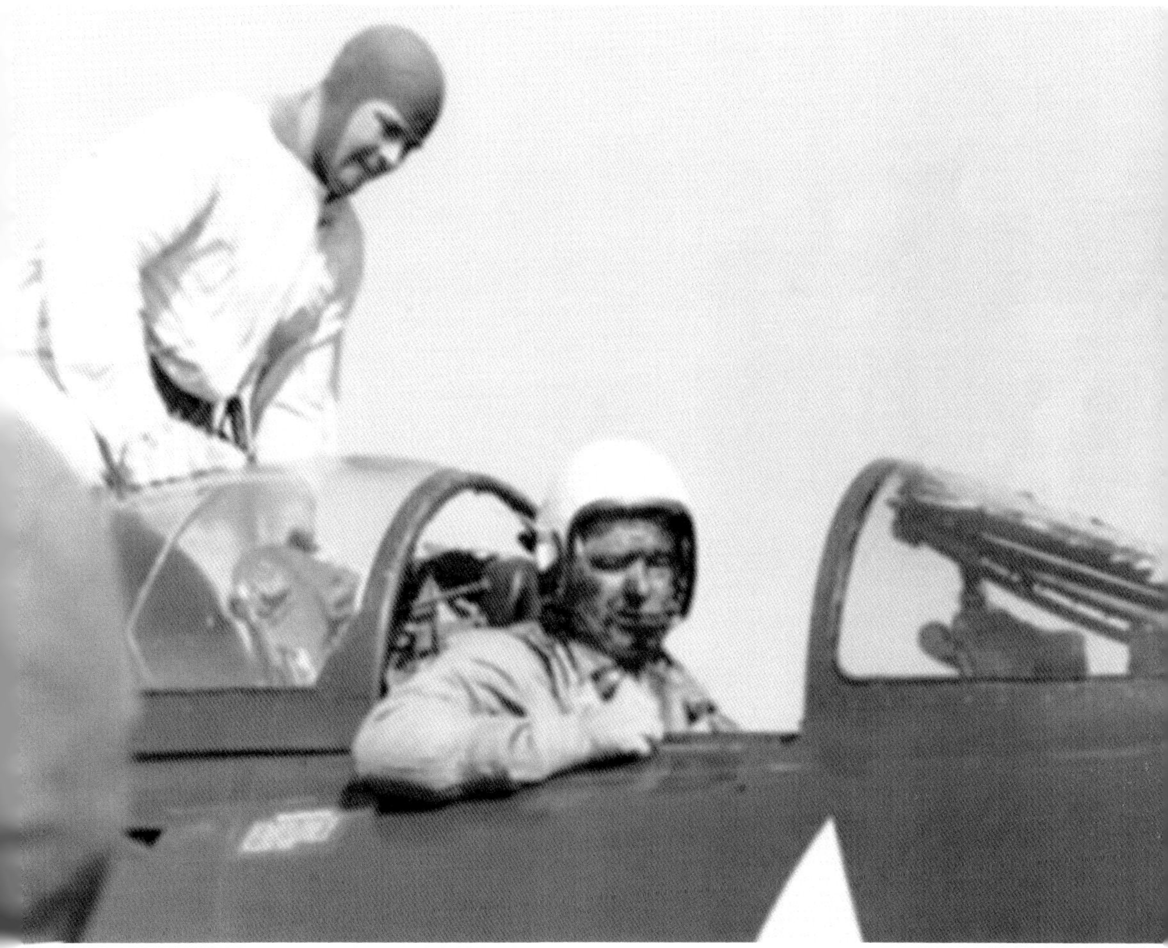

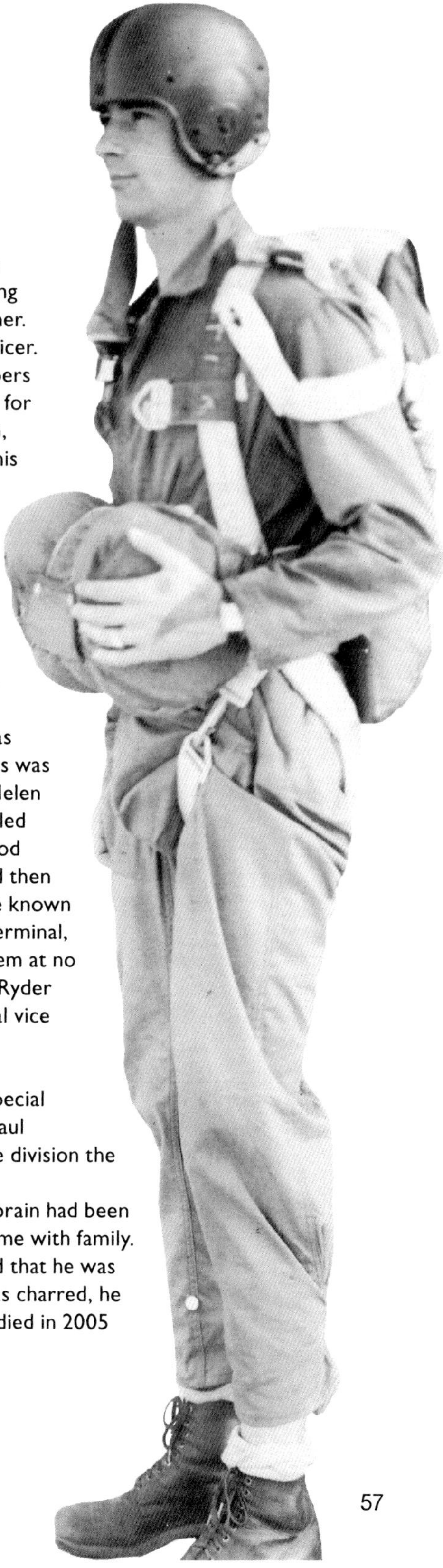

### LeGrand "Legs" King Johnson

When LeGrand "Legs" King Johnson graduated from North Carolina State University, he held a degree in civil engineering in one hand and orders to report to Fort Benning in the other. His ROTC experience opened the door to training as an officer. Newly married to "Petey" Graham, he joined the paratroopers for the extra $100 a month. Legs was company commander for F Company of the 101st Airborne in the Normandy invasion, where enemy fire blew off the back of his head, destroying his optic nerve. He was left in "the dead pile" at the battalion aid station. When retrieving his captain's dog tags, Sgt. Charles Dohun discovered him breathing and forced a field surgeon to work on him at gunpoint. Later, his commanding officer asked Dohun if he understood that his action qualified for a court-martial. Dohun said yes, and the officer arrested him for exactly one minute before sending him back to his unit, reportedly the shortest court-martial on record.

Although Legs survived, he needed long-term care and was sent back to the States. With his optic nerve destroyed, Legs was blind, and he learned to read braille from none other than Helen Keller. After a very brief stint as a counselor for other disabled veterans—his "quit your belly-aching" attitude was not a good fit—Legs worked as an estimator for a cement company and then as a safety man for Roadway Express truck lines. He became known for his "get it done" efficiency. As manager of the Chicago terminal, the firm's biggest and busiest, he solved the high theft problem at no cost by having drivers park their rigs back-to-back. In 1964, Ryder Truck Lines hired him, and they eventually made him regional vice president based out of Jacksonville.

After a call from the federal government requesting help transporting rockets to Cape Canaveral, Legs created the special commodities division and secured the permits required to haul oversize loads. Influenced by his Army service, he named the division the Ryder Rangers.

A brain scan in the 1990s showed that the left side of his brain had been destroyed, but it never stopped him from success, golf, or time with family. Even with his can-do, will-do approach, his daughter recalled that he was also always positive. Once when he was served food that was charred, he replied, "Oh, the burns are my favorite part." Legs Johnson died in 2005 with Petey at his side. (Courtesy of Kathy Johnson Vann.)

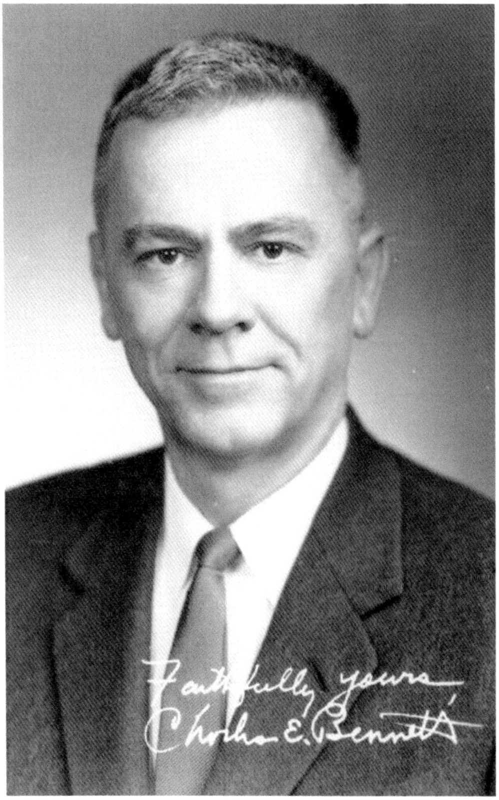


### Charles E. Bennett

Any of Charlie Bennett's pursuits would set his life apart. He wrote nine books on North Florida's history and worked to preserve local treasures such as Fort Caroline and the Timucuan Preserve. He received the Distinguished Eagle Scout Award for at least 25 years of service after attaining the level of Eagle Scout. He was a devoted family man, churchgoer, lawyer, and wounded World War II veteran. Elected to the Florida House of Representatives in 1941, Charlie is better remembered for his service as Jacksonville's beloved congressman in the US House of Representatives from 1949 to 1993. His constituency elected him to the office 23 times. (Courtesy of State Archives of Florida, *Florida Memory*, www.floridamemory.com/items/show/43730.)

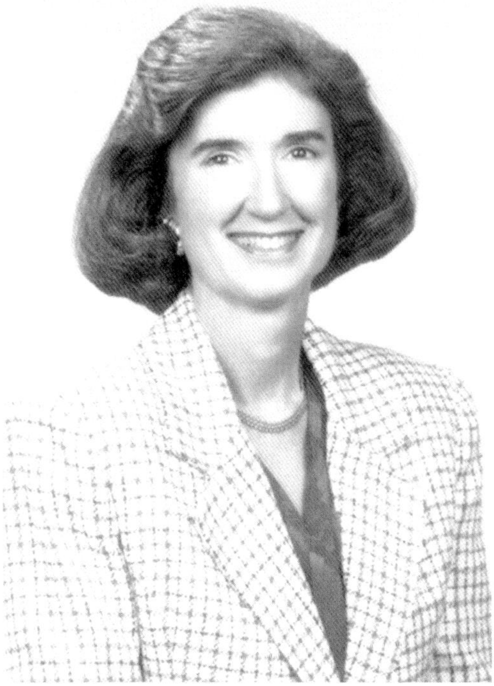

### Tillie Fowler

When Tillie Fowler died in 2005, the *Washington Post* referred to her as a "Steel Magnolia." She was often "described as a hybrid of a Southern belle and a Marine drill sergeant." These were words the former congresswoman and top-ranking woman in the Republican Party considered compliments. The first female president of Jacksonville's city council, Tillie won the seat of Congressman Charlie Bennett when he retired. She pledged to serve no more than four terms, a pledge she honored. In Congress, she championed higher defense budgets and served as the deputy majority whip for six years. (Courtesy of State Archives of Florida, *Florida Memory*, www.floridamemory.com/items/show/20780.)

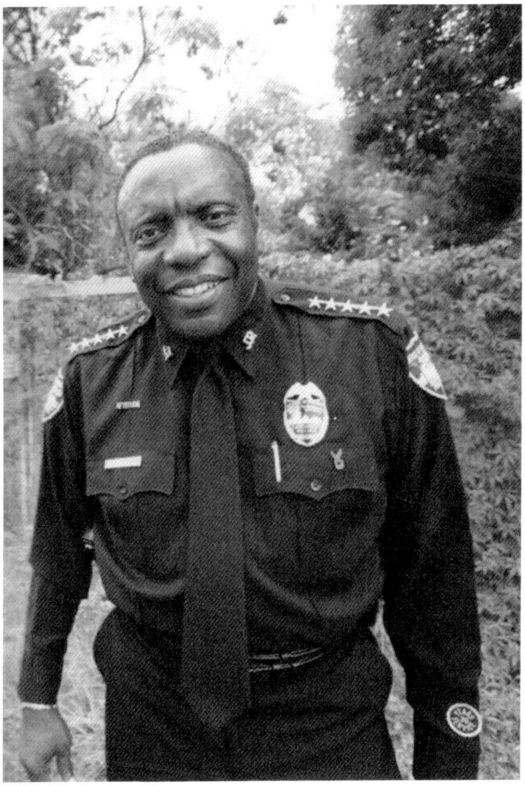

**Nat Glover**

Although a bogus arrest threatened his dream of becoming a police officer, Nathaniel "Nat" Glover not only joined the force, but he also became what many consider to be one of Jacksonville's most effective sheriffs of all time. As a boy in the inner city, Glover listened to tales of the FBI, Private Eye Michael Shayne, Gangbusters, and Dragnet on the radio, tales that instilled respect of and appreciation for "the good guys." One night in the 1960s, as he left his college job as a dishwasher at a downtown cafeteria, the police stopped him to ask about food theft at the restaurant. When he could not give them any information, they arrested him for two napkins in his back pocket.

The judge dismissed the case, but his arrest record remained, thwarting his chance of joining the force. Officer Marvin Young promised to take him to see the mayor, a promise that Glover viewed cynically until Mayor Lou Ritter greeted Young and Glover warmly. Ritter also told the Civil Service Board that if Glover passed the exams and was not hired, he would appoint a new board. Glover joined the force in 1966 and quickly rose through the ranks.

About 10 years later, Detective Glover negotiated the release of 32 passengers from an armed hijacker of a Greyhound bus. He eventually became director of police services. In 1995, Glover became the city's first black sheriff. For the eight years he was sheriff, Glover continued the practice of walking Jacksonville's neighborhoods, which he started during his campaign.

"It kept me in touch with the people and intimidated the bad guys," he said. "The city has 51 subsectors, and I walked every one of them every year I was sheriff. That's a total of 408."

On Saturdays, Sheriff Glover would pull a team together to go back to the neighborhoods where people "seemed to have given up." The sheriff, fellow officers, inmates from the jail, citizens, and neighborhood residents picked up trash and cleaned up streets.

Glover was sheriff until 2003, when he ran an unsuccessful campaign for mayor. He now serves as president of his alma mater, Edward Waters College, where he was a starting linebacker and captain on the football team. (Courtesy of Nat Glover.)

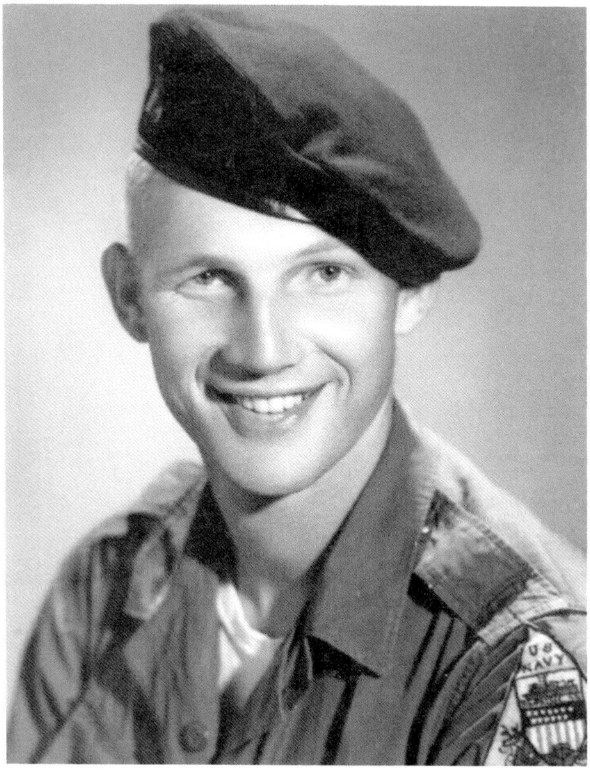
US NAVY

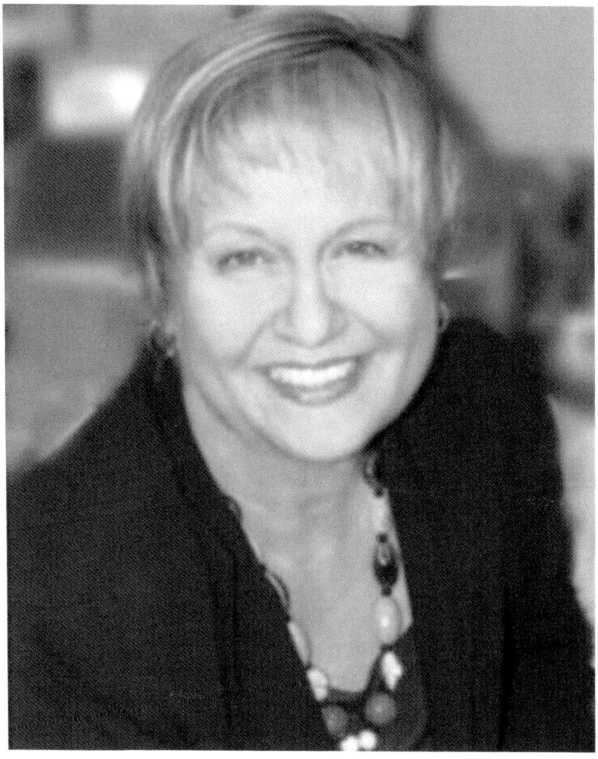

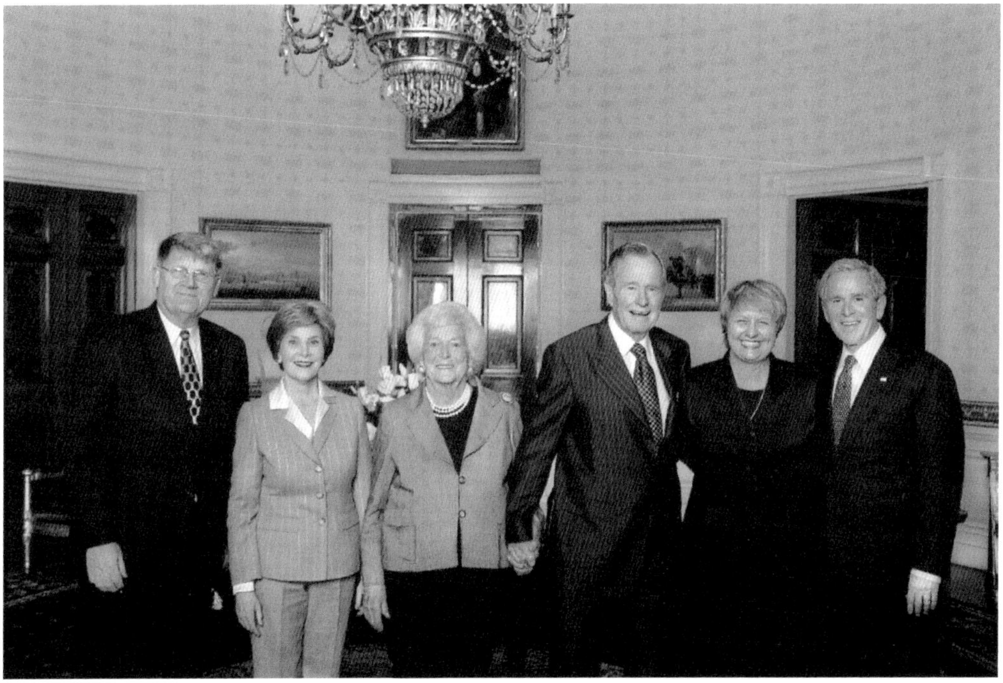

**The Smiths Come to Jacksonville** (OPPOSITE PAGE AND ABOVE)
When the Navy stationed Chester B. "Chet" Smith and his wife, Judy, in Jacksonville in 1986, they were not thrilled. But when citizens lined the streets for miles to honor the families of the sailors killed in the attack on the USS *Stark* in the Iran-Iraq War in 1987, they both knew it was home.

Chet was no stranger to war, having commanded a patrol boat in the Mekong River during the Vietnam War, where he earned the Navy Cross, Silver Star, and Purple Heart. In 1993, he retired as a Navy captain and reentered civilian life with the same dedication. As the interim executive director for Habitat for Humanity of Jacksonville, he integrated marketing efforts, increased donations significantly, enhanced record-keeping, and secured a computer network while the organization searched for a permanent leader. He then served as chief of Jacksonville's Veteran Services and as the mayor's military liaison under Mayor John Delaney. Chet made significant improvements in helping veterans receive the benefits and services they deserved. When asked what makes him proudest, Chet doesn't hesitate: "The Silver Star because I got that for saving lives."

Judith A.M. "Judy" Smith is a natural leader as comfortable with US presidents as she is with friends and neighbors. After retiring as a Navy commander in 1995, she became the president and CEO of HandsOn Jacksonville (Volunteer Jacksonville at the time). Under her leadership, Volunteer Jacksonville transitioned from a nonprofit resource center into a hands-on project management center that inspires, equips, and mobilizes people to take action that changes the community. HandsOn Jacksonville has been recognized consistently as one of the Best Places to Work in Northeast Florida by the *Jacksonville Business Journal*.

In 2014, the Mayor's Commission on the Status of Women recognized Judy for her work to create a stronger community. In her acceptance remarks, Judy said she hopes everyone will realize "that all successful lives include service to others, that service bridges our differences, and that what unites us in our humanity is far more powerful than what divides us." On the opposite page, Chet and Judy visit with Pres. and Mrs. George H.W. Bush and Pres. and Mrs. George W. Bush at the Bush compound in Kennebunkport, Maine. (All courtesy of Judy Smith.)

## Blue Angels

The Mississippi Delta may have given birth to the blues, but Jacksonville is proud to be the birthplace of the US Navy's Blue Angels. The flight demonstration squadron was formed in 1946 at NAS Jacksonville, on the Westside. The team of precision pilots thrills spectators with low-flying maneuvers performed in tight formations, keeping something in front of the crowds at all times.

The original team, under the direction of Lt. Cmdr. R.M. "Butch" Voris, developed its maneuvers over the Florida Everglades to avoid publicity if any accident occurred. The Korean War drained the Navy's aviation resources, and the Blue Angels became the core of Fighter Squadron 191, perhaps better known as Satan's Kittens.

Now based out of Pensacola, the Blue Angels' six demonstration pilots fly the F/A-18 Hornet in more than 70 shows at 34 locations throughout the country each year. They still employ many of the same practices and techniques used in their aerial displays from 1946. An estimated 11 million spectators view the squadron during air shows each year. The Blue Angels also visit more than 50,000 people in a standard show season. Since 1946, the Blue Angels have flown for more than 260 million spectators.

Pictured from left to right are members of early Blue Angels teams: Lt Cmdr. R.M. "Butch" Voris, the first Blue Angels flight leader; Lt. Maurice "Wick" Wickendall; Lt. Cmdr. Bob Clarke, who created the Blue Angels' signature diamond formation; Lt. Al Taddeo; and Lt. Jg. Billy May. (Courtesy of NAS Jacksonville).

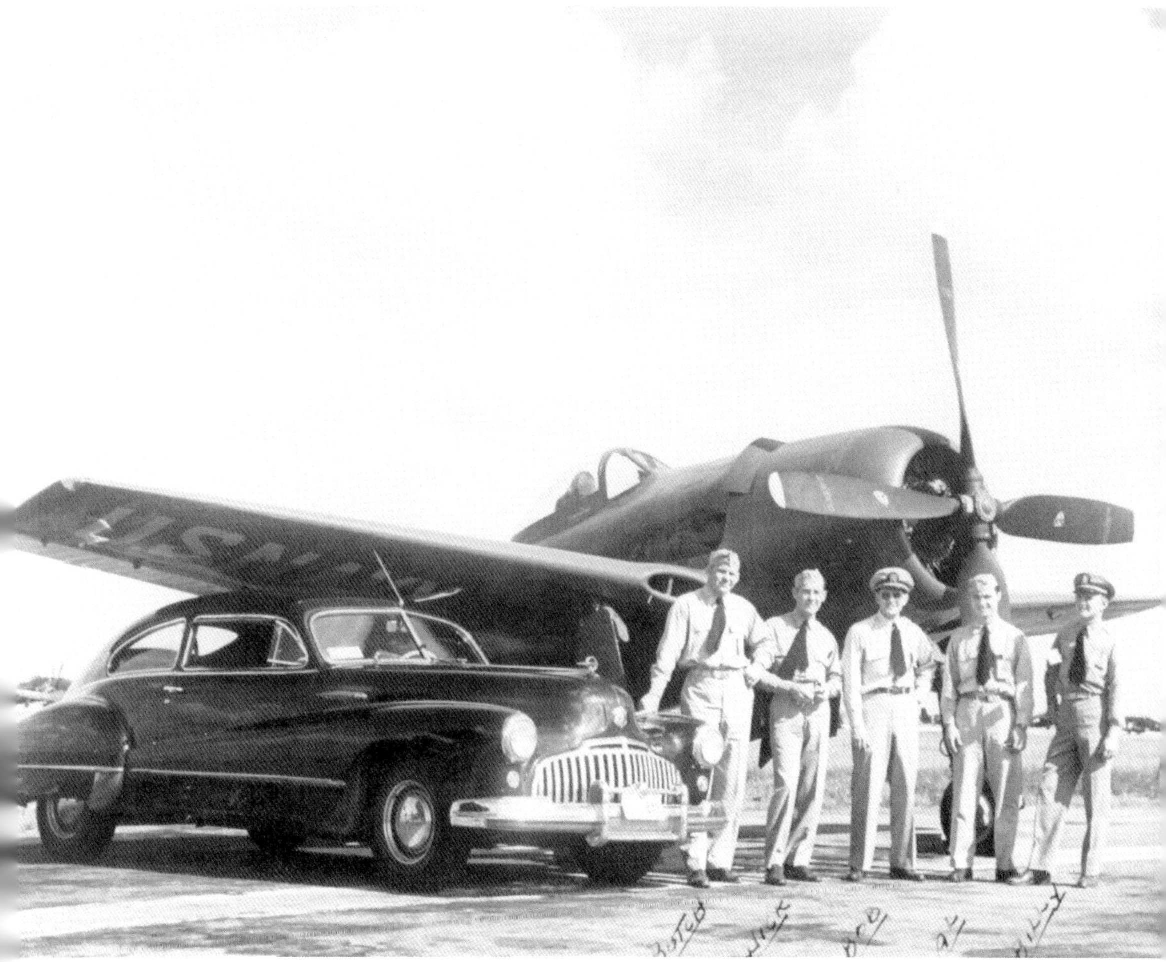

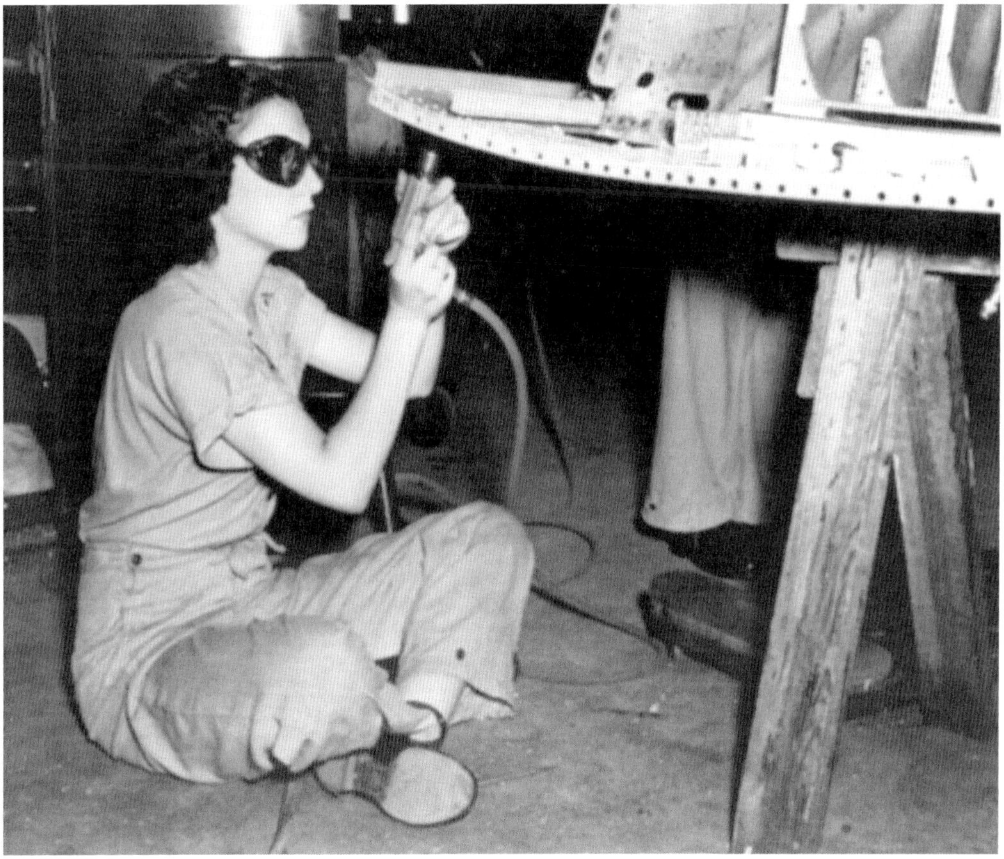

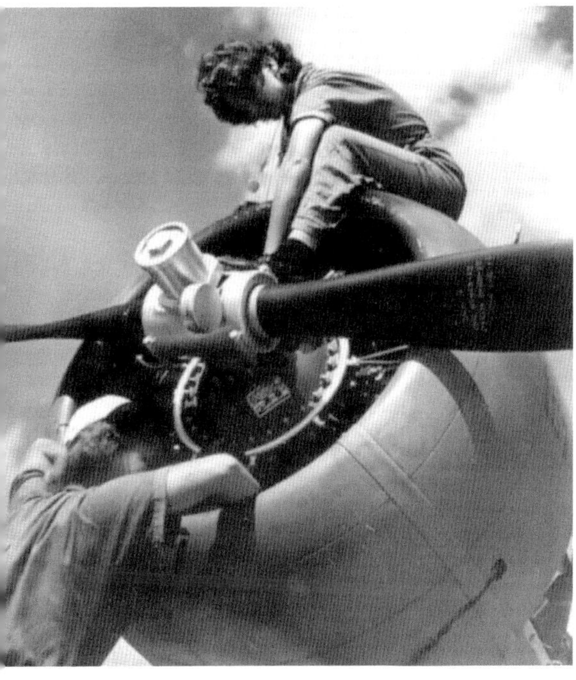

## WAVES

With extra personnel needed during World War II, women were recruited under the WAVES program (Women Accepted for Volunteer Emergency Service). As military service in the Naval Reserve had previously been limited to men, the legislation had to be changed. On July 30, 1942, Pres. Franklin D. Roosevelt signed into law the emergency services law for women, also known as WAVES. Within a year, more than 27,000 women joined the program, and, by the end of World War II, there were more than 8,000 female officers and an estimated 80,000 WAVES enlisted.

Above, A1c. Barbara Stroud is riveting an aircraft structure in the assembly and repair department at NAS Jacksonville. Left, also at NAS, aviation machinist's mates work on the Pratt & Whitney R-1340 radial engine of a SNJ-4 training plane. (Both courtesy of the US Navy, National Archives Collection.)

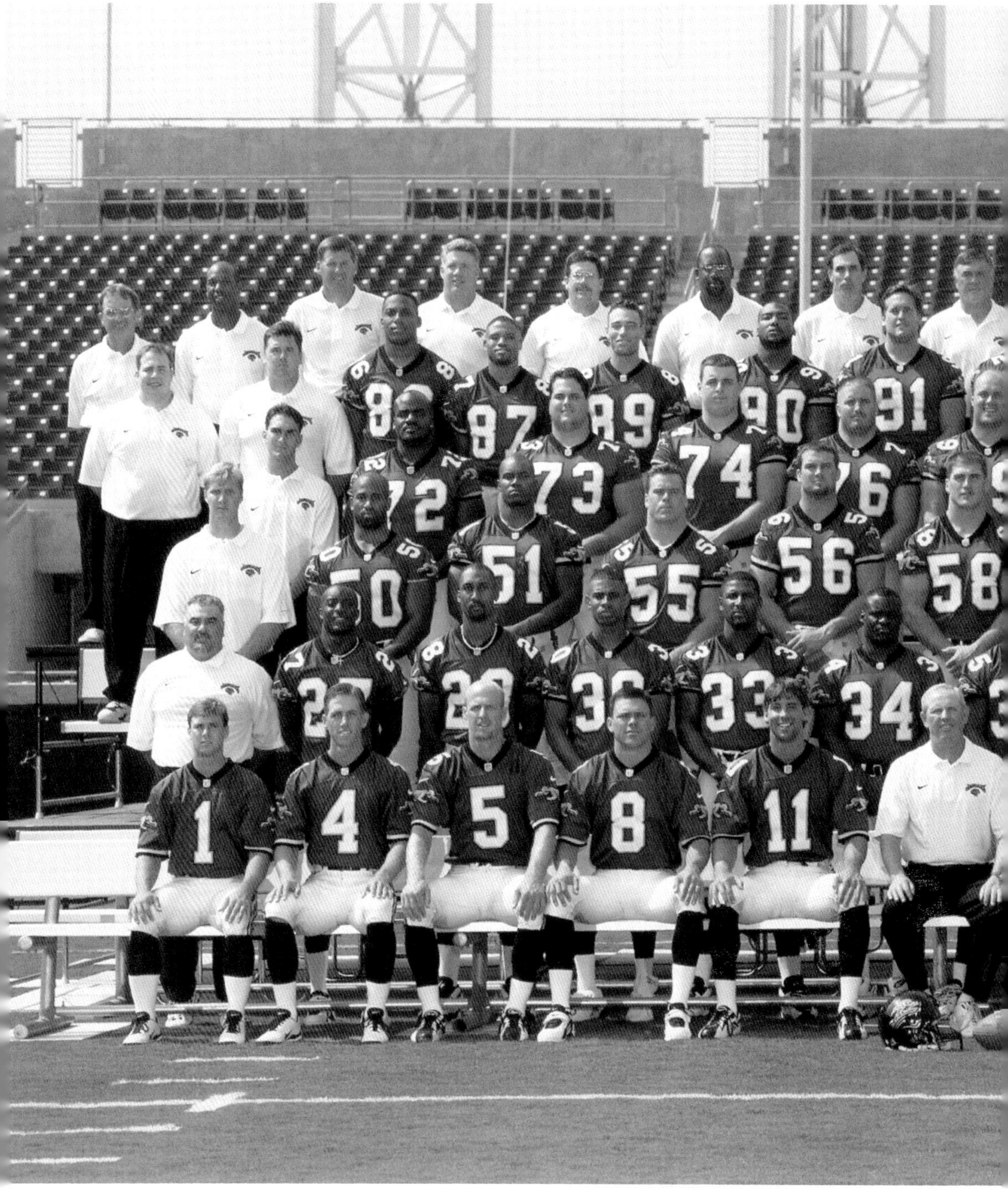

**One Game Away from the Super Bowl**

After closing out its first season with only four wins, the Jacksonville Jaguars, a second-year expansion team in the National Football League (NFL), won six of its last seven games for a 9-7 record in 1996. The Jaguars played the Buffalo Bills in their first-ever playoff game, winning 30-27. They followed that with another 30-27 victory, this time over the Denver Broncos. When they returned home after that win,

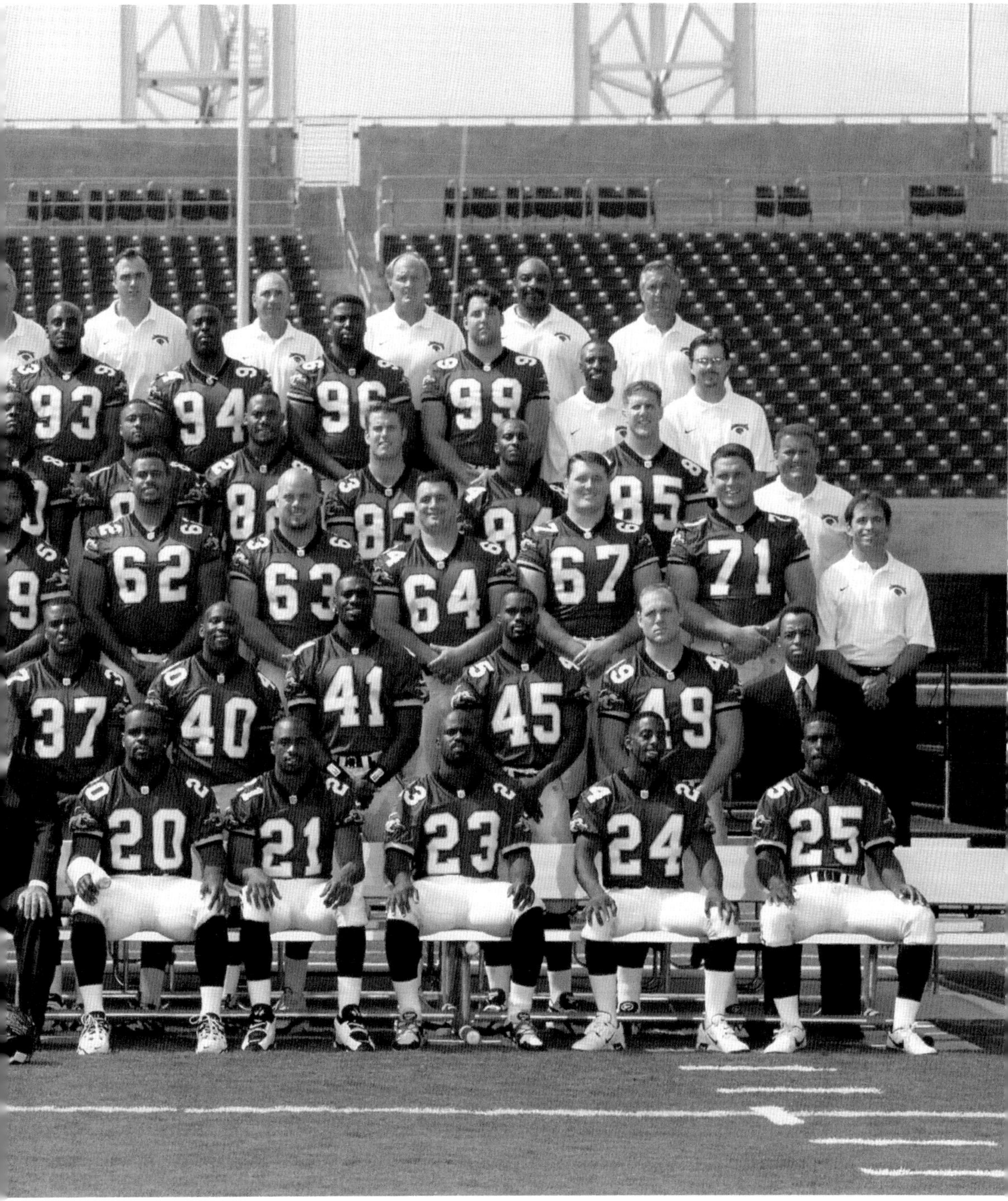

40,000 cheering fans in the stadium greeted them in the early-morning hours. The Jaguars lost the AFC Championship game to the New England Patriots 20-6, leaving them one game away from the Super Bowl. However, it was the start of a four-season era in which the team twice finished with the Super Bowl one game beyond its reach. (Courtesy of the Jacksonville Jaguars.)

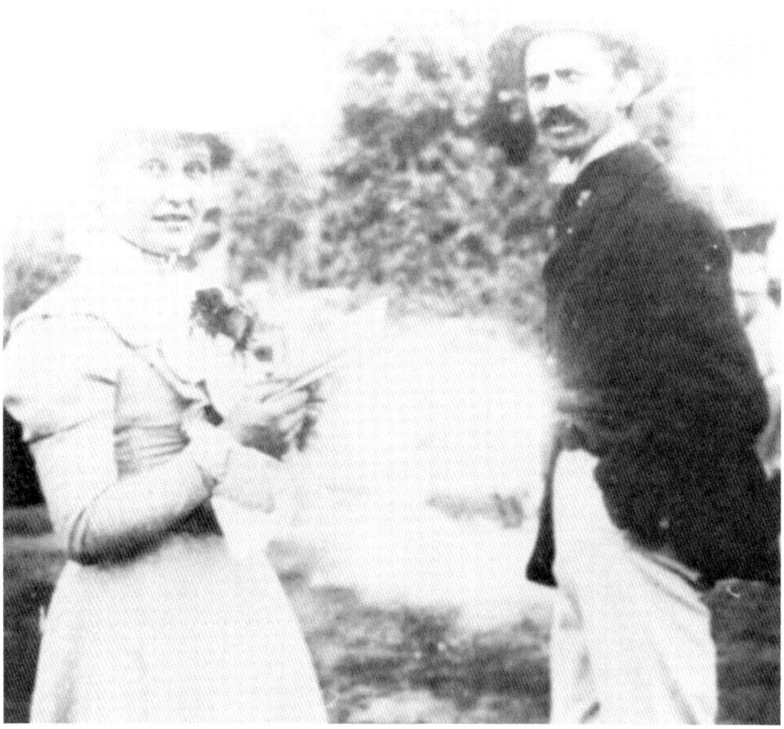

**Cora Taylor Crane**

Cora Taylor Crane's colorful life does not constitute the usual tale of Jacksonville women. While many know Cora was the wife of journalist and writer Stephen Crane, few know that they had a common-law marriage or that she had a reputation as a brothel owner.

According to the website *Jacksonville Story*, the Boston native, born in 1865, grew up in refined society and was well educated. Cora gained recognition as a short-story writer. When she moved to New York, she married a British captain named Steward and went into business, running munitions and a gambling house. She then moved to England, where she became fast friends with fellow American Jennie Churchill, the mother of Winston. When Steward was ordered to India, Cora remained in England and had a notorious affair.

With an alienated husband and a damaged reputation, Cora sailed to America on a private yacht. After a lovers' quarrel with the ship's captain, Cora jumped ship and swam to shore, landing in Jacksonville. Taking the name Cora Taylor, she bought and remodeled a hotel into a popular nightclub where the specialty was connecting men with women of the night.

She met writer-journalist Stephen Crane in 1896 during his stay at Jacksonville's St. James Hotel on his way to cover the Spanish-American War. Cora became the first female war correspondent when she traveled with Crane to cover the Greco-Turkish War for the New York press, using the pen name Imogene Carter. From there, the Cranes settled in England. Cora immersed herself in the middle of a battle between a wronged widow and an ex-mistress, who was jailed because of the prominent widow's efforts. Cora took the illegitimate children while their mother was in jail and raised funds for their support, actions that prompted writer Joseph Conrad to call her "the only Christian in sight."

Five years after Stephen Crane's death in 1900, Cora married again for a brief time but then divorced and reverted to using Crane as her last name. She spent much of her last three years in Pablo Beach (now Jacksonville Beach), but she maintained a home in the city. In September 1910, she died of a stroke after helping get a stranded car out of the sand. She is buried in Jacksonville's Evergreen Cemetery. This 1899 photograph shows Cora and Stephen Crane. (Courtesy of State Archives of Florida, *Florida Memory*, www.floridamemory.com/items/show/403.)

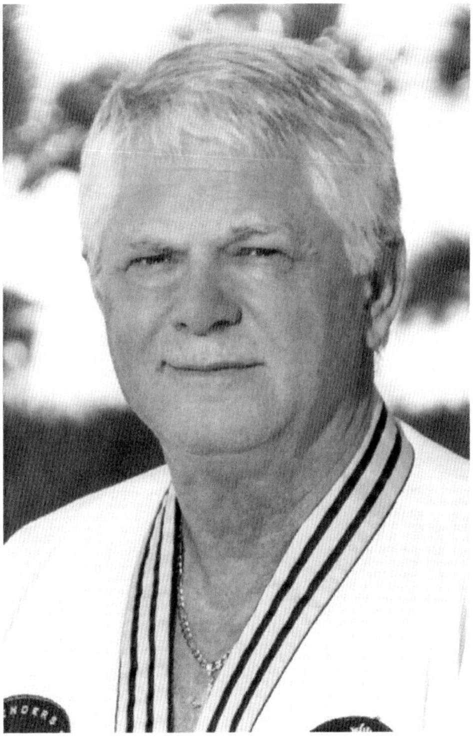

**Chuck Coker**

The founder of Yeshá Ministries, Chuck Coker is a seventh-degree grandmaster with an impressive Tae Kwan Do pedigree. Yeshá Ministries is a parent's dream: the highest caliber martial arts training available, at no cost. That training has produced more than 250 Olympic, Junior Olympic, national, and state champions. In his professional life, Dr. Coker is an expert in personal development, talent management, sales, safety intervention, change, and individual accountability. Corporations throughout the world have embraced his Personal Formations Process, which helps grow organizations through full-cycle developmental programs (applicant to retirement) to solidify productivity and profitability. (Courtesy of Chuck Coker.)

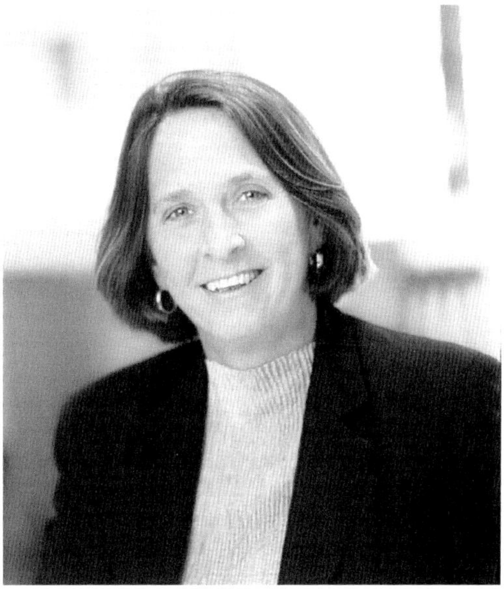

**Nancy Seely**

The daughter of Mayor Lou Ritter, Nancy Seely grew up with expectations of improving her community. She broke through the male-only restrictions of the old Seminole Club and serves on important local commissions and boards, including the Mayor's Council on the Status of Women. In the 1980s, Nancy joined a rising ad agency. Three decades later, she is considered the city's maven of public relations, and the agency, the Robin Shepherd Group, is the go-to firm for integrated marketing communications. To help balance her busy life, Nancy surfs every day in warm weather. (Courtesy of Nancy Seely.)

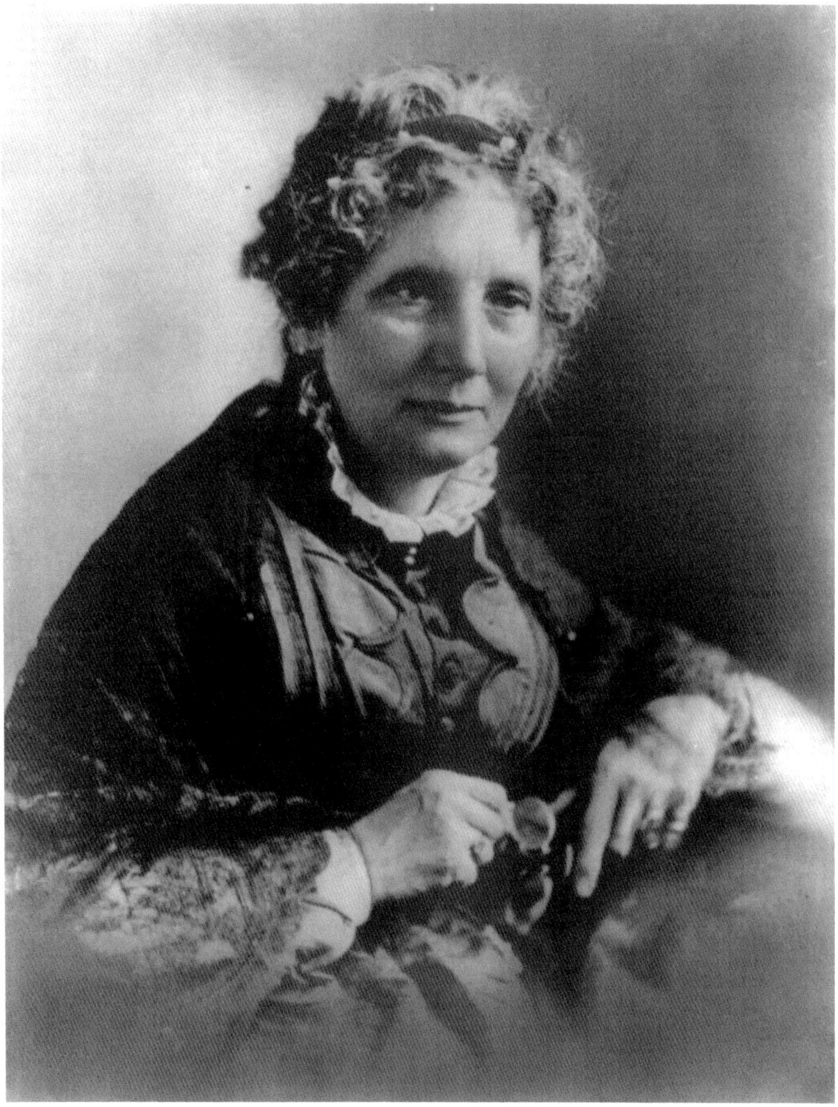

**Harriet Beecher Stowe**

After the Civil War, abolitionist and novelist Harriet Beecher Stowe bought a house on the St. Johns River in Mandarin, which she used as her winter home. She had promised her publisher a second novel to follow *Uncle Tom's Cabin*, but instead submitted *Palmetto Leaves*, a memoir and travel guide about her winters in Mandarin. She described life here as "a tumble-down, wild, panicky kind of life—this general happy-go-luckiness which Florida inculcates." Although the book was one of Stowe's minor works, *Palmetto Leaves* was one of the first travel guides about Florida and stimulated Florida's first boom of tourism and residential development in the 1880s.

Stowe's son Frederic had been wounded in the war and developed an addiction. The Stowes purchased a cotton plantation in Orange Park that had been owned by Zephaniah Kingsley and his ex-slave wife, Anna Madgigine Jai, believing the climate would hasten his recovery. Later, they bought property in Mandarin just across the St. Johns River as their own winter home. Sadly, her son disappeared, and Harriet never learned what happened to him. The Stowes' Mandarin home no longer stands, but a marker memorializes the site. (Courtesy of the Library of Congress.)

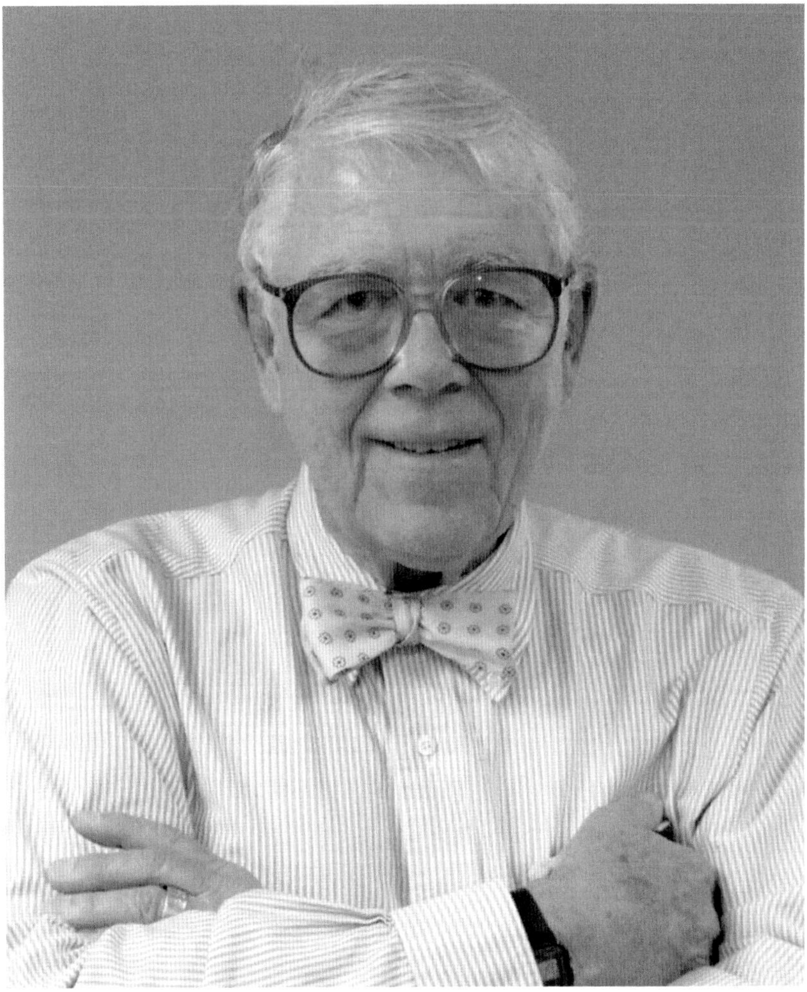

**The Historian**

Few people in Jacksonville know the city's history as well as Doug Milne. A lawyer, Milne has earned the nickname "City Historian" and is often the speaker of choice for development programs such as HandsOn Jacksonville's Blueprint for Leadership or the Jacksonville Women's Lawyer Association.

His interest started as a boy growing up in Riverside. He was "always fascinated by the stories of others" as his boundaries expanded to other areas of the city. Sharing fossils and arrowheads he found in the Suwanee River, he leaves no doubt of his excitement that human hands had not touched them for thousands of years until his.

Another of Milne's passions is community involvement, whether it is with the YMCA, the Ida M. Stevens Foundation, Edward Waters College, Jacksonville Area Legal Aid, Rotary Club, the Florida Sierra Club, the University of North Florida College of Health Advisory Council, or the Ritz Theatre, to name a few. Milne credits his parents with nurturing his passion for community involvement. "They always told us, 'You're here for a purpose and that purpose is to help other people.' We learned there is no limit to the ways you can help. The real measure of success is how many lives you've touched and made better."

Milne, who holds a law degree from the University of Florida and practices general commercial law, was admitted to the Florida Bar in 1968. He and his wife, Nora, have six children and 11 grandchildren. (Courtesy of Doug Milne.)

### Nancy Hogshead-Makar

Ask Nancy Hogshead-Makar what she wants to be most remembered for, and it is not that at the age of 14, she was the only American swimmer to be ranked No. 1 in the world. It is not her three gold medals and silver medal from the 1984 Los Angeles Olympic Games. Nor is it her induction into 12 halls of fame. Nancy wants to be remembered for her civil rights work.

Nancy started swimming at Episcopal School of Jacksonville, where she trained with brothers Eddie and Randy Reese. By the age of 12, Nancy was smashing national records, and she set her sights on the 1980 Olympics. When the United States boycotted those games, Nancy enrolled at Duke on a full swimming scholarship.

After competing and winning in the 1984 Olympics, Nancy tried her hand at broadcasting before enrolling at Georgetown University Law Center. She then moved back to Jacksonville to be closer to her family.

She practiced privately for a few years and taught at the Florida Coastal School of Law, and she now works for the Women's Sports Foundation. Before she became officially employed by them, Nancy worked for the organization for more than 25 years. She promotes equality in sports and works to prevent discrimination against women, the disabled, homosexuals, and minorities under Title IX. She has also testified in front of Congress more than a dozen times, fighting for equality.

Locally, she worked with John Delaney, president of the University of North Florida, to prevent the women's swim and dive teams from closing. She says that collaborating with John has helped improve sports for all women at the university. In 2009, the Florida High School Athletic Association wanted to discriminatorily cut girls' competitive seasons, and Nancy brought a successful legal challenge under Title IX.

Nancy's passion is driven by years of discrimination. As a muscular woman from her elite training, Nancy's sexuality was questioned. She pinpoints that as a reason she wholeheartedly believes in gay and lesbian rights. To her, people's sexual orientation does not matter, but they should never face inequality because of it. During her second year at Duke, Nancy was brutally attacked and raped while out for a run. She goes to work every day trying to prevent the sexual assault of other athletes. "Until it gets better for everyone, it will impact me," she says. "There's no individual escaping it." (Courtesy of Nancy Hogshead-Makar.)

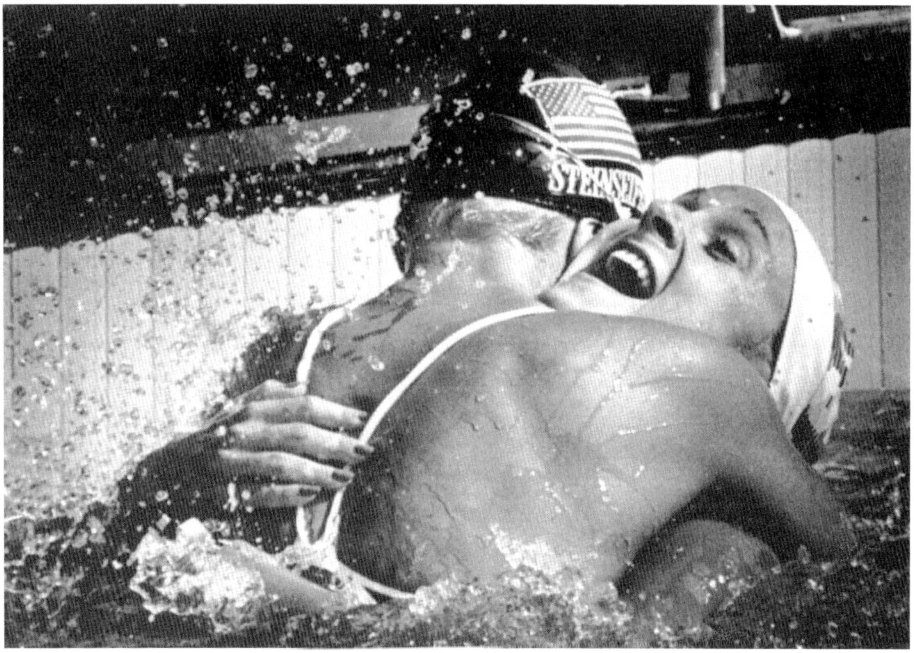

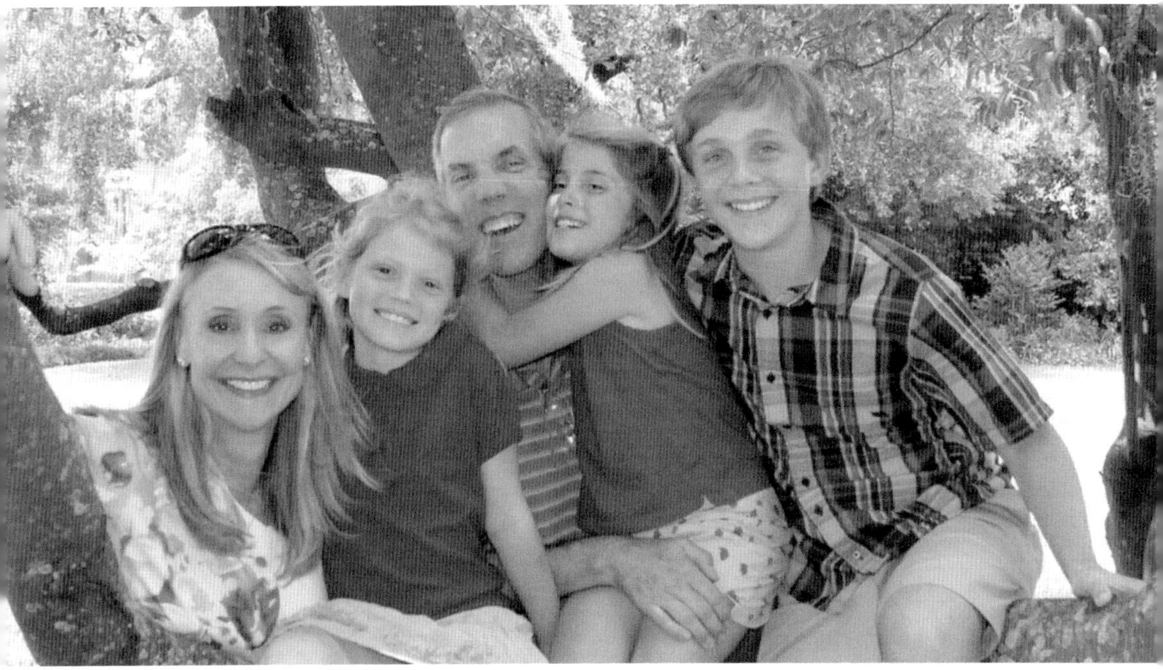

**Her Real Gold Medals**

For Nancy, family comes first, and she loves raising her children near her parents. Her father, Dr. Howard Hogshead, started the Jacksonville Orthopedic Institute.

Modeling how she was raised, Nancy and her husband, Scott, are academically oriented with their children. She notes that if she ever made a bad grade, her parents would have yanked her out of swimming. They wanted her to finish her education and have many options for her future.

None of her children are swimmers, because Nancy wants them to discover their own passions, set goals, and develop leadership skills. Nancy is pictured here with Scott and their three children, Millicent, Helen Clare, and Aaron. (Courtesy of Nancy Hogshead-Makar.)

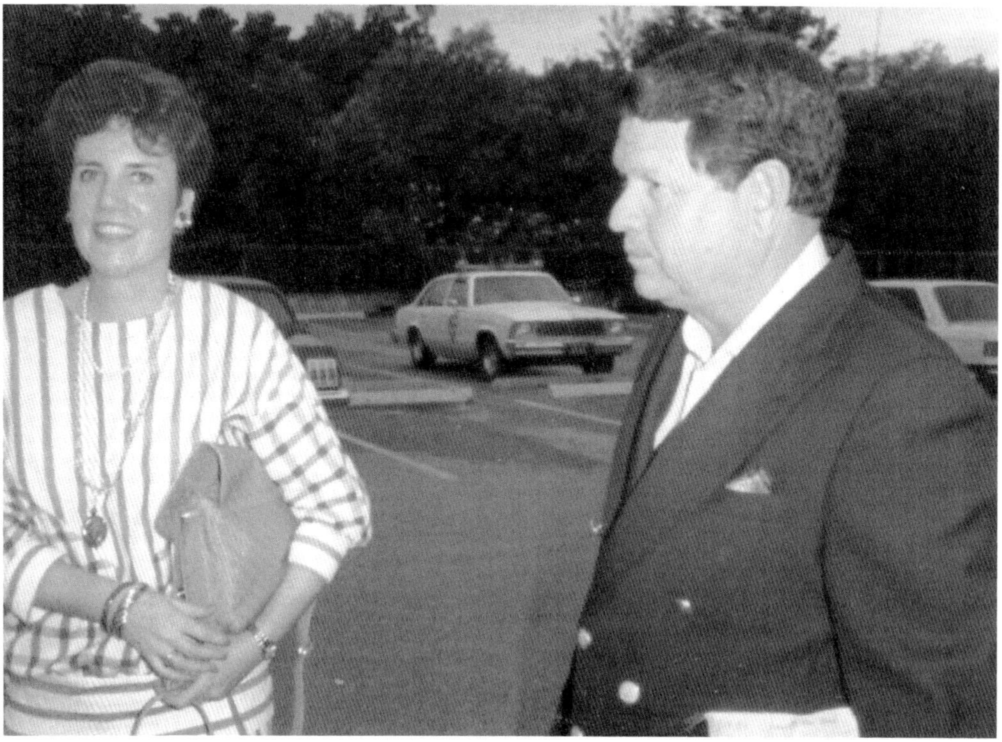

### Martha Barrett

Armed with degrees in political science and education, Martha Barrett carved the most fitting of careers. Early on, she realized that, while she loved education, she was not "meant to be in the classroom," because "you've got to be magical to reach students." Martha redirected her career to politics.

Her list of bosses is a literal who's who of important leaders: Pres. Jimmy Carter, US senators Ed Muskie and Dick Stone, Mayor Jake Godbold (above), and city councilman and Florida senator Jim King. She herself served on the Duval County School Board for 11 years. Along the way, she built a solid reputation as the business development officer for a staffing company and as vice president of market development for Bank of America's Jacksonville office. (Courtesy of Martha Barrett.)

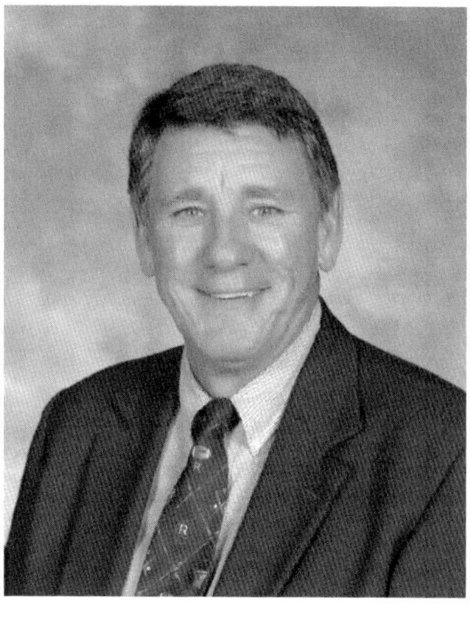

### Working behind the Scenes

In 1979, Rick Catlett went to work for Mayor Jake Godbold and helped start the Jazz Festival. Two years later came "Colt Fever," when the city expected 3,000 people to come welcome Baltimore Colts owner Bob Irsay. A total of 53,000 came to show support for having an NFL team in Jacksonville. Under Mayor Tommy Hazouri, Rick focused on removing tolls and cleaning the air. Next, Rick helped Touchdown Jacksonville land the Jaguars NFL franchise in 1993. Then, Rick took the helm at the Gator Bowl, helping rebuild it from an also-ran to a top-tier bowl game with a minimum payout of $5.2 million. (Courtesy of the Gator Bowl Association.)

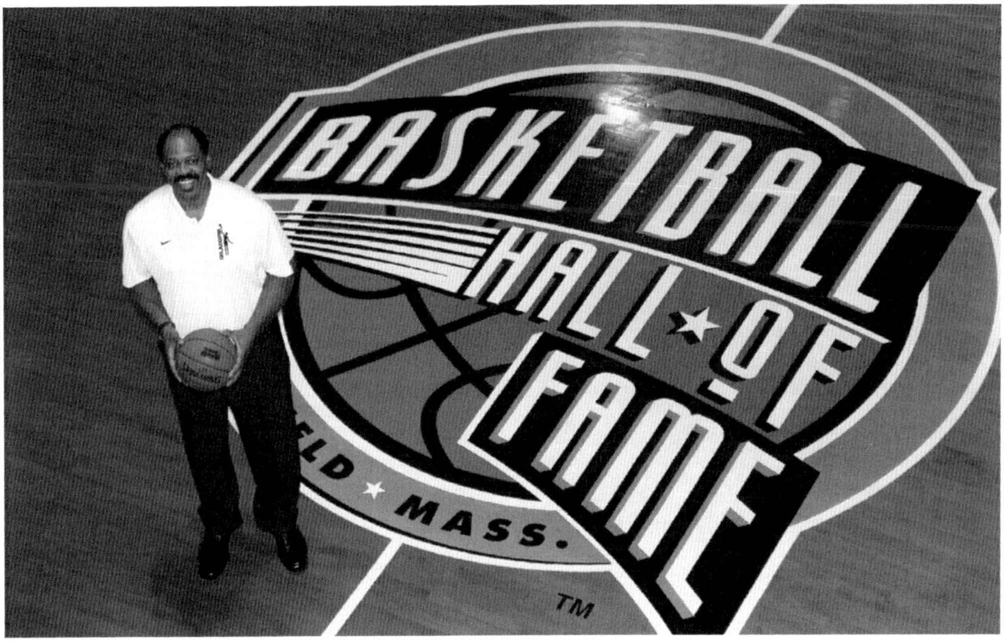


**Artis Gilmore**

It is hard to miss Artis Gilmore's 7-foot-2-inch frame on Jacksonville University's campus. In 1970, Gilmore led JU's basketball team to the NCAA Division I Championship. Although the Dolphins lost to the UCLA Bruins, Gilmore's history on campus was sealed.

He played professionally with several teams, including the Chicago Bulls, and was the American Basketball Association's (ABA) MVP and an 11-time all-star. Returning to Jacksonville to raise his family, Gilmore volunteered with the NBA's Read to Achieve Program, assisted in coaching girls' basketball teams, and worked with foundations of other sports professionals. Today, Gilmore works as special assistant to JU's president and still attends Dolphins basketball games, where he is an inspiration for students and athletes alike. (Courtesy of Jacksonville University.)

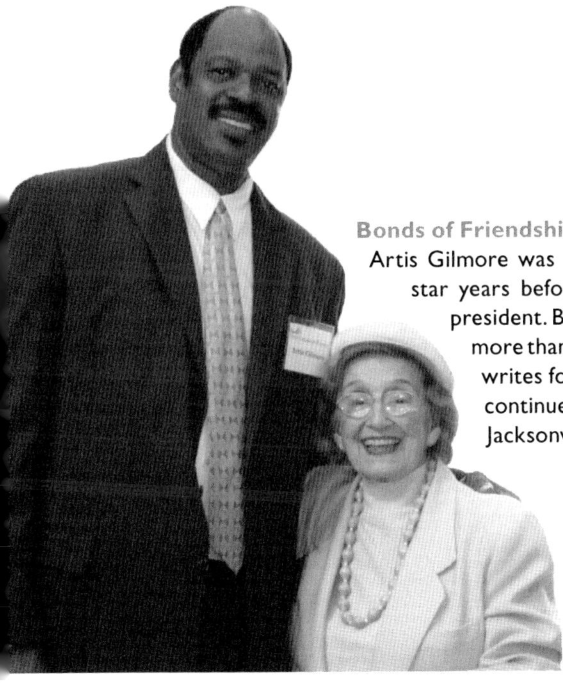

**Bonds of Friendship**

Artis Gilmore was a Jacksonville University basketball star years before Dr. Frances Kinne became JU's president. But they formed a bond that has lasted more than 40 years. In her autobiography, Fran writes fondly of their friendship, saying Artis continues to call her "mom." (Courtesy of Jacksonville University.)

### Charles Ponzi

Charles Ponzi, the father of the Ponzi scheme, fell into some serious trouble during his time in the River City. After fleeing Boston when he was released on bail for larceny charges, Ponzi arrived in Jacksonville with his wife, and with his eye on the booming real estate market.

Ponzi spent some time as a sign painter before setting up the Charpon Land Syndicate in 1925, a real estate business that sold swampland to unsuspecting buyers.

In 1926, Ponzi was charged and found guilty of violating Florida's securities laws, but he skipped out of town after making bond. He was captured in New Orleans and sent back to Massachusetts to serve out his sentence. (Courtesy of the Library of Congress.)

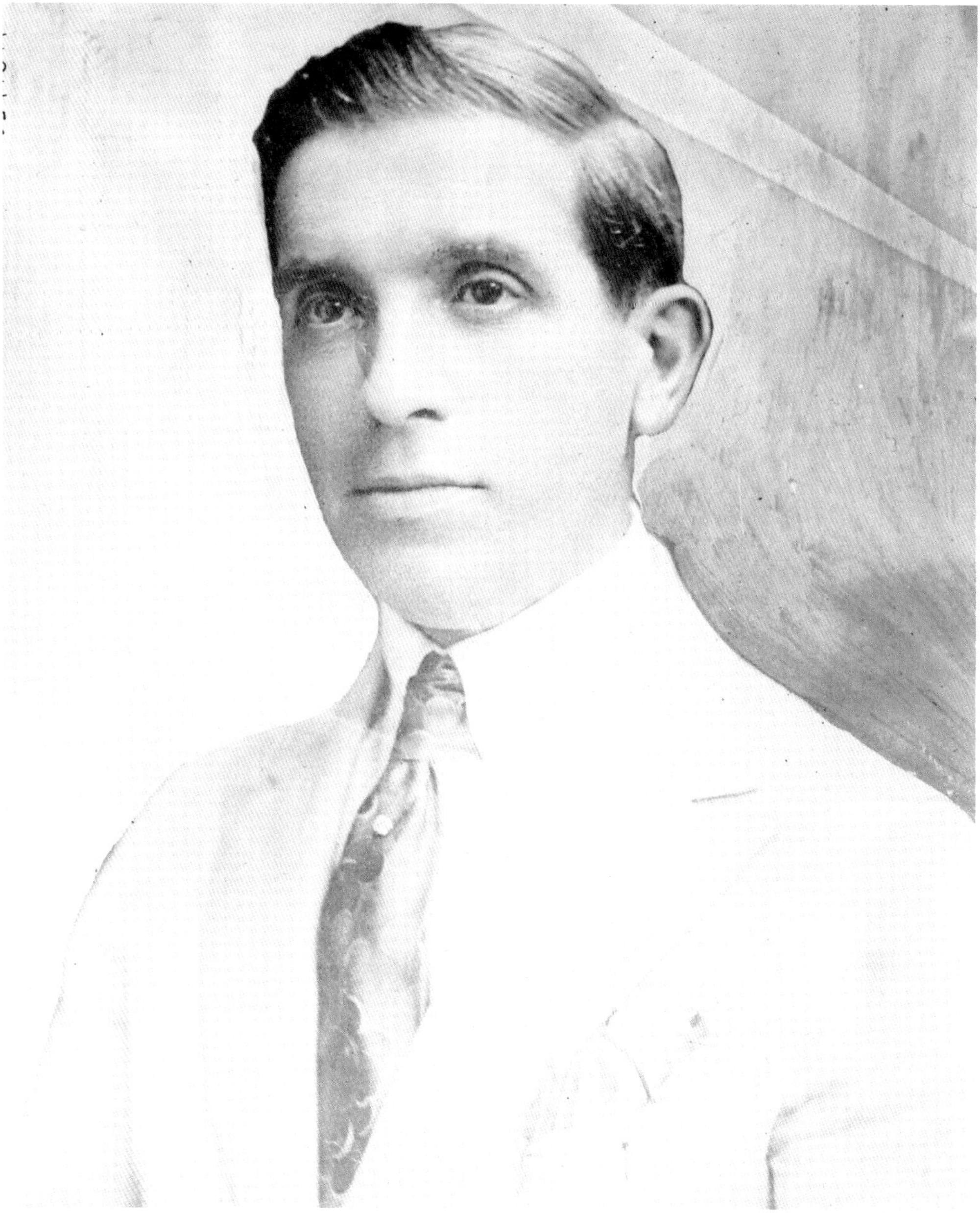

# CHAPTER FOUR

# Music and the Arts

As a business city, Jacksonville has become the beloved home of many corporate transferees, who treasure it as an underappreciated gem. The city has also served as a temporary home to executives from densely populated urban areas, some of whom have said it lacks culture. Those same executives overlook the gems shining right before their eyes: a symphonic orchestra of national renown; the longest-running professional dinner theater in the country; a harmony chorus that consistently places in international competitions; and the birthplace of Southern Rock.

Perhaps the city's vast size and natural beauty make it more difficult to find the art and culture that abound here.

Lack of culture? The Johnson brothers, Jacksonville natives, wrote and composed "Lift Ev'ry Voice and Sing," more commonly called the Black National Anthem. They also contributed significantly to the rich period of American literature known as the Harlem Renaissance.

Frank Slaughter, a local surgeon, published his first novel, *That None Should Die*, dealing with a young doctor's view on socialized medicine, in 1941. That book has never been out of print. Harriet Beecher Stowe wintered at her Mandarin home on the St. Johns River. And Al Letson won a competition sponsored by National Public Radio and now captivates listeners with "driveway stories" featured on his show, *State of the Re:Union*.

No arts? Visual and performing artists fill Downtown with their displays and performances on the first Wednesday of every month, and the city overflows with people visiting these venues.

When a converted warehouse in a virtually forgotten part of town opened its doors, artists filled the spaces so quickly that it gave birth to a young and growing arts district.

No one can deny that Jacksonville is a business city. And people who pay attention to the life around them cannot ignore the beautiful and vibrant pulse that gives pitch, color, and texture to the way of life for the one million people who call Jacksonville home.

### John Rosamond Johnson

The Internet Broadway Database credits John Rosamond Johnson, who was born in Jacksonville in 1873, as a composer, performer, lyricist, musical director, and conductor. The site also lists more than 30 performances and productions of his, including *Porgy and Bess*. According to the Florida Artists Hall of Fame, Rosamond was an accomplished classical pianist by the time he was four years old. His first music teacher was his mother, a public school teacher. He studied at the New England Conservatory in Boston and was the musical director at Bethel Baptist Church in Jacksonville for a time.

His passion for musical comedy drew him to New York, where he and his older brother James Weldon Johnson joined forces with Bob Cole. The trio toured with great success, performing many songs written and composed by Cole and the Johnson brothers. The three men's music reached beyond the stereotype of African American music to Broadway musical productions. Rosamond set one of Weldon's poems to music, "Lift Ev'ry Voice and Sing," more commonly known as the Black National Anthem. Rosamond also toured with the Oriental American Opera Company, thought to be the first all-black show on Broadway that was not a burlesque house act.

In 1912, he became the first African American musical director of a white theatrical company, Oscar Hammerstein's Grand Opera House in London. Rosamond returned to New York in 1914 with his new wife to found the Music School Settlement for Colored People. He continued to perform, direct, compose, and teach until his death in 1954. This photograph shows Bob Cole (seated) and Rosamond. (Courtesy of John Kenrick and www.Musicals101.com.)

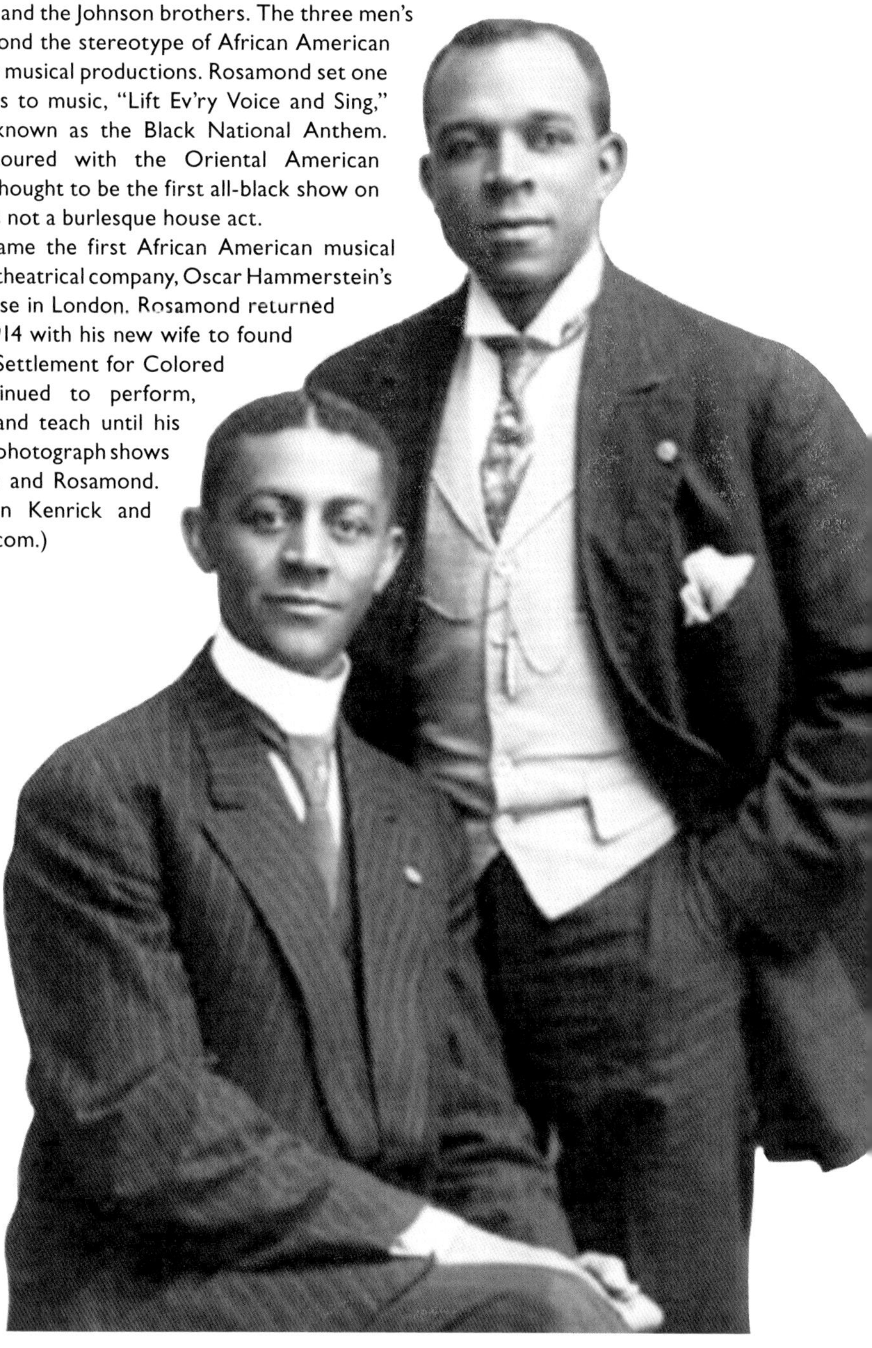

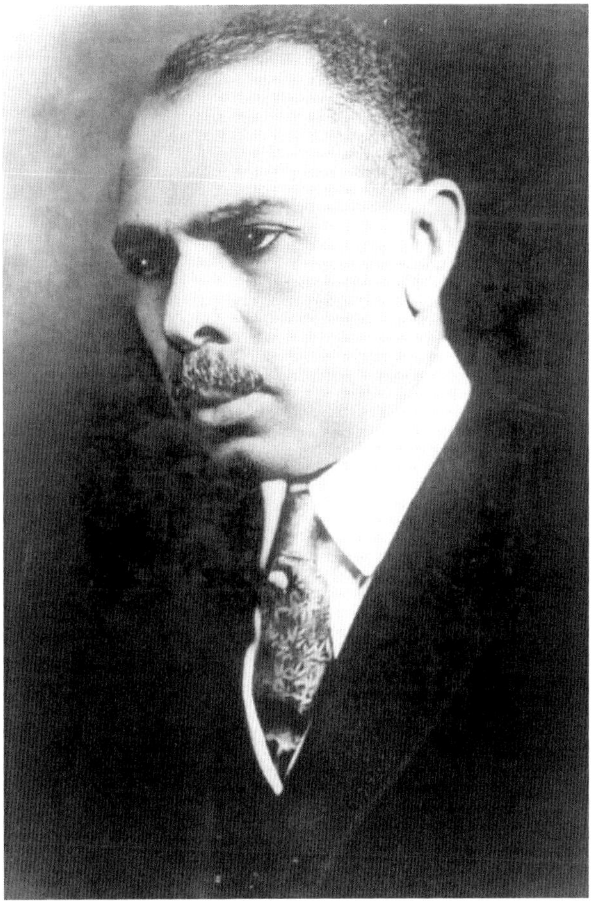

**James Weldon Johnson**

Although he died in 1938 at the age of 67, the impact of James Weldon Johnson's life as a writer, diplomat, lawyer, and civil rights activist continues to influence citizens across the nation.

Born in Jacksonville in 1871 to a headwaiter and Florida's first black female public school teacher, Johnson led a remarkable life. He was the first African American to be admitted to the Florida Bar after Reconstruction, but he yielded to his talent for writing and music and joined his younger brother Rosemond in New York in 1901. Weldon toured with his brother and Bob Cole, writing many of their songs, including "Lift Ev'ry Voice and Sing."

According to a biography of Weldon on the Florida Artists Hall of Fame website, he spent a brief tenure as principal of his alma mater, the all-black Stanton School. Weldon made profound improvements to the curriculum of what was then Jacksonville's largest public school before being tapped by Pres. Theodore Roosevelt for diplomatic posts in Venezuela and Nicaragua. During that time, he published poetry and the famous book *The Autobiography of an Ex-Colored Man*, published anonymously in 1912.

He returned to New York in 1914 as the editor of a black newspaper, where his powerful editorials captured the attention of emerging national civil rights leaders. Two years later, he moved to Washington, DC, to work for the newly created National Association for the Advancement of Colored People (NAACP), an organization he led for 14 years. In 1930, Weldon joined Fisk University in Nashville as a professor in creative literature.

His contribution to American literature comprises many notable works of the Harlem Renaissance, including *God's Trombones: Seven Negro Sermons in Verse*, *The Book of American Negro Poetry*, and two volumes of spirituals. (Courtesy of the Library of Congress.)

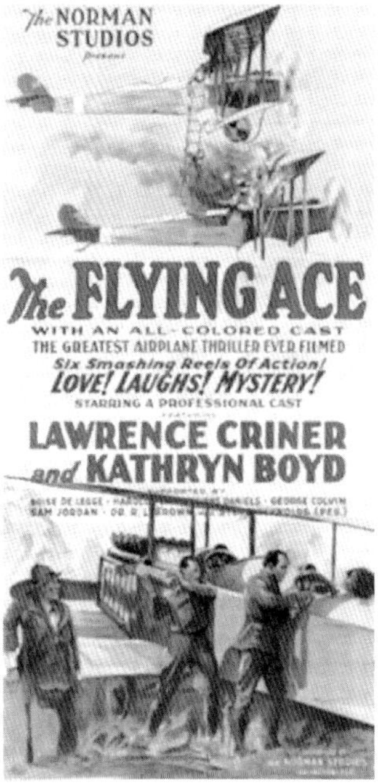


## The Flying Ace

Richard Norman's race film *The Flying Ace* featured black fighter pilots long before the military allowed black pilots. But the film inspired young African Americans by showing men who looked like them in heroic roles. World War II historians credit *The Flying Ace* with influencing the future members of the Tuskegee Airmen. It is the only one of Norman's eight full-feature race films still in existence. (Courtesy of the Norman Studios and the Norman family.)

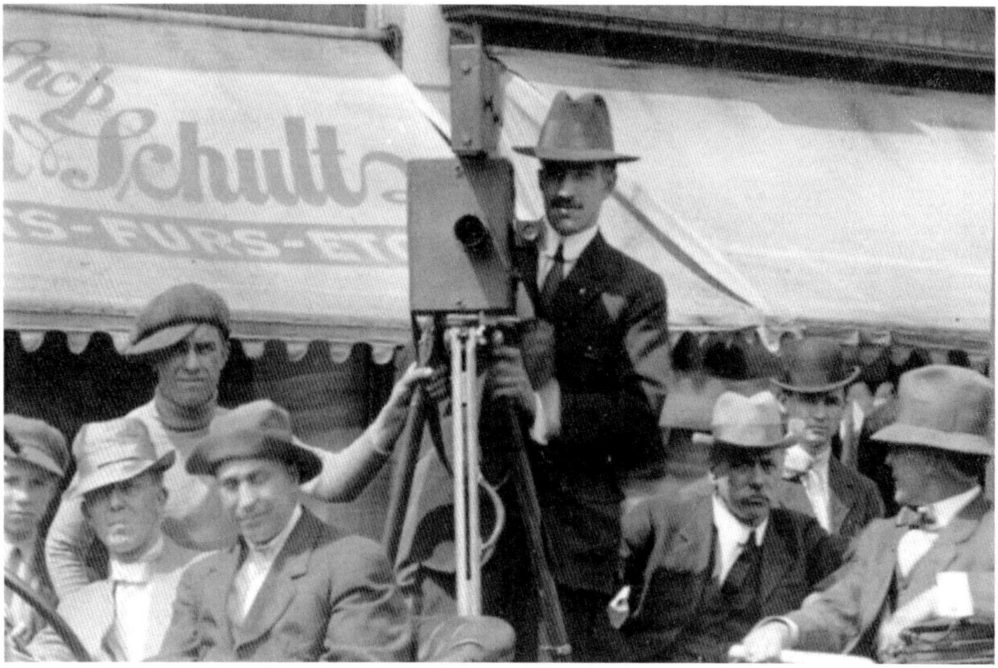

## Race Films

Politicians rallied against movie production techniques, like setting off false fire alarms in public places, and drove the industry out of Jacksonville by 1920. But one white producer, Richard E. Norman, spent the next 10 years making "race films," with all-black casts in positive roles. Richard, a Middleburg native, also invented a system to synchronize sound with film, popular until sound-on-film systems became available. Norman's five-building studio complex still stands in Old Arlington. (Courtesy of the Norman Studios and the Norman family.)

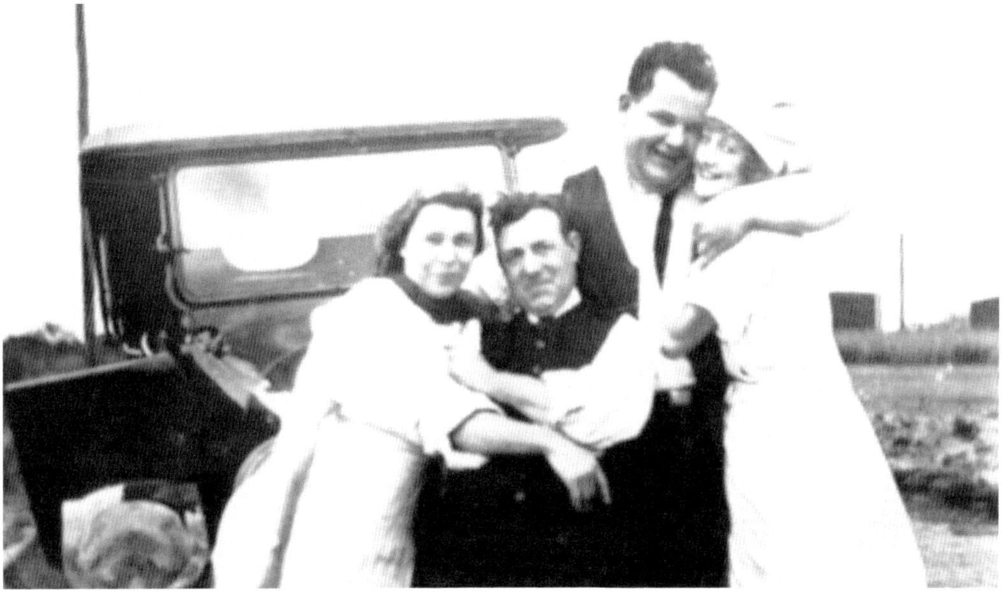

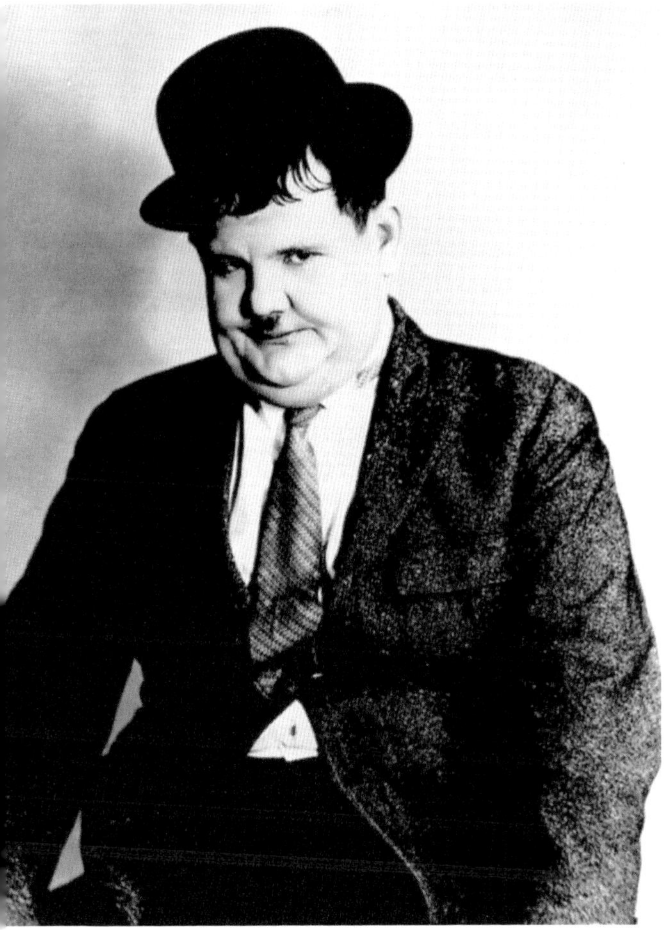

**Oliver Hardy**

Try as she might, Oliver Hardy's mother could not get him to focus on school or the future. His father died before his first birthday, and an older brother died in his arms. He was a "difficult child." All that changed when a movie theater opened in his hometown in Georgia. The 18-year-old got a job at the theater and became obsessed with the new motion picture industry. He moved to Jacksonville in 1913 when a friend told him about the growing film industry here. It was seven years before he and Stan Laurel met and became partners. He made 50 one-reel films here. This photograph, taken in Jacksonville, shows early film actors (from left to right) Pearl Bailey, Budd Ross, Oliver Hardy, and Ethel Burton (later Palmer). (Both courtesy of the State Archives of Florida, *Florida Memory*, www.floridamemory.com/items/show/144866 and www.floridamemory.com/items/show/35615.)

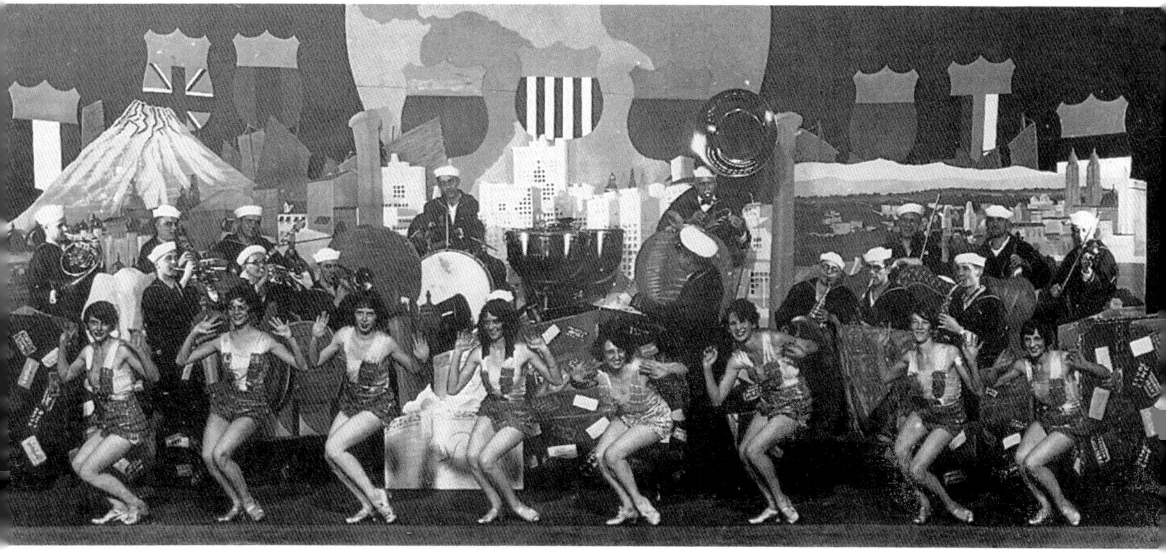

## Eleanor King

Though most people in the community associate Eleanor King with the philanthropic work she has done for music, her heart belonged to dance.

At the age of 13, she rode the streetcar from Springfield to the Florida Theatre, Downtown, where she was a dancer. She danced four shows a day, four days a week, and she did her homework between sets. Eleanor remembers making $35 if she was in the chorus line for the week and $50 if she was the soloist. She saved her money to pay for college.

Above, Eleanor is second from the right, and her friend Thelma Johnston Baggs, who was instrumental in bringing *The Nutcracker* to Jacksonville, is third from the right.

Below, Eleanor is pictured dancing an Irish jig for the Florida Theatre's *Around the World Show.* (Both courtesy of Eleanor King.)

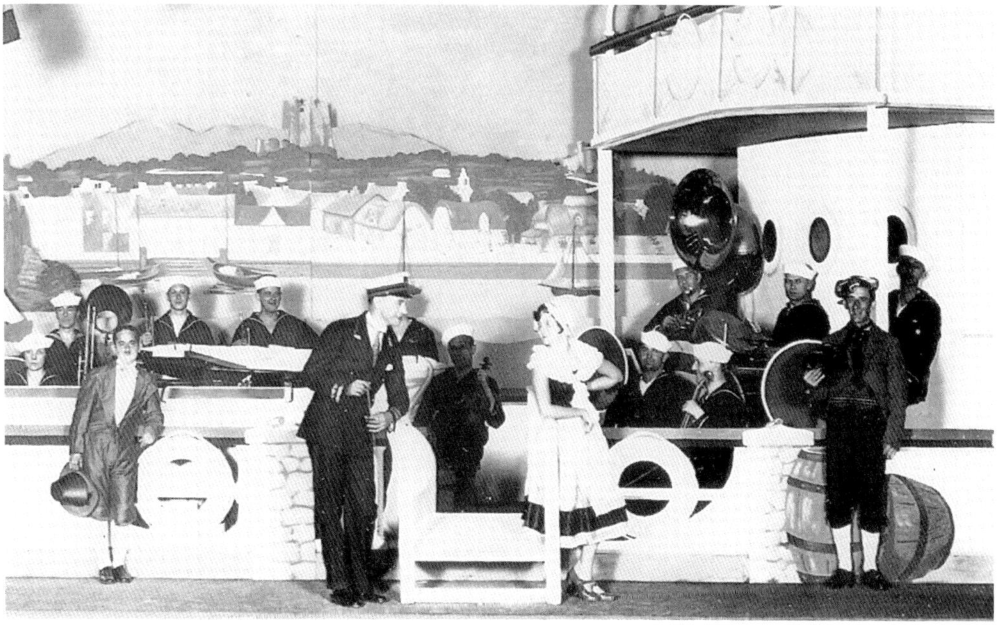

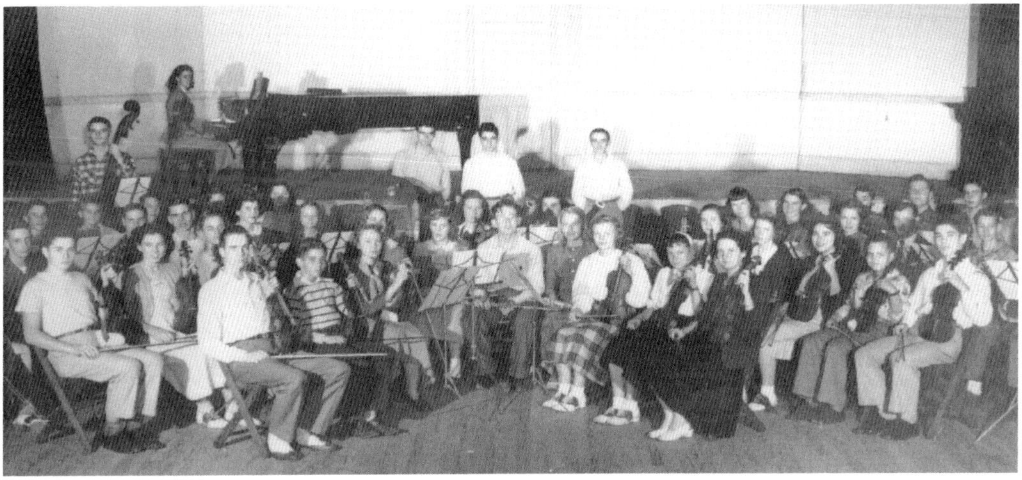

### Heart to Serve

When asked what she is proudest of, Eleanor says it is organizing the symphony orchestra for more than 65 middle-school students in 1947. At that time, there were not many opportunities for children to play in classical ensembles. Above is Friday Musicale's Junior Symphony Orchestra.

Eleanor has been president of many organizations, including the Children's Museum of Jacksonville (now the Museum of Science and History). She was on the board of the Mary L'Engle Trust, the Children's Home Society, and the Jacksonville Symphony Orchestra. She says she was called to serve her community.

Eleanor has volunteered with countless other organizations, including her church's Sunday school. She recalls running into one of her previous Sunday school students as a grown adult, and he was still able to recite the Beatitudes to her all those years later.

Below, Eleanor is seated center as Friday Musicale's president with other members in front of her home. (Above, courtesy of Eleanor King; below, courtesy of Friday Musicale.)

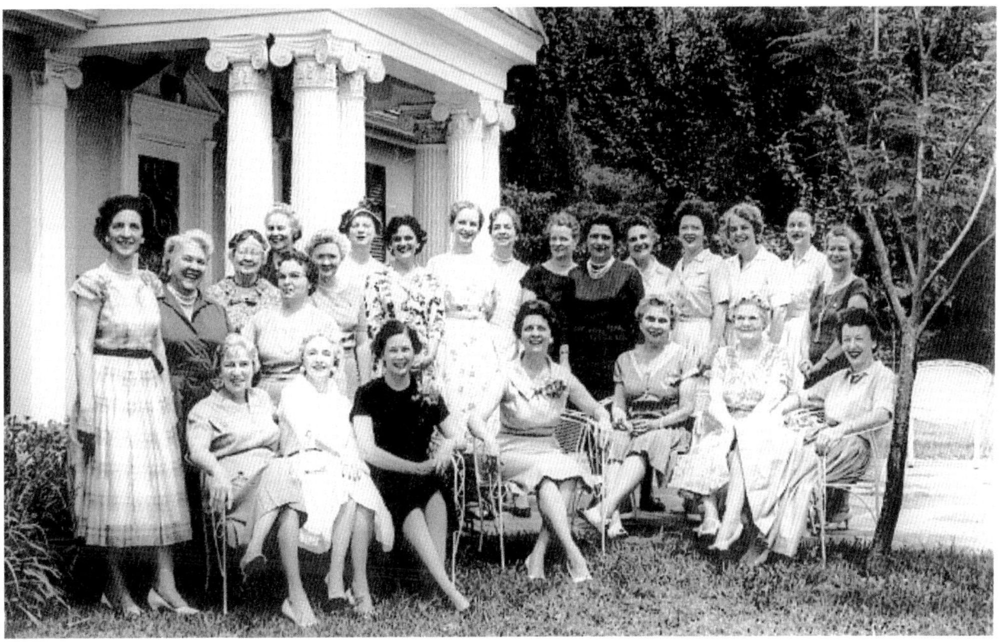

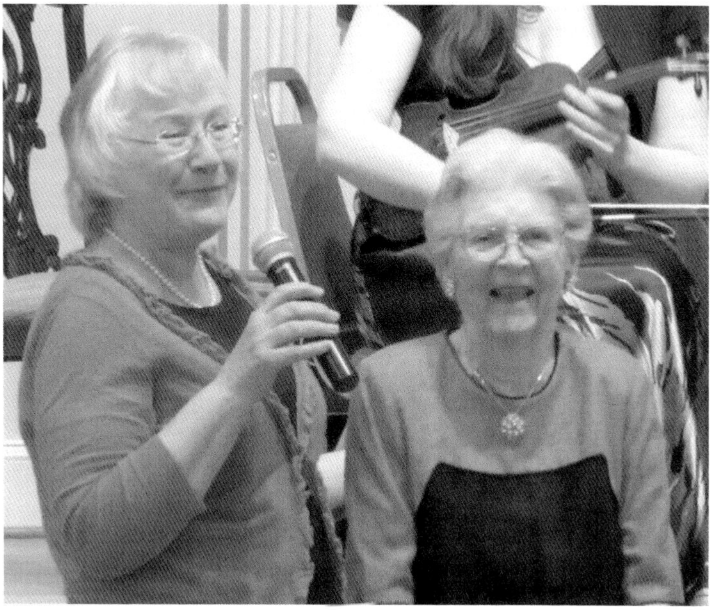

### A King's Century

Eleanor King has seen many changes in her 100 years. She attended Florida State University when it was a woman's college. She remembers using streetcars to get around the River City and vacationing in Havana, Cuba.

After her husband passed, Eleanor went back to finish her bachelor's degree at the University of North Florida, graduating as an English major just shy of her 80th birthday. She was then a substitute teacher for a few years in the public schools.

Eleanor's strongest memories are the love of her husband and children, the companionship of friends, and the melody of life. Eleanor laughs as she says, "I never thought I'd have Happy Birthday played to me on a Stradivarius!" Here she is at her 100th birthday celebration at Friday Musicale. (Both courtesy of Friday Musicale.)

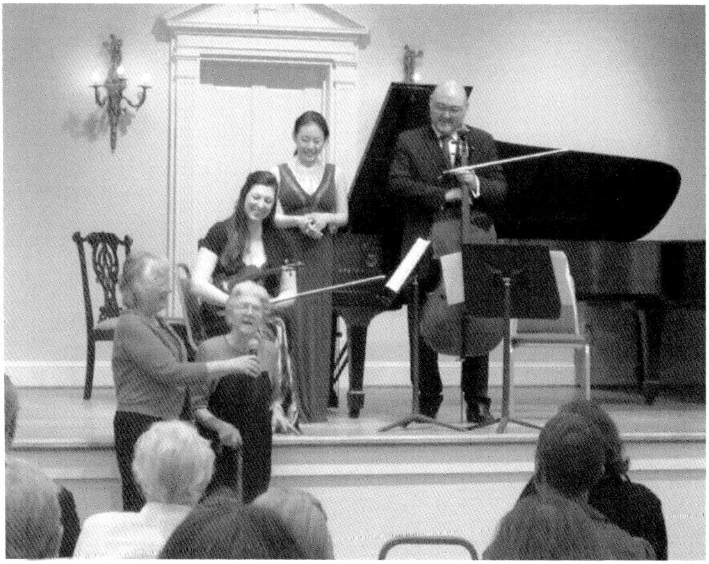

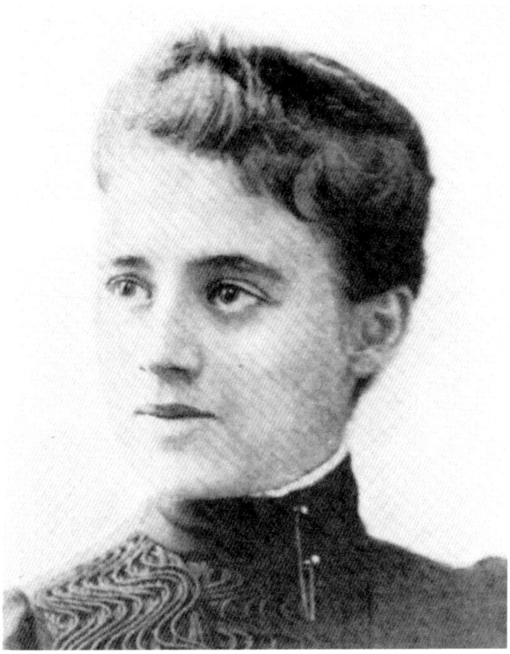

**Claudia L'Engle Adams**
Claudia L'Engle Adams moved to Jacksonville from Baltimore with her husband at age 25. A classical pianist trained at the Peabody Conservatory of Music, Claudia gathered 11 friends in her parlor one Friday afternoon in January of 1890 to celebrate music.

These Friday gatherings became formalized in 1893 as the Ladies' Friday Musicale. Although Claudia died in 1895, the club continued to grow. In 1923, the bylaws were changed to allow men, creating Friday Musicale. (Courtesy of Friday Musicale.)

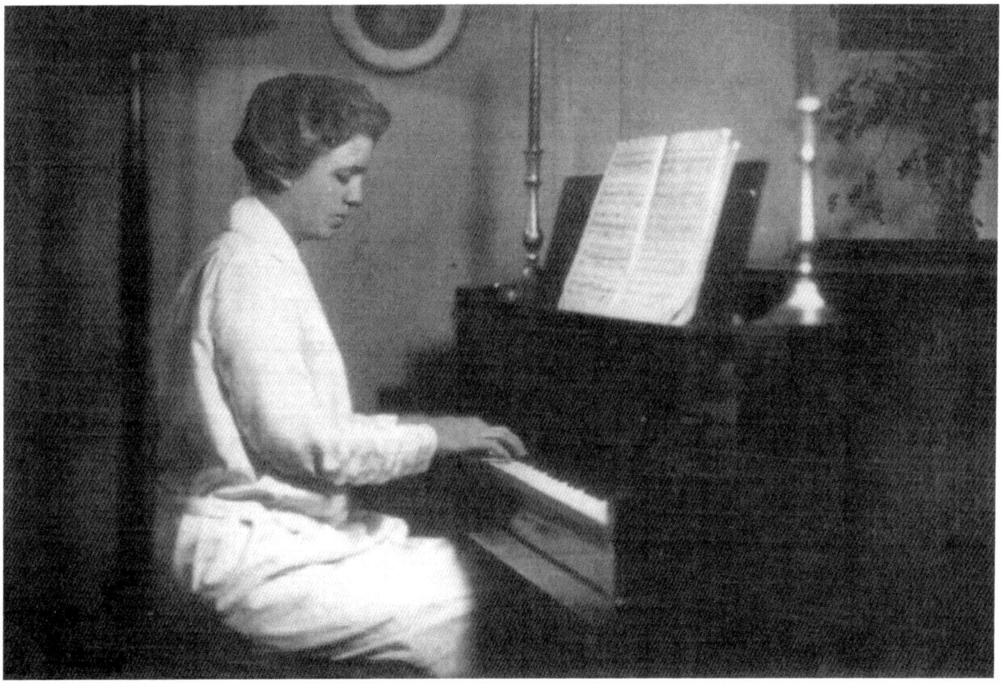

**Mary L'Engle**
Mary L'Engle, Claudia's little sister, was also a musician. Affectionately known as "Miss Mary," she worked to foster a love of music in young children, and she bequeathed her trust to Jacksonville schools. Little did anyone know until her will was read in 1948 that she left more than $100,000 for an orchestra fund. The Mary L'Engle Trust was instrumental in building strong orchestral studies for the students of the River City. (Courtesy of Friday Musicale.)

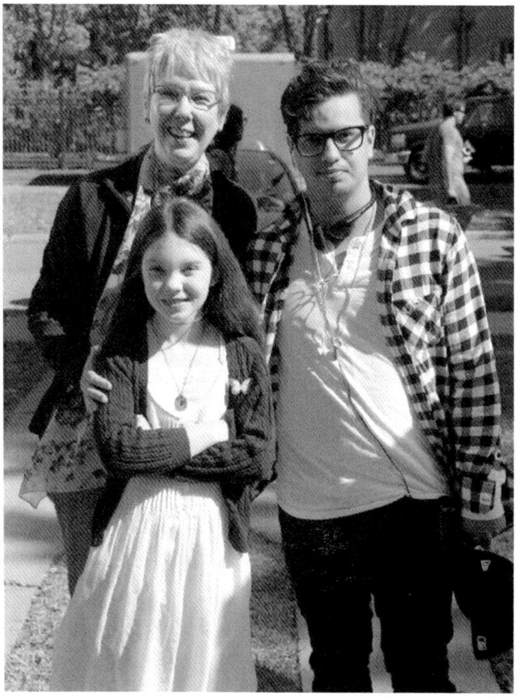

### The Screenwriter

Sharon Cobb liked the idea of writing but worked as a graphic artist. While living in Key West, she met Tennessee Williams, and she asked him for writing advice. He said, "Just write, goddamnit! Just write!"

She took writing classes and heeded the advice. She moved to Los Angeles in 1993, where she launched a successful screenwriting career—credits include *Lighthouse Hill*—before moving to Jacksonville to be closer to family. Sharon wrote *False Confessions of a True Hollywood Screenwriter* and created www.FunnyFixx.com.

She teaches screenwriting classes and participates in the 48 Hour Film Project, where she found a writing partner in L. Gustavo Cooper. They cowrote the movie *June*, which Gustavo directed. This photograph from the set of *June* features, from left to right, Sharon, star Kennedy Brice, and Gustavo. (Photograph by Robert J. Ward.)

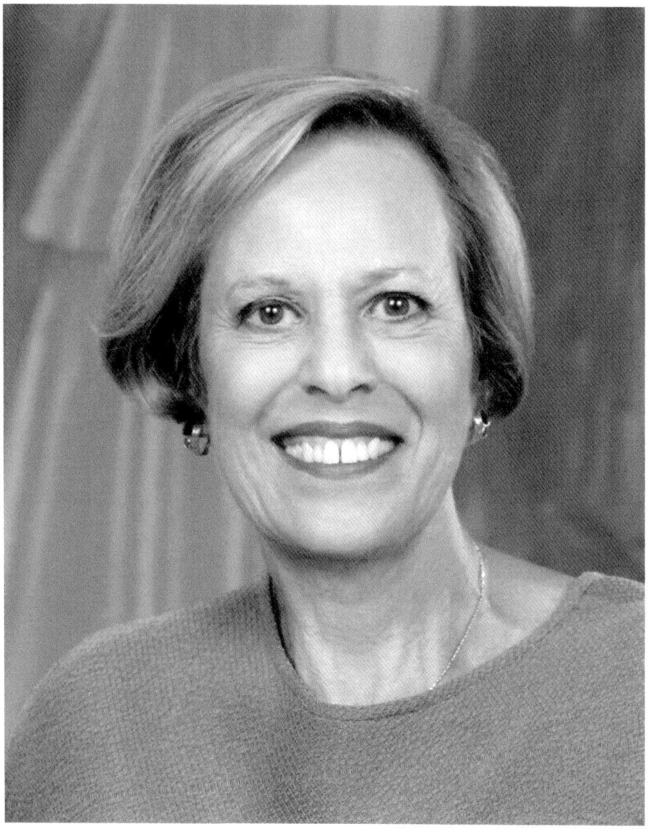

### E.L. Konigsburg

Elaine Konigsburg did not begin to write until her youngest child entered kindergarten, and then she wrote up a storm. She is the only children's author to both win the Newbery Medal and place as runner-up in the same year, for *From the Mixed-Up Files of Mrs. Basil E. Frankweiler* and *Jennifer, Hecate, Macbeth, William McKinley, and Me, Elizabeth*, respectively. Almost 30 years later, she again won the Newbery Medal for *The View from Saturday*. She and her family lived in Jacksonville from the mid-1950s to 1962, when they moved to New York. They returned in 1968 to live on the beach. She died in 2013 at the age of 83. (Photograph by Ron Kunzman; courtesy of Simon & Schuster.)

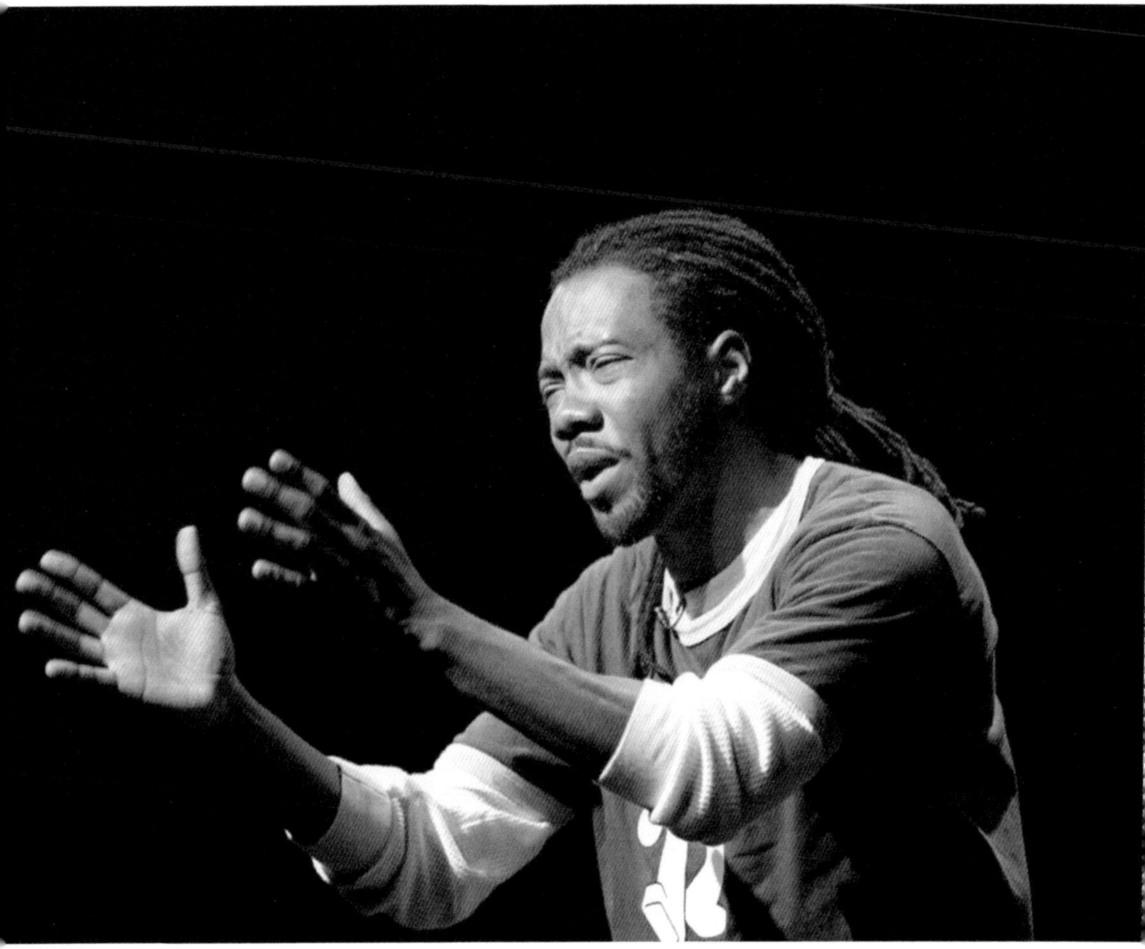

**The Storyteller**

Al Letson is no mere performance poet, playwright, or public radio host; he is a storyteller.

Traveling across the country as a flight attendant, he recognized that everyone has a story. During this time, he performed in poetry slams in various venues and crashed on couches, letting these experiences shape his view of America.

His first poetry performance was in Five Points in 1995; within three years, he ranked third in the National Poetry Slam. Soon after, Al began working on his one-man show *Essential Personnel.* He has performed on many public stages, including HBO's *Def Poetry Jam* and CBS's *Final Four PreGame*, in 2004.

Al entered the Public Radio Talent Quest competition in 2008 not thinking he would even place in the top 10, let alone win. From a pool of 1,500 entries, Al was chosen as the winner, and he now hosts *State of the Re:Union*, *Freestyle: A Mixtap*, and *Reveal*, an investigative journalism show, on National Public Radio.

Being the host of three radio shows has not stopped him from pursuing other projects, including developing two comic book series and writing and performing the autobiographical piece *Summer in Sanctuary*, which is told through monologues, poetry, and song.

Early in his career as a storyteller, Al created a guiding principal that his work has to stand for something: "Art without purpose is vanity." (Courtesy of Al Letson.)

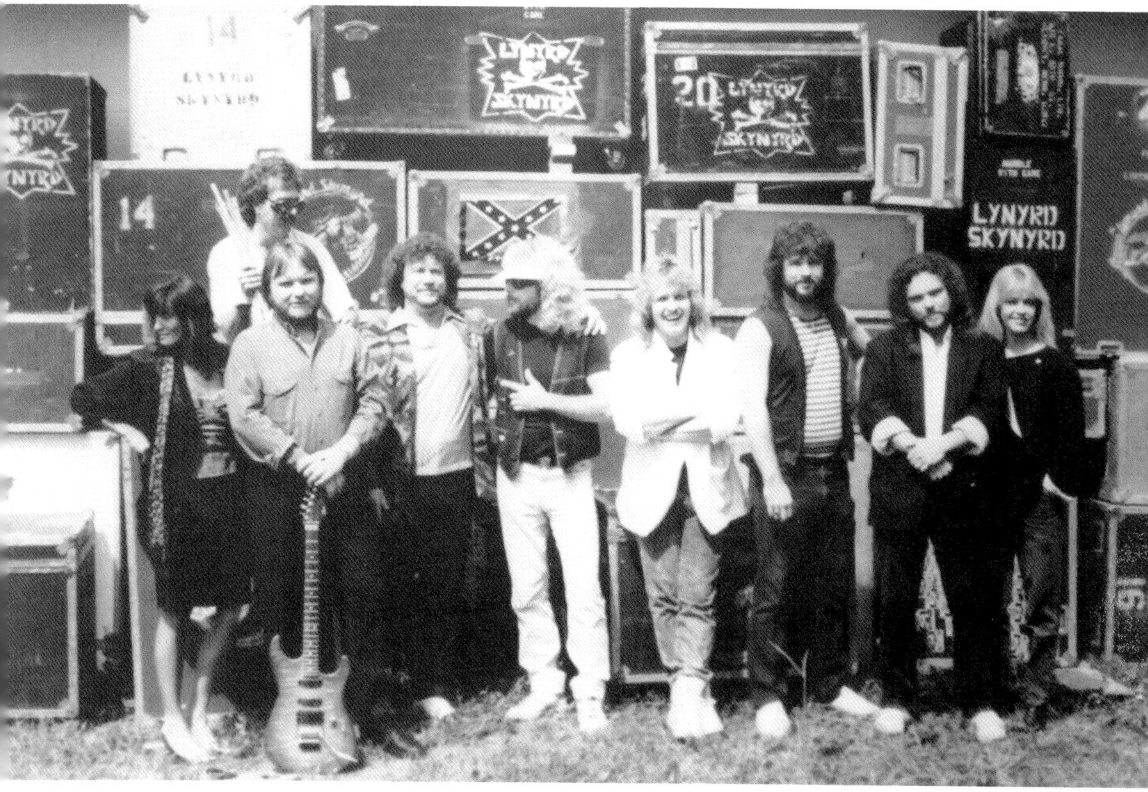


**Lynyrd Skynyrd**

First formed as the Noble Five in Jacksonville in 1964, Jacksonville's Southern Rock pioneers went through several names before settling on Lynyrd Skynyrd. Ronnie Van Zant was in high school when he recruited Allen Collins, Gary Rossington, Larry Junstorm, and Bob Burns to form a band. They eventually became the American equivalent of the Rolling Stones. What happened would alter music history.

They changed their name in 1970 as a mocking tribute to strict gym teacher Leonard Skinner. Along with another legendary Jacksonville group, the Allman Brothers Band, Lynyrd Skynyrd created the tone and sound for Southern Rock. Lynyrd Skynyrd's "Sweet Home Alabama" and "Free Bird" are considered classics in rock music. Tragedy struck the band at the height of its success, in 1977. Returning from a gig in Louisiana, the band's plane crashed, killing three of its members, including Ronnie Van Zant and the road manager. The band has evolved and reformed over the years, and, in 2012, Lynyrd Skynyrd released its latest studio album. In this photograph are, from left to right, Carol Bristow, Artimus Pyle, Ed King, Billy Powell, Leon Wilkeson, Johnny Van Zant, Randall Hall, Gary Rossington, and Dale Krantz Rossington. (Publicity photograph distributed by MCA Records.)

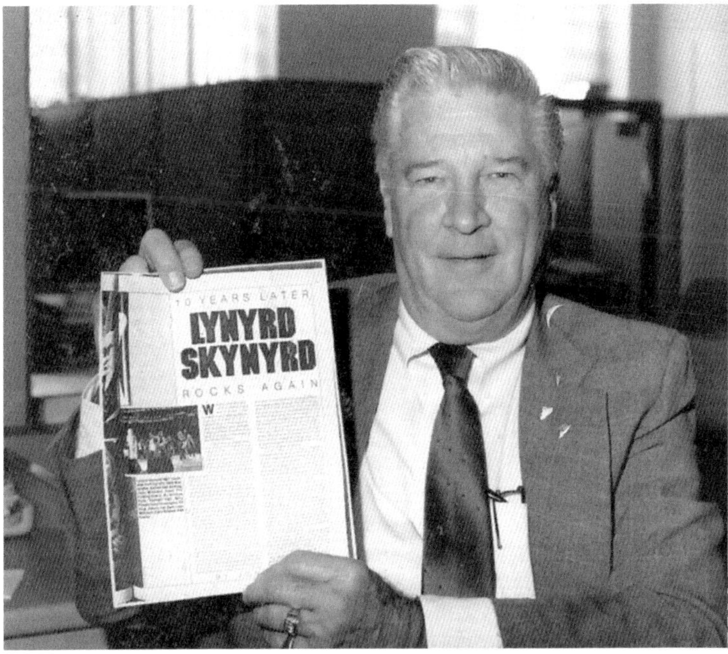


**The Enforcer**
Leonard Skinner graduated from Robert E. Lee High School in 1951, eventually returning as basketball coach. But that is not why the *New York Times* called Coach Skinner "arguably the most influential high school gym teacher in American popular culture" when he died in 2010 at age 77. Enforcing the ban on long hair for male students in the 1960s, Leonard sent members of a teen band to the dean's office. The band played under several names, but when Ronnie Van Zant introduced the band as "Leonard Skinner," the crowd loved it. The band altered it to Lynyrd Skynyrd to avoid legal issues. (Courtesy of Rosemary Skinner.)

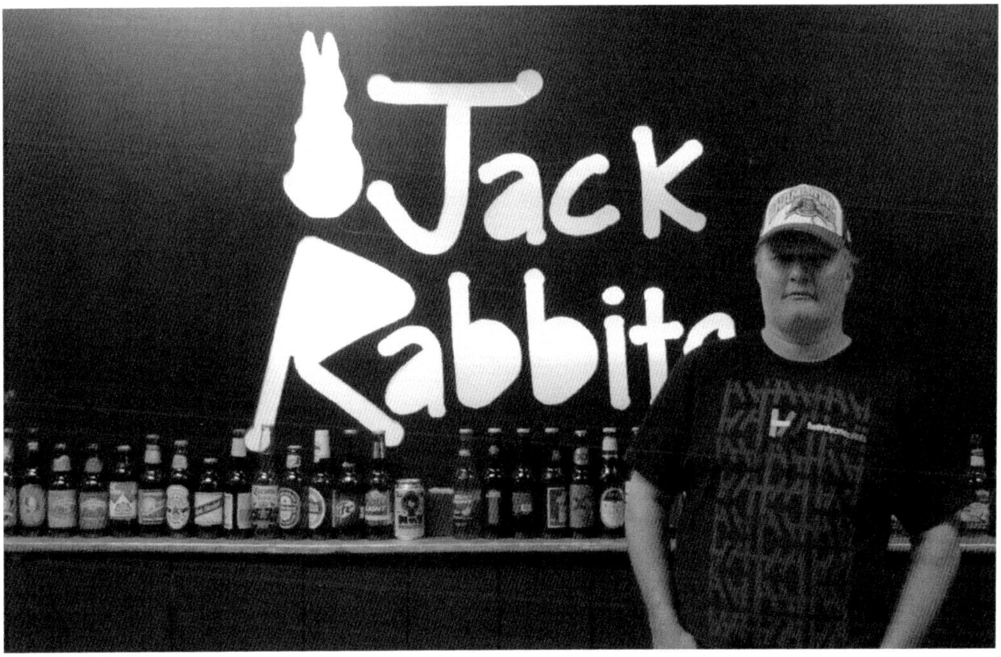


**Tim Hall**
Tim and Anne Hall knew the music business long before they moved here from San Diego in 1998. Tim had booked big music names in the business, including Eddie Vedder of Pearl Jam. Their first year here, Tim booked acts for local clubs, but then he and Anne started Jack Rabbits in San Marco, which has introduced Jacksonville to emerging music greats such as Le Tigre, Flogging Molly, and John Mayer. Running Jack Rabbits is hard work, but when asked why he keeps going, Tim quickly responds: "For the love of music." (Photograph by Kendall Brunson.)

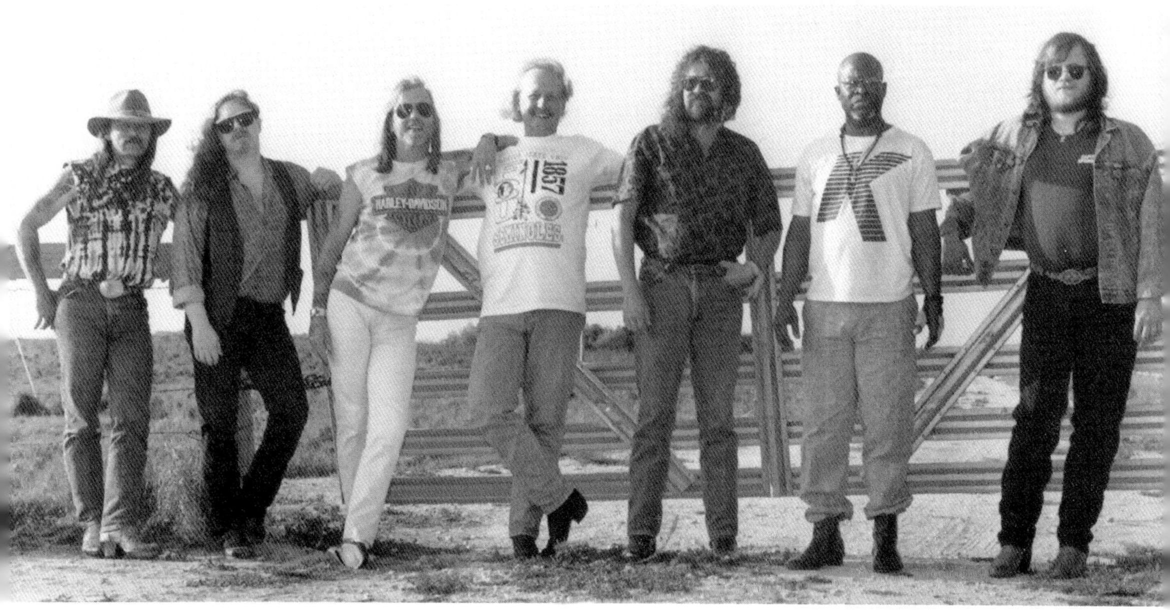

**Allman Brothers Band**

Brothers Duane and Gregg Allman, along with Dickey Betts, Berry Oakley, Butch Trucks, and Jai Johanny "Jaimoe" Johanson formed the Allman Brothers Band in Jacksonville in 1969. The band is one of the founding bands of Southern Rock and established a lasting impression on the local music scene. Known for hits such as "Ramblin' Man" and "Jessica," the band survived the deaths of two of its members early on, losing both Duane and Berry in separate motorcycle accidents. In 1995, the band was inducted into the Rock and Roll Hall of Fame, and *Rolling Stone* ranked the band number 53 on its list of 100 Greatest Artists of All Time in 2004. (Publicity photograph by Kirk West; distributed by Epic for the release of *Seven Turns.*)

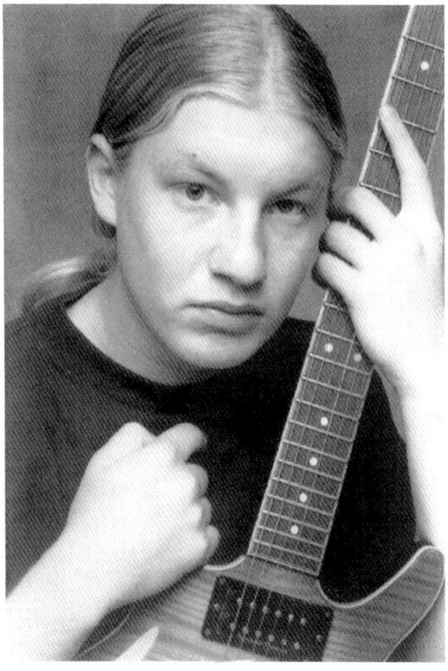

**Derek Trucks**

The youngest person ever named in *Rolling Stone*'s list of the greatest guitarists of all time, Derek Trucks was headlining shows by age 11. By 13, he had played with Buddy Guy and toured with the Allman Brothers Band, which as cofounded by his uncle Butch Trucks.

In 1999, he joined the Allman Brothers Band and also started his own band, the Derek Trucks Band. He met his wife, Susan Tedeschi, when she opened for the Allman Brothers Band, and together they formed the critically acclaimed Tedeschi Trucks Band. In 2014, Trucks resigned from the Allman Brothers Band to focus on his family and band with his wife. (Publicity photograph distributed by Entourage Talent Associates.)

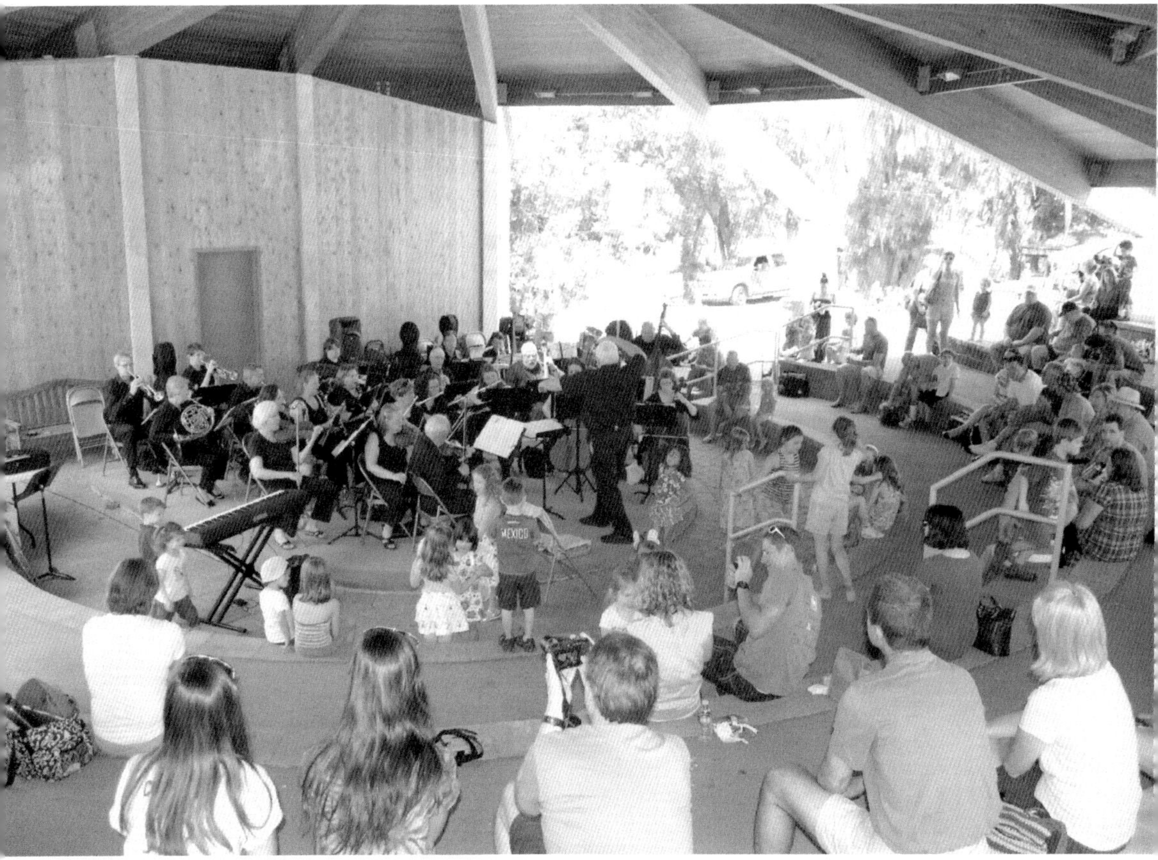

**Pops Symphony**

Formed in 1989, the Pops Symphony Orchestra is filled with volunteer musicians, amateur and professional, who want to play and perform for the community.

The Pops numbers about 40 players at any given time, with one musician acting as musical director. The group rehearses for two hours every week, except for summers, and players practice in trios and duets throughout the week as well.

Weekends are busy, with shows all over the city, at churches, retirement communities, and nature preserves. The Pops Symphony Orchestra is busiest during the holidays, with at least two shows a week leading up to Christmas.

Why all of this hard work? The members say they do it for the pleasure of playing.

This photograph of a Pops Symphony performance was taken at the Butterfly Festival at the Tree Hill Nature Center. (Photograph by Kendall Brunson.)

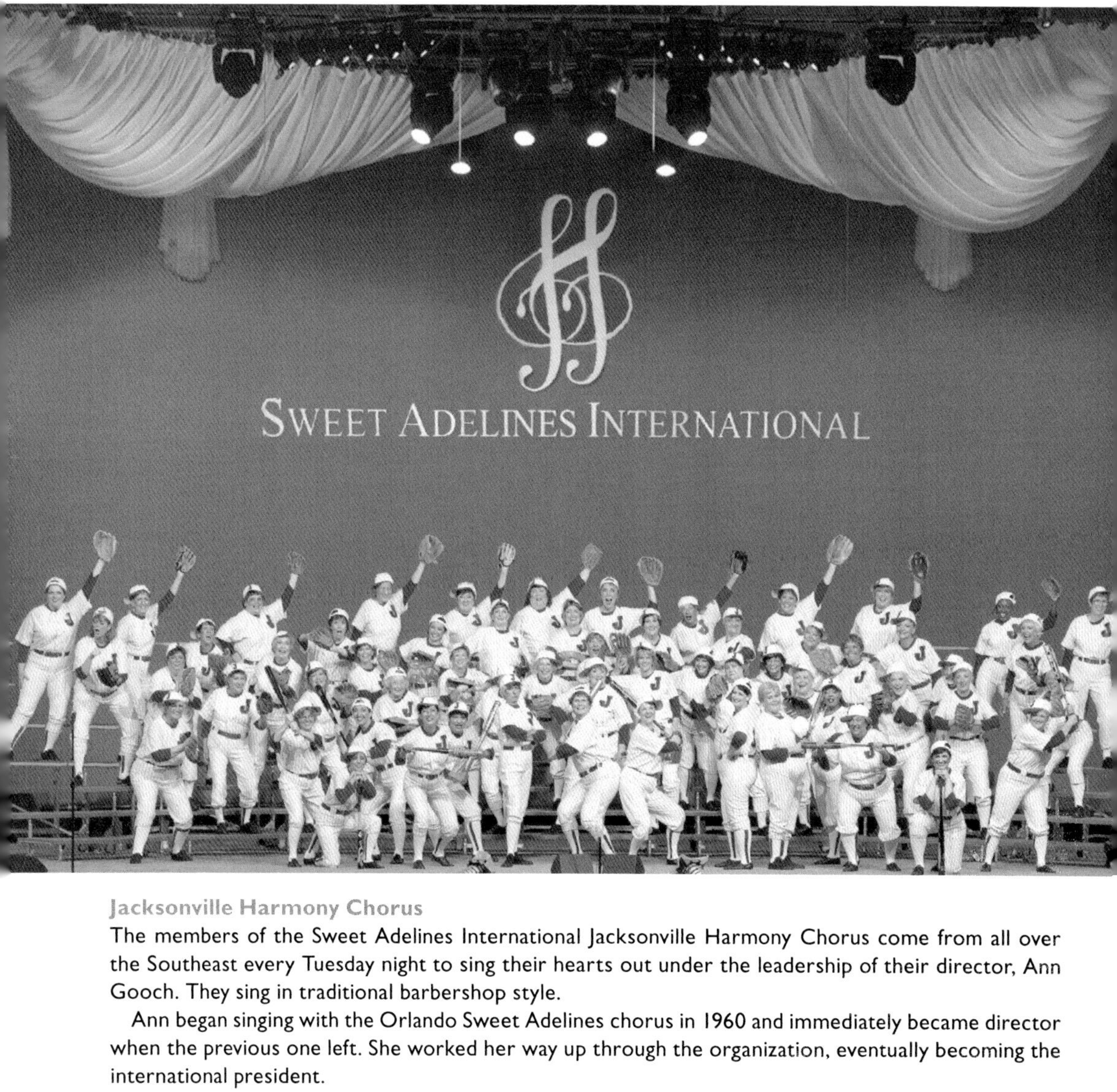


### Jacksonville Harmony Chorus

The members of the Sweet Adelines International Jacksonville Harmony Chorus come from all over the Southeast every Tuesday night to sing their hearts out under the leadership of their director, Ann Gooch. They sing in traditional barbershop style.

Ann began singing with the Orlando Sweet Adelines chorus in 1960 and immediately became director when the previous one left. She worked her way up through the organization, eventually becoming the international president.

When she moved to Jacksonville in 1971, she realized their theme song, "Harmonize the World," was not reaching women everywhere. She was soon organizing choruses in England, Sweden, and Australia, all while directing the chorus here and teaching at Florida State College at Jacksonville (FSCJ). Under Ann's leadership, the chorus has been invited to over a dozen international competitions. They are seen here at Worlds, in Hawaii, in 2013, where they took second place in the mid-size chorus category. (Photograph by Lilley Photography.)

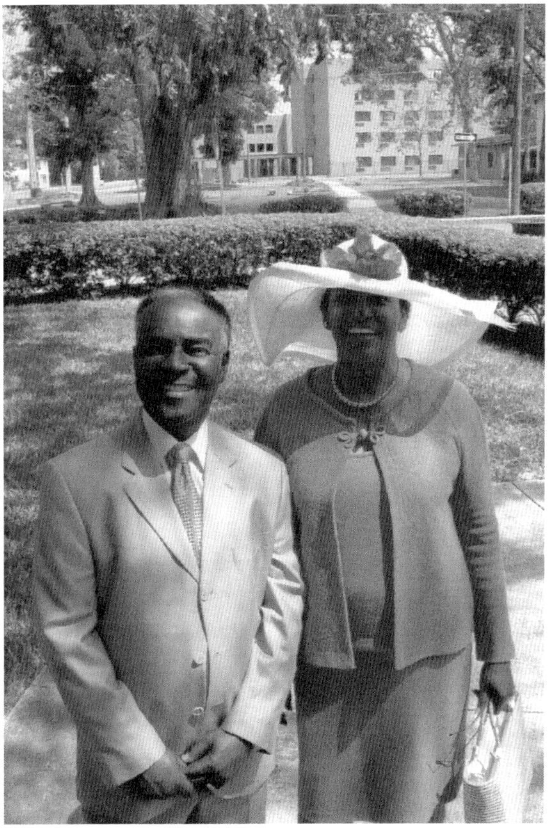

### Irene Lumpkin

Born and raised in Arlington, Irene Lumpkin sang gospel with her mother when she was 5. Irene mimicked sirens growing up, which expanded her vocal range. At 19, she learned she was a soprano, not an alto, which, except for her husband, John's, death in 2010, has been her greatest challenge. Weyerhaeuser heiress Kay Sweeney heard Irene perform at Bethune-Cookman College and became her benefactor, providing her with opera training at Julliard and Aspen Music Festival. Irene, shown here with John, sings at many local functions and at her church. (Courtesy of Irene Lumpkin.)

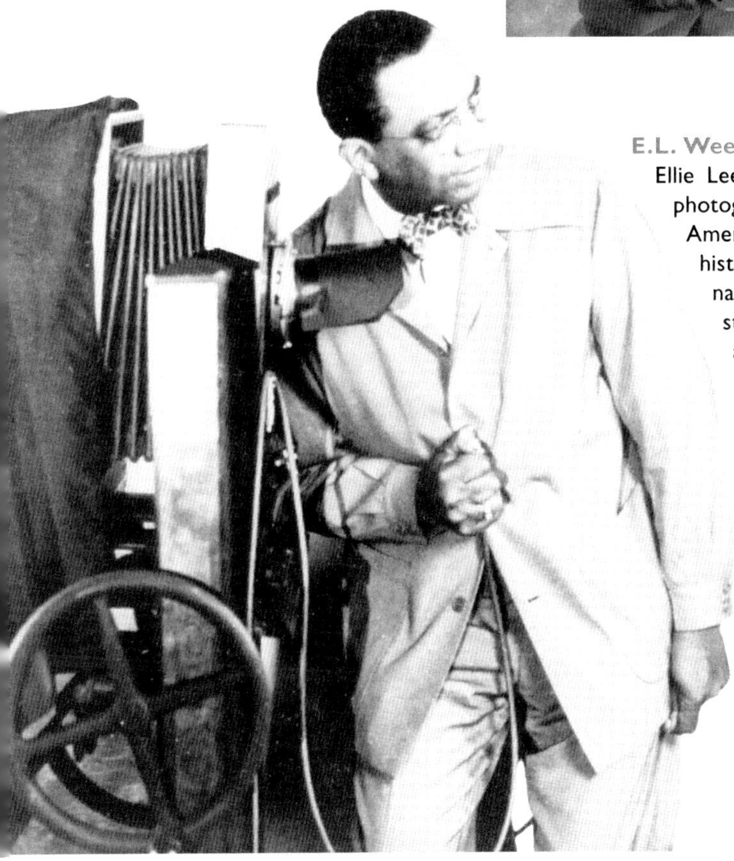

### E.L. Weems

Ellie Lee Weems spent half a century photographing Jacksonville's African American community, documenting historical moments. The Georgia native moved to Jacksonville after studying at the Tuskegee Institute and serving an apprenticeship with an Atlanta photographer. Weems captured much of the life of Eartha White as White cared for the less fortunate. The second floor of the Clara White Mission, on Ashley Street, features a museum of E.L. Weems's photography studio. (Courtesy of the Eartha M.M. White Collection, Thomas G. Carpenter Library, University of North Florida, Jacksonville, Florida.)

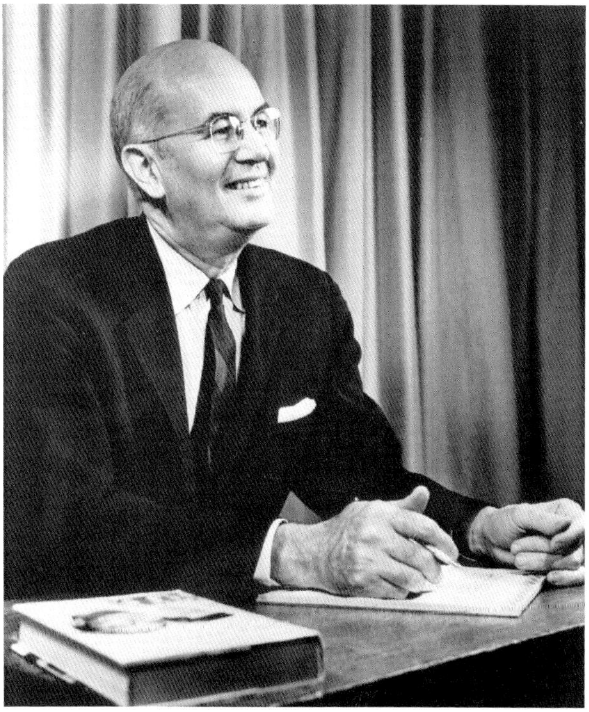

**Frank Slaughter**
Frank G. Slaughter successfully combined two loves, medicine and writing. His first novel, *That None Should Die*, addressed socialized medicine. It has never been out of print since being published in 1941. Dr. Slaughter practiced surgery at Riverside Hospital until 1942, when he began writing full-time. He also taught writing as an adjunct professor at Jacksonville University. When he died in 2001 at the age of 93, the surgeon had published 56 books, which sold a total of nearly 60 million copies. (Publicity photograph by Allan Walker; courtesy of Doubleday & Co.)

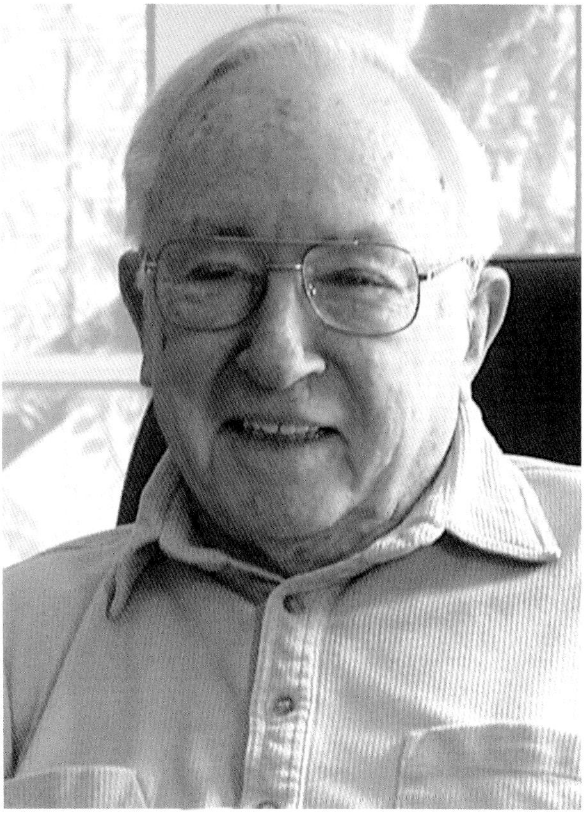

**Jack Hunter**
After World War II, Jack D. Hunter worked as a journalist, public relations executive, and speechwriter during the day. At night, he wrote on a yellow legal pad. The result was *The Blue Max*, a wartime novel that has mesmerized readers for decades. He went on to write 16 more novels. In the 1980s, Jack coached the journalists at the Florida Publishing Company. He died in 2009 and is interred in Jacksonville National Cemetery. (Courtesy of the Jack D. Hunter estate.)

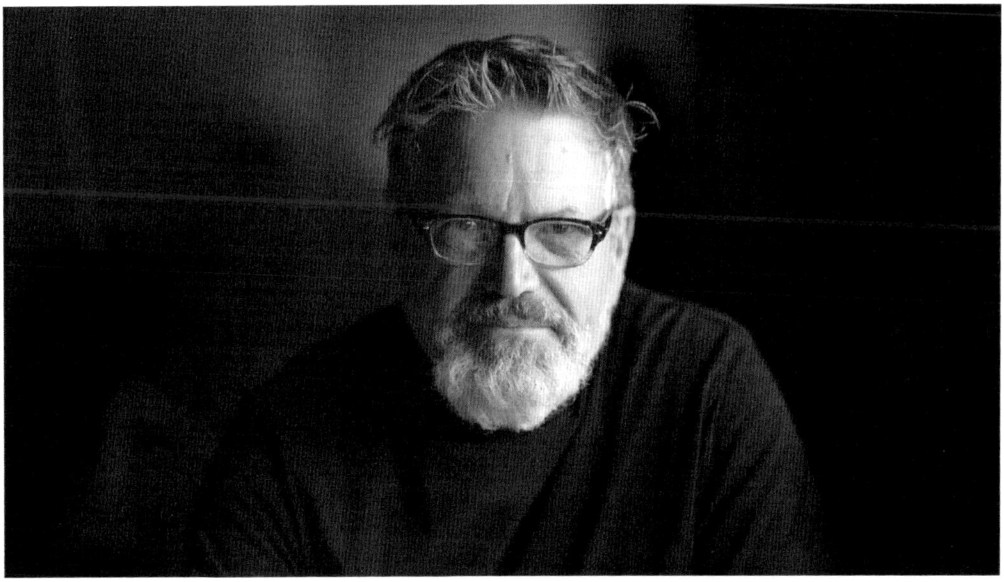

**Jim Draper**

It is well known that a local art collection is incomplete without a work by Jim Draper.

A trained artist with his master's in fine arts from the University of Georgia, Jim worked multiple retail jobs until he was 40. He then decided he no longer wanted to work for anyone else and pursued painting as his full-time career. Teaching adjunct art classes supplemented his income, and he opened his first studio in Edgewood.

Although Jim's work has explored the human figure, he is best known for his palm tree paintings and *Feast of Flowers* exhibition. Jim believes one can learn a lot about humanity by exploring the natural world, which is why he leaves the city once a week to paddle in the Okefenokee, Suwanee, or Ichetucknee River. This respect for nature translates into action. He was on the board of the St. Johns Riverkeeper, and he advocates for environment preservation, saying, "We shouldn't take more than we need."

With his studio now in the CoRK Arts District, Jim's creativity is evolving toward writing short stories. His childhood in Mississippi and admiration for Southern Gothic authors such as Flannery O'Conner and Tennessee Williams influence his writing. If this next chapter reflects the first, there will be many patrons flocking to read Jim's work. (Both courtesy of Jim Draper.)

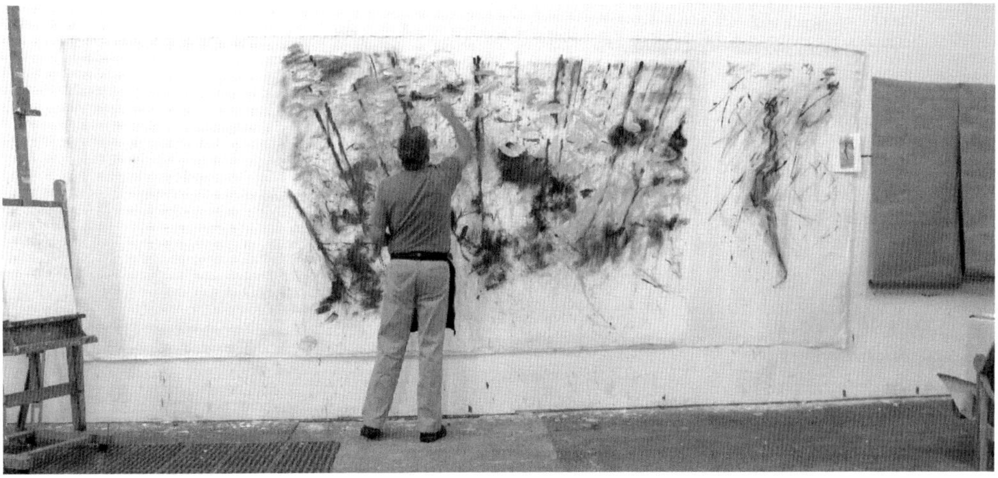

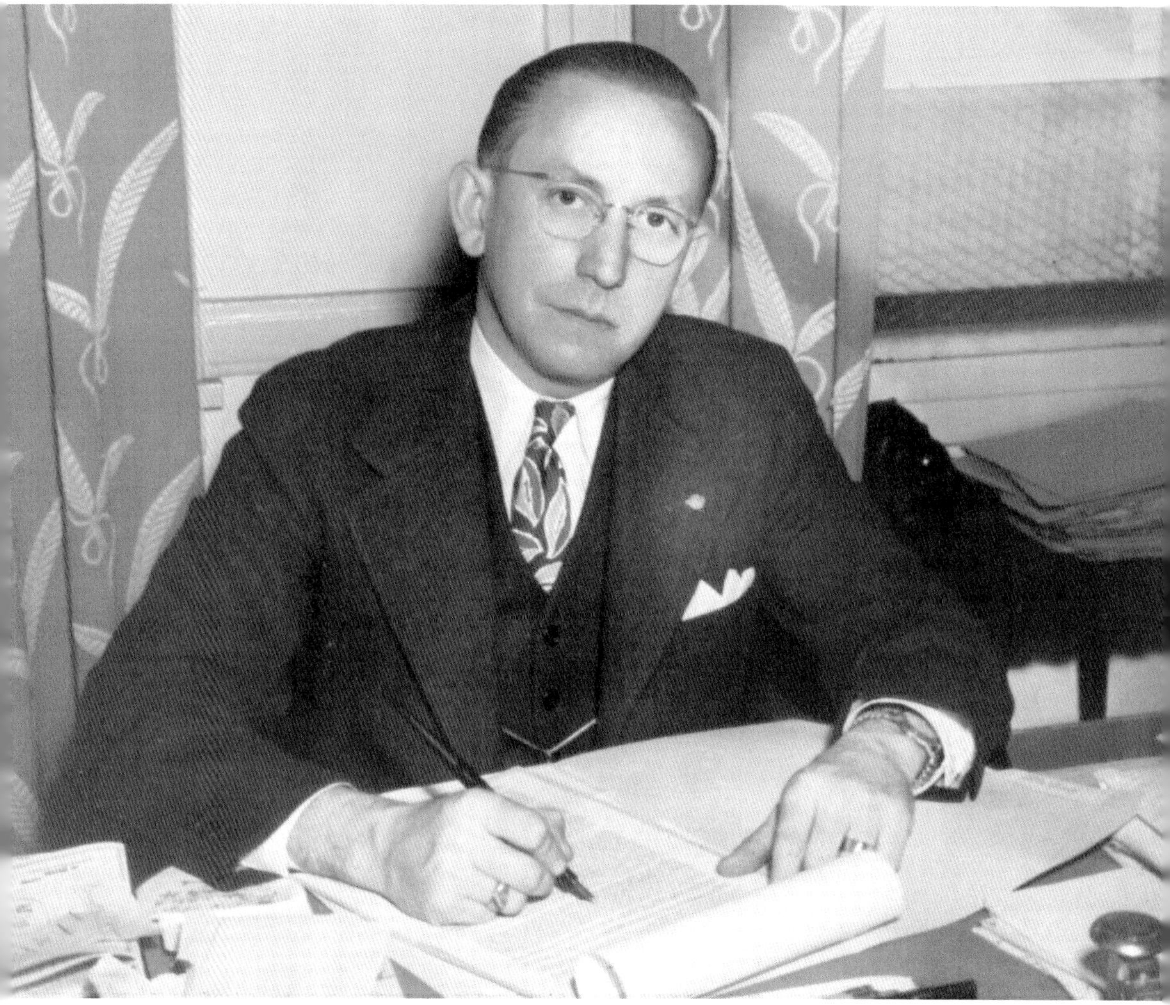

### Judge Gooding

Jacksonville juvenile judge Marion Gooding never expected to make national headlines. He was a World War II veteran, husband, and father of six children. But, in August 1956, Judge Gooding responded to the concern of citizens who petitioned the court after reports of youth reaction to Elvis Presley, who was slated to headline six shows at the Florida Theatre over a two-day period. Judge Gooding's son Mack said Elvis was on a "Train Tour" from Tampa to Miami to Daytona Beach and then to Jacksonville. At each stop, teen rowdiness grew into violence. In Tampa, the teenagers tore up the theater. In Miami and Daytona Beach, the theaters were damaged and violence spilled into the streets, leading to arrests. By the time the train reached Jacksonville, Elvis's performance was as much an issue of public safety as it was "morality."

Judge Gooding ordered Elvis Presley to cease from his trademark hip gyrations or go to jail for impairing the morals of minors. He sat through the next show to make sure Elvis complied. (Mrs. Gooding, their three teenage daughters, and their 10-year-old son also watched the show—that was six tickets for the judge!) The incident resulted in coverage in *Life* magazine. According to his son, Judge David Gooding, Judge Marion Gooding also became an Elvis fan and enjoyed watching "the King" when he performed on television. (Courtesy of Mack Gooding.)

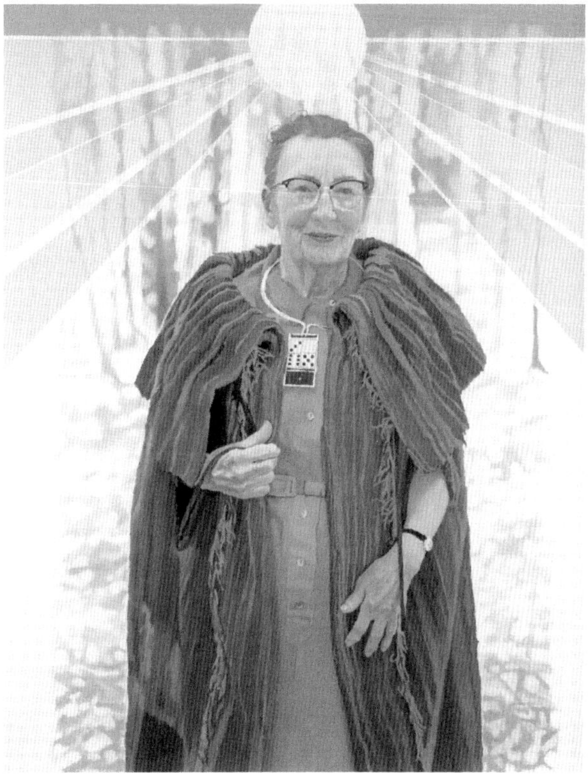

### Jacksonville's First Lady of Art

People may not know they are familiar with the work of the city's "First Lady of Art," as the Museum of Contemporary Art Jacksonville calls Memphis Wood. But her unmistakable sculptural fiber art hangs in many buildings. She worked more than six decades as an artist and teacher, influencing generations of artists. She encouraged local accountant and painter Charlie Brown to take a pottery class. It changed his life. She died in 1989 at the age of 87. (Courtesy of Museum of Contemporary Art Jacksonville; portrait of Memphis Wood by Mary Ann Bryan, 1977; gift of Ms. Memphis Wood.)

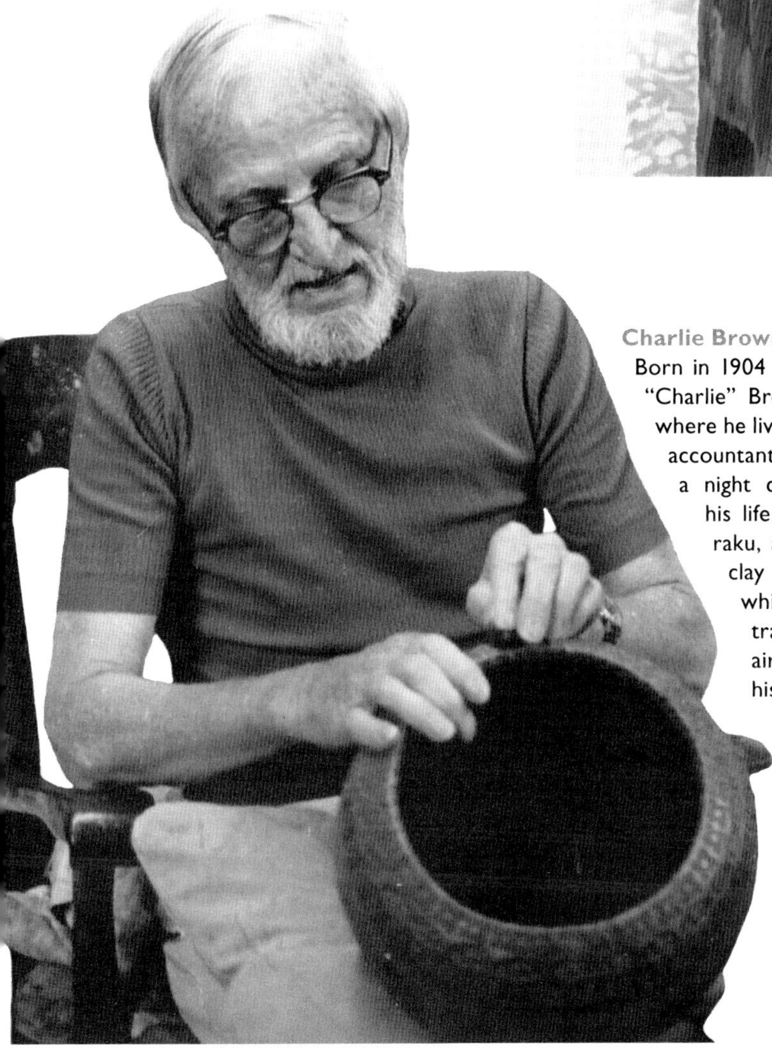

### Charlie Brown

Born in 1904 in Mayport, Charles Moses "Charlie" Brown grew up in Mandarin, where he lived until he died in 1987. The accountant painted until 1951, when a night course in pottery changed his life. In the 1960s, he adopted raku, a low-fire method in which clay is removed from the kiln while still hot. Abandoning the traditional Japanese open-air method, Charlie cooled his in a container filled with combustible material, such as dried leaves. (Courtesy of the Mandarin Museum and Historical Society.)

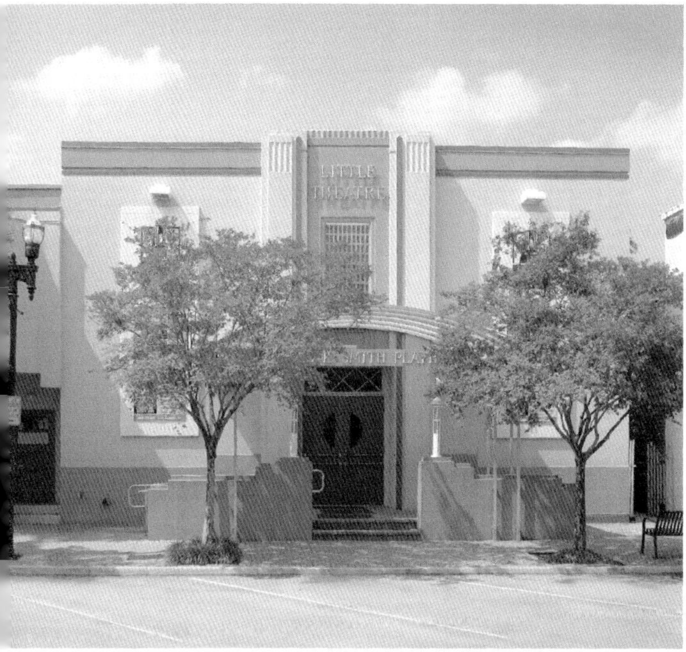

**Theatre Jacksonville**
Theatre Jacksonville is one of the oldest continually operating community theaters in the country. Founded as the Little Theatre in 1919, it had no permanent home until it settled into San Marco Square in 1938. The first show in the new space was *Boy Meets Girl*. In 1969, it was reincorporated as Theatre Jacksonville. All Jacksonville mayors have recognized the playhouse as the city's official theater since 1972. (Courtesy of Theatre Jacksonville.)

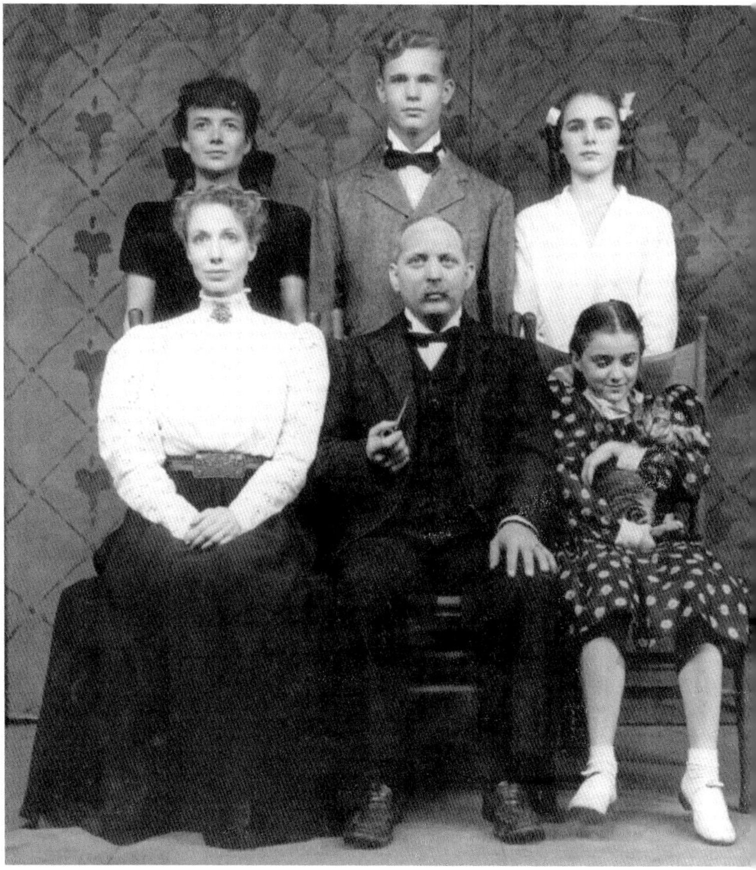

**Marion Conner Price**
Some call her the grand dame of Jacksonville theater, others call her its first lady, but one thing is sure: Marion Conner Price shaped local theater. Several generations of actors studied with her at the Storybook Players, including Theatre Jacksonville executive director Sarah Boone.

Marion's first play here was *Angel Street* at Theatre Jacksonville, and she was known for her one-woman shows portraying famous women such as Helen Keller, Eleanor Roosevelt, and Emily Post. In this photograph, Marion is pictured front left in the play *I Remember Mama* at Theatre Jacksonville. (Courtesy of Theatre Jacksonville.)

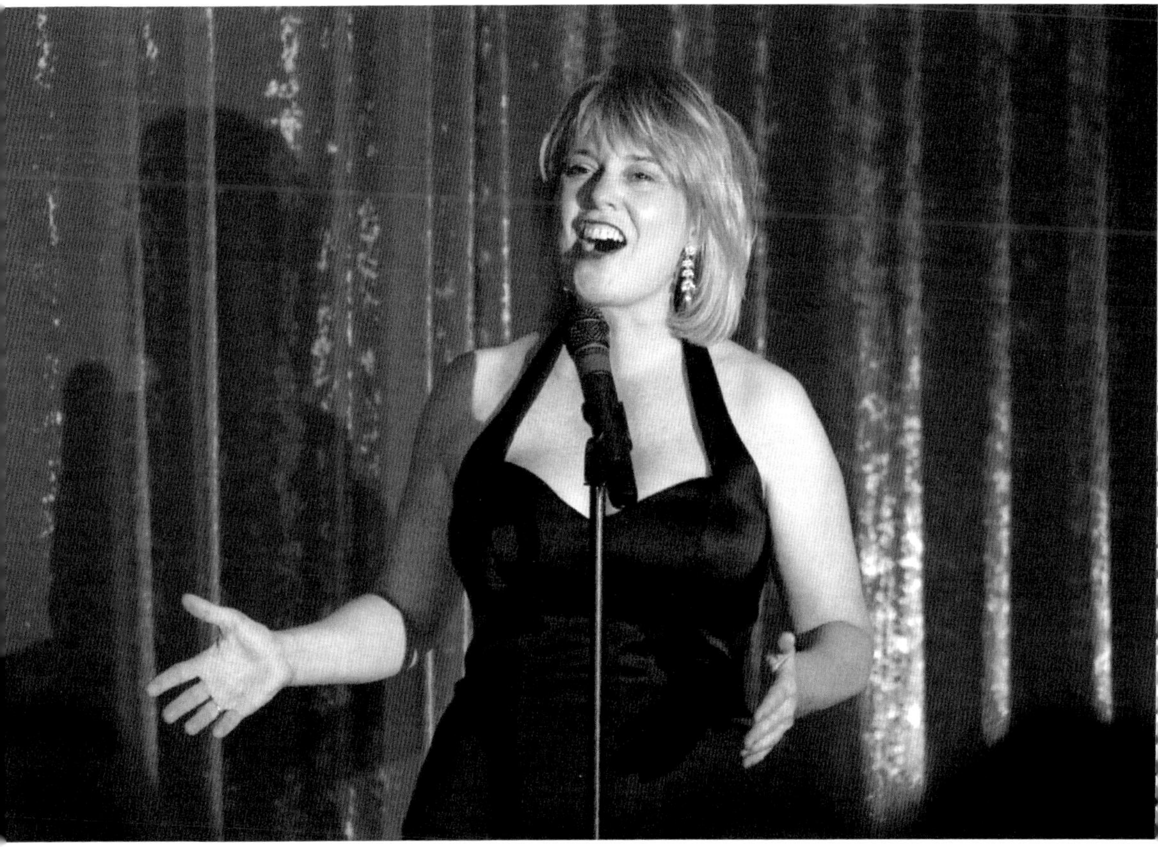

**Sarah Boone**

Sarah Boone feels a strong responsibility to the city as Theatre Jacksonville's executive director. She has to strike a balance of maintaining the history of the theater while keeping the productions relevant to a contemporary audience.

The Jacksonville native attended the Bolles School and studied with actress and acting teacher Marion Conner Price. After studying theater at Florida State University, Sarah continued her education in New York City before earning her master's in arts management and communications at American University. She has managed and acted in playhouses from New York to Los Angeles.

Sarah returned to Jacksonville for an intended brief stay in 2000. However, once the executive director position opened at Theatre Jacksonville, her plans changed. It is fitting that Sarah found her place here. After all, her very first show was in the historic theater when she was cast in *Cat Princess*, directed by Marion Conner Price.

Because of the community support, Sarah thinks Theatre Jacksonville stands above the rest. Under her leadership, the theater has added edgier, guerrilla shows and a playwriting competition. She wants to use art to move people and create discussions within the community. (Photograph by Laura Evans.)

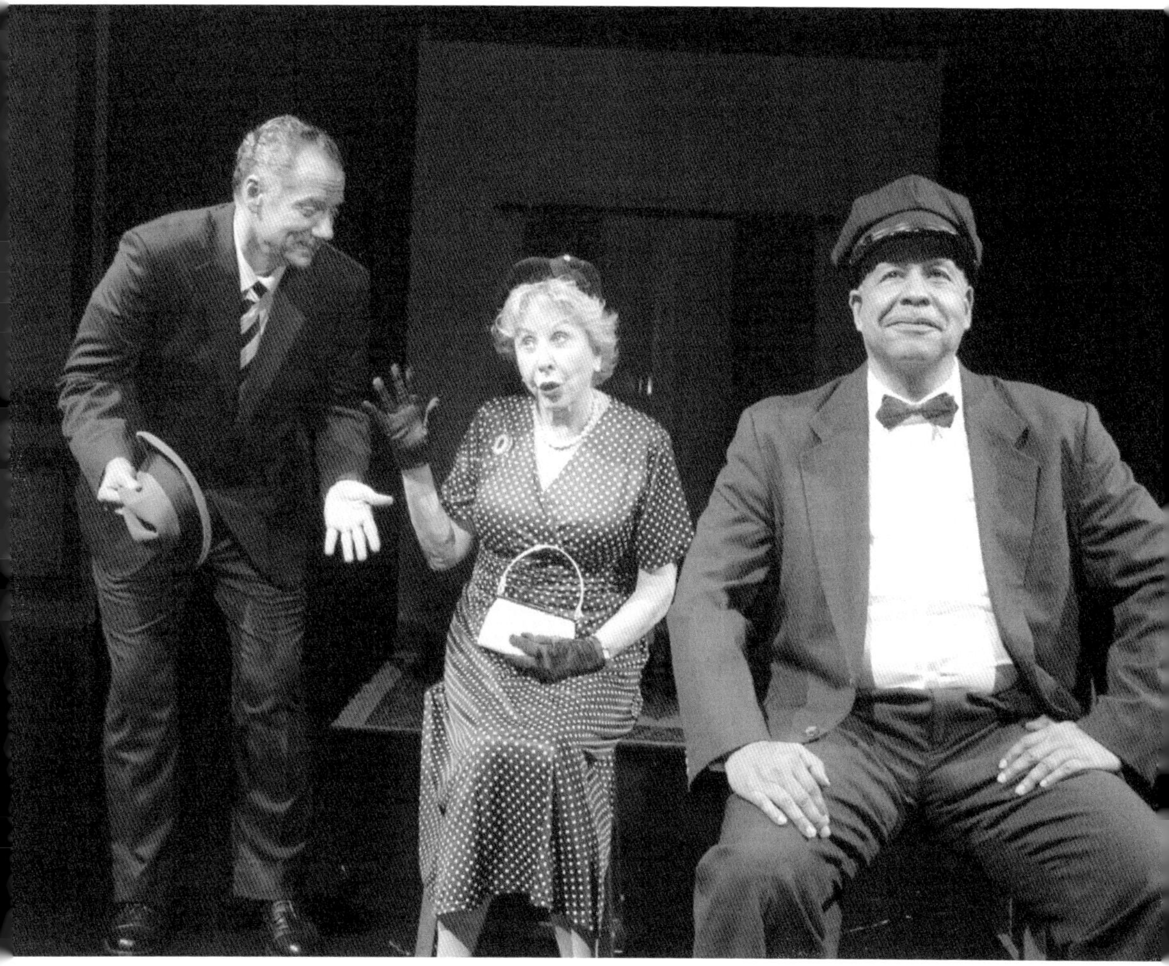

**The Alhambra**

Generations in Jacksonville saw their first Broadway show at one of the city's gems: Alhambra Theatre & Dining. The country's longest-running professional dinner theater, the Alhambra has featured performers such as Dorothy Lamour, Frank Gorshin, and Cyd Charisse. It was also the site of Betty Grable's last live performance.

In addition, generations of actors have graced the Alhambra stage. Former owner and now executive producer Tod Booth says he is often called "Papa" or "Grandpa" by child actors whose parents have acted in his productions there. Alhambra performers are members of the Actors' Equity Association.

Built in 1967, the venue features a bar, a restaurant, and an open stage that provides theatergoers seats on three sides. Here, Michael Learned (center) stars in the Alhambra production of *Driving Miss Daisy.* (Courtesy of Alhambra Theatre & Dining.)

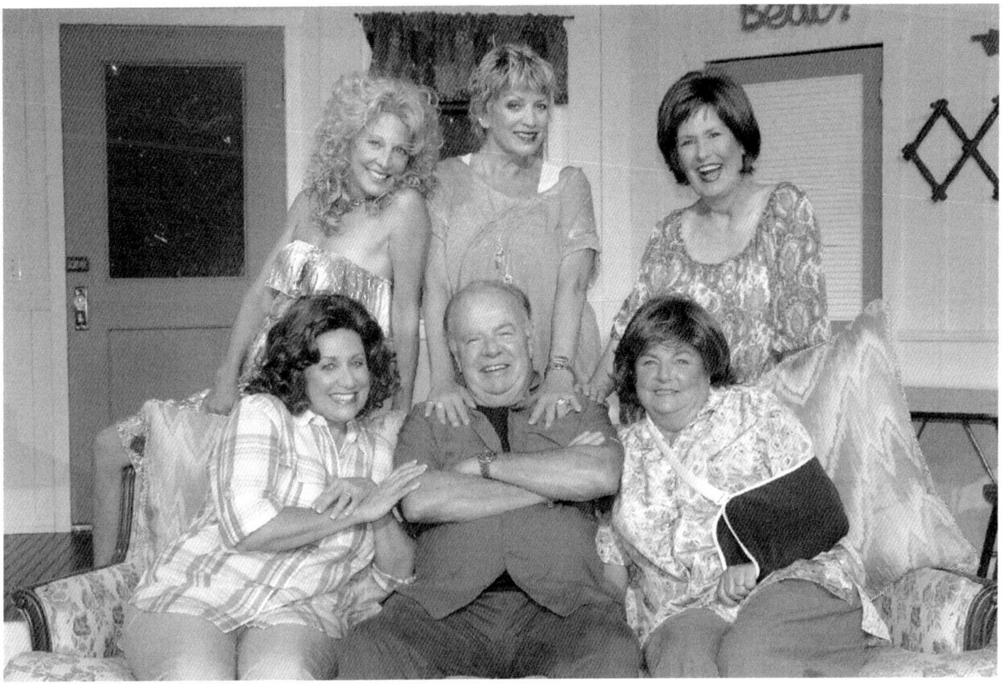

**Tod Booth**

Tod Booth has worked with many notable actors of the 20th century over dinner, including Don Ameche, Vera Miles, Sally Struthers, Barbara Eden, Mickey Rooney, Imogene Coca, John and Keith Carradine, and Claude Atkins.

Working for Chicago's five Drury Lane dinner theaters, Tod produced many shows that toured dinner theaters nationwide. In 1984, Claude Atkins asked him to do a show in Jacksonville, where Atkins represented a bulletproof vest company. Tod produced *You Ought to Be in Pictures*, starring Atkins, at the Alhambra Dinner Theatre (now Alhambra Theatre & Dining), owned by Leon Simon. Over dinner, Simon mentioned being tired of the business, and Tod bought the Alhambra "on a napkin for $1 million."

The world of dinner theater changed dramatically since the Alhambra opened in 1967. In 2014, only five professional dinner theaters remain, down from a high of 176. In 2009, after a quarter of a century, Tod brought in investors and now works as Alhambra's executive producer and director. In this photograph, Tod joins the cast of *The Dixie Swim Club*. (Courtesy of Alhambra Theatre & Dining.)

**Craig Smith**

Entrepreneur Craig Smith grew up in Jacksonville, where he enjoyed dinner and a show at the Alhambra, an experience he shared with his daughter. In 2009, he was dining with Tod Booth Jr., whose father owned the theater. When Tod mentioned the struggles faced in the new market, Craig's first thought was that the Alhambra cannot go away. So he did what any successful entrepreneur would do: he bought the Alhambra. And he has brought a few changes. Despite the long days and seven-day workweeks, he says he has to pinch himself to make sure it is real. Here, Craig is pictured with Jamie Farr, known for playing Klinger on *M*A*S*H*. (Courtesy of Alhambra Theatre & Dining.)

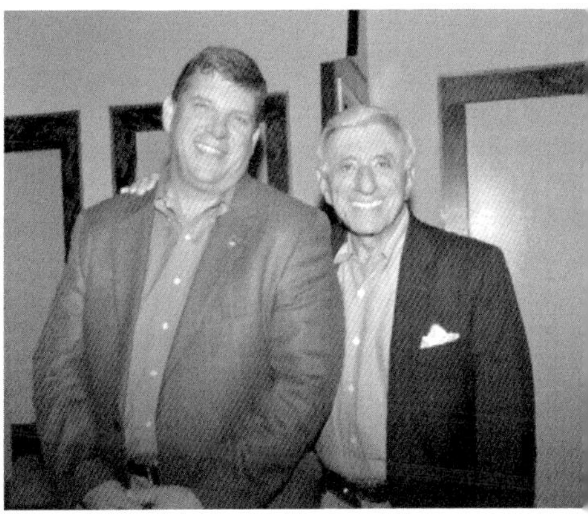

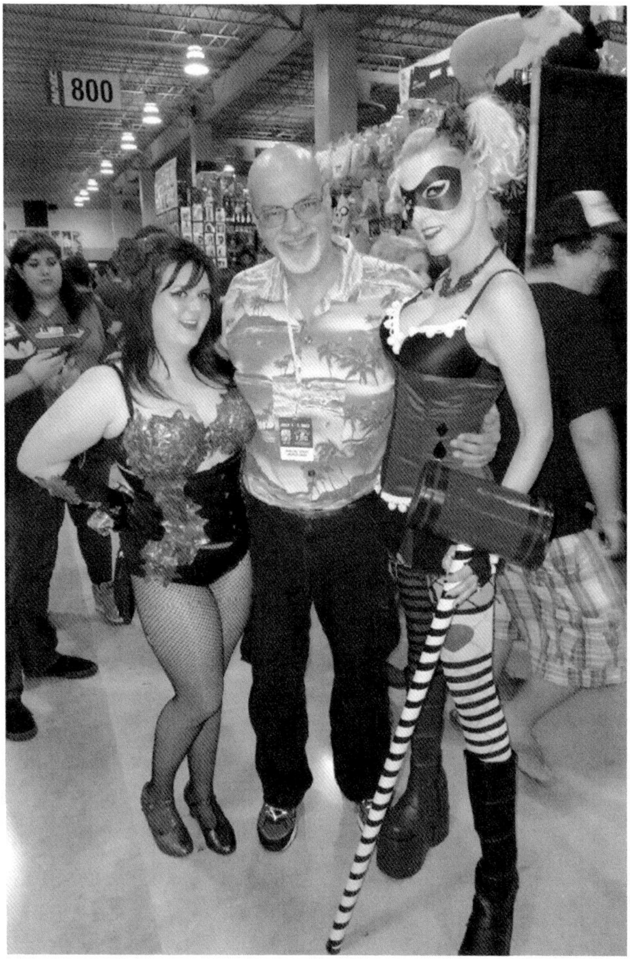


## Dressing for Success

Candy Keane cannot remember a time when she was not making costumes. She learned at the sewing machines of her mother and grandmother for the purpose of winning costume contests as a child. She took that love of costuming with her to college, when she studied at the University of Florida's School of Journalism.

Candy and her husband, Sean, moved to the West Coast for work, and she expanded costume-making into more challenging ideas. On a whirlwind trip to Jacksonville, the couple purchased a house and flew back to San Diego to pack their things. Having to fit all their possessions into their car and a small U-Haul, Candy decided to downsize her costume collection. She sold her Princess Leia costume for $501 on eBay, sparking the idea for a new career.

Three Muses Costumes started out of her house in May 2005, selling solely online, and she opened the physical location in January 2009. Candy travels all over the country attending comic book and sci-fi conventions such as Comic-Con and Dragon Con. Her costumes have appeared on the cover of magazines and on the movie poster for *Fanboys*. She was interviewed in the documentary *Jedi Junkies*, and she appears on the cover of the film in her notorious Princess Leia slave costume. In 2013, *Entertainment Weekly* photographed her transformation into Wonder Woman for Comic-Con.

Her custom costumes are shipped far and wide, including Greece, Latvia, and Scotland.

Pictured at SuperCon from left to right are Brema Ebbing, who helps Candy run the business; George Perez, one of Candy's favorite comic book artists; and Candy. (Photograph by Sean Keane.)

# CHAPTER FIVE

# Visionaries

It is no wonder that Jacksonville is and has been home to visionaries. However, the range of visionaries the city has generated is indeed a surprise.

A former slave and widowed mother, Clara White collected surplus food to serve meals out of her two-room home to hungry neighbors and homeless people. Her daughter Eartha White expanded her work to include housing, training, and other needed services.

Evelyn Nehl, the daughter of a Baptist preacher, worked tirelessly to bring the AIDS quilt to Jacksonville at a time when people spoke of the disease only in whispered tones.

Mayor Lou Ritter believed in and worked for Jacksonville's consolidation for years. Voters defeated the proposals six times. Less than two months before citizens passed consolidation, a new mayor took the keys to the city and guided it through the process of becoming the world's largest city in the area, at that time.

Mayor Jake Godbold reached out to political opponents from the business sector to join forces with him to build a "Bold New City of the South." His charisma drew thousands of residents to fill the football stadium with little notice when the owner of the Baltimore Colts (now Indianapolis Colts) agreed to visit.

In early 1962, US government meteorologist George Winterling changed the way TV news presented weather reports. He suggested to a station manager that a meteorologist broadcasting the weather would benefit viewers. Winterling also invented weather maps before the days of satellite.

Jacksonville's Bonnie Upright is one of those rare public relations professionals who helps people while generating awareness. Her creative spark has not only dotted Jacksonville's landscape with large, colorful sculptures of manatee, sea turtles, and jaguars, but it has also raised more than $500,000 for community organizations.

A crystal ball would reveal that Jacksonville's visionaries have not sought fame, but rather a flame for their passion. And, in seeking that flame, they have made Jacksonville's past, present, and future brighter, warmer, and more relevant.

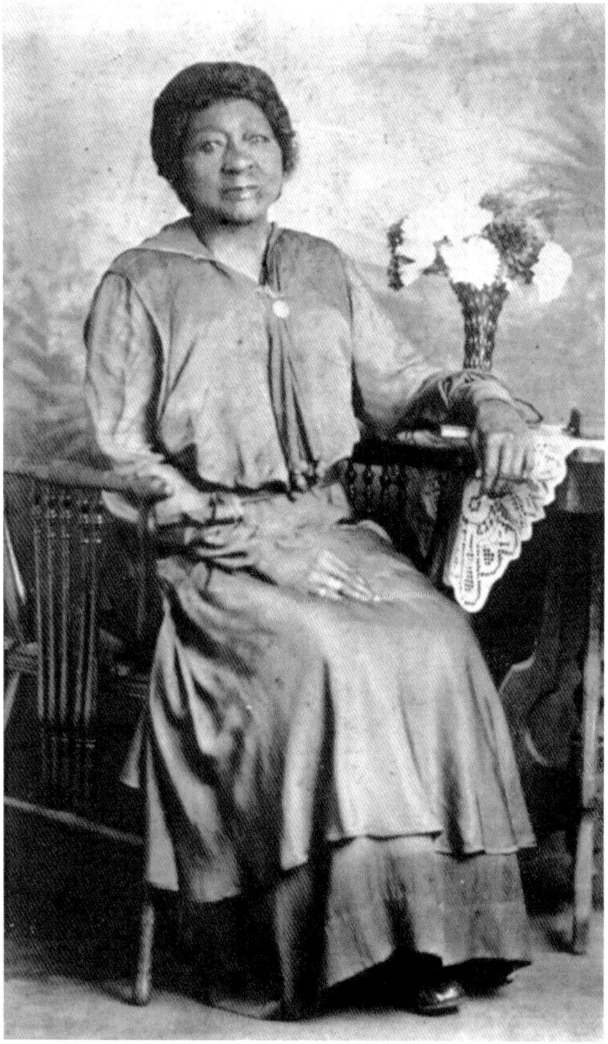

### Clara White

Born a slave on Amelia Island, just north of Jacksonville, Clara was only nine when she saw her mother sold to a new owner who lived in another town. Clara married at the age of 19, and the couple moved to Jacksonville. Sadly, none of their 12 natural children lived, but Clara and her husband adopted a baby girl, who was only five when Clara was widowed.

After Clara's husband died, she worked as a stewardess on a steamboat that ran between Jacksonville and New York City. At the time, Jacksonville was the steamboat's last stop in Florida. The city's Subtropical Exposition drew tourists and dignitaries, including Pres. Grover Cleveland. When Clara was not working aboard the ship, she took care of others. Children in the neighborhood believed in Santa Claus because of the stockings filled with candy and homemade toys that "Aunt Clara" hung over her fireplace. She collected food from the steamboats and restaurants to feed the homeless and very poor out of her two-room house on Clay Street.

Clara and her daughter Eartha started the very first soup kitchen in Jacksonville, which today is the Clara White Mission. In 1902, Clara and Eartha founded the Old Folks Home, the forerunner of the Eartha White Nursing Home. Clara died in 1920. (Courtesy of the State Archives of Florida, *Florida Memory*, www.floridamemory.com/items/show/837.)

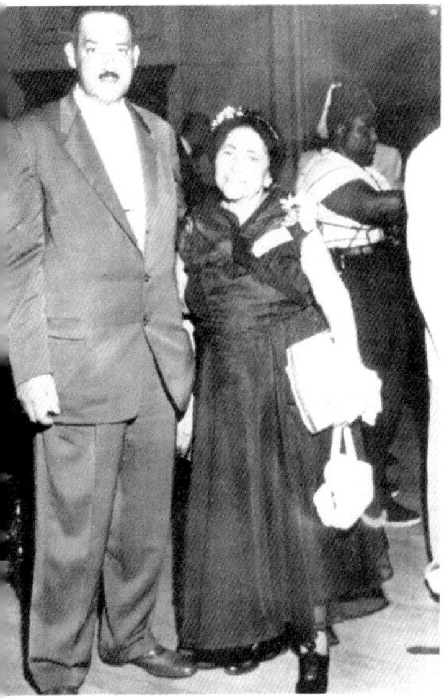

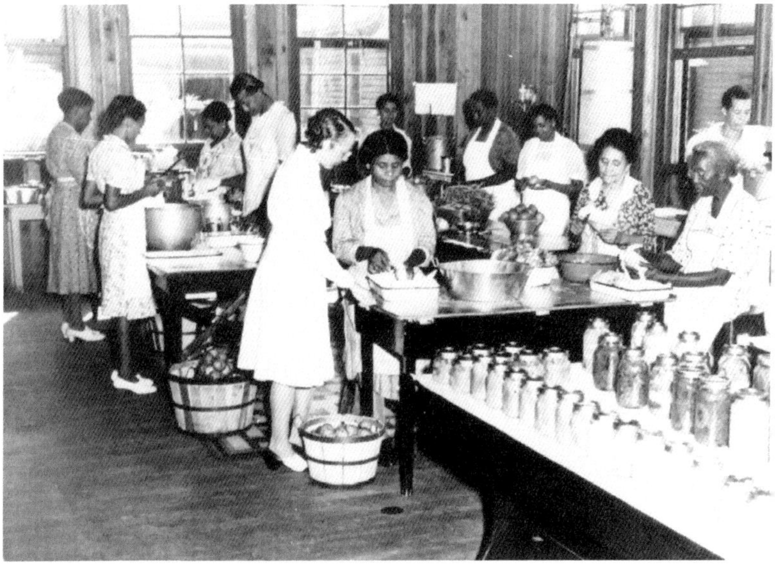

**Eartha M.M. White**

Born in 1876, Eartha was adopted by former slaves and taught from the earliest age to care for her neighbors in the heart of Jacksonville. Fatherless from the age of five, she worked at her mother's side to help feed the hungry in her neighborhood and care for the poor. Eartha trained at the National Conservatory and was an opera singer with James Rosemond Johnson in the Oriental American Opera Company. The company toured throughout the country and in Europe and Asia. Eartha became engaged, but her fiancé died a month before the wedding. Heartbroken, Eartha returned to Jacksonville and enrolled in the Florida Baptist Academy. After graduation, she taught for 16 years, all the while working part-time at the Afro-American Life Insurance Company. Through the insurance work, Eartha gained keen business insight and made connections with prominent leaders, both black and white. She applied her knowledge and entrepreneurial skills and used them to finance her philanthropic and volunteer work.

In the early 1900s, Eartha worked with prison inmates, started an orphanage, and founded a daycare center for working mothers. She secured a permanent home for the Clara White Mission and expanded its work to include educational programs. Men learned to cook, and women learned to sew. With her mother, she started the Old Folks Home, which became the Eartha White Nursing Home. For years in Downtown Jacksonville, the children's Christmas party at the mission was a highlight of the year. A special focus of the mission was veterans. Her work was so renowned that dignitaries, including presidents and congressmen, came to visit Eartha White in her home quarters, above the mission on Ashley Street. Eartha White died in 1974 at the age of 97. (Both courtesy of the Eartha M.M. White Collection, Thomas G. Carpenter Library, University of North Florida, Jacksonville, Florida.)

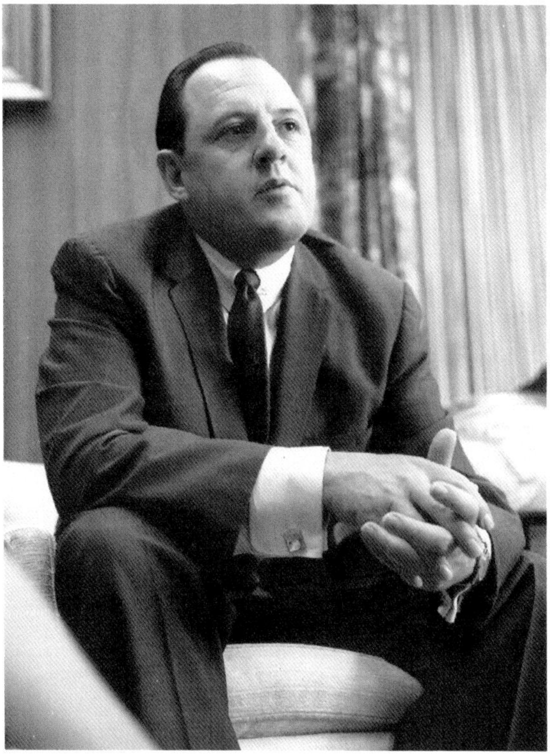

### Lou Ritter

Lou Ritter was a friend of Pres. John F. Kennedy and worked for Pres. Lyndon Johnson. But his political career grew from humble roots planted in 1951 when he took the oath of council member of the City of Jacksonville at the age of 25.

Ritter, who held a degree in public administration from the University of Florida, also held forward-thinking ideas. He believed in government efficiency and access, and he excelled at policy work and consensus building. Anticipating the city's growth, he realized the need for a new airport and secured the location and funds for the facility, which has easily expanded to meet increased demand. After befriending Kennedy at a conference in Daytona Beach, he was tapped to run his presidential campaign in North Florida. While Kennedy did not carry the state, he won North Florida hands down.

When the sitting mayor, Haydon Burns, won the election for governor in 1964, the council appointed Ritter to finish the three years left on his term. Ritter was the perfect man for the job, as the country and the city struggled with civil rights. He appointed African Americans to advisory boards, allowed them to take tests for civil service jobs, and started the Greater Jacksonville Economic Opportunity program, which became a nationwide model. Among Ritter's treasures is a letter from a constituent: "If not for you, Lou Ritter, we would be a Selma, Alabama."

Ritter also initiated the study for consolidation, which would increase the size of Jacksonville 20-fold, from 39.38 square miles to 841. Voters had turned down consolidation six times, but, less than a year after the study was released, they passed the referendum nearly two-to-one. However, Ritter did not win his bid for reelection, and the next mayor oversaw the day of consolidation for Jacksonville. Ritter never ran for office again.

He did, however, work for the Office of Economic Opportunity as Sargent Shriver's executive assistant during Pres. Lyndon Johnson's administration. He returned to Florida to become secretary of the Florida Department of Professional and Occupational Regulation for Gov. Reubin Askew, and he later started a lobbying firm.

Lou Ritter died in 2010 at the age of 84. (Courtesy of Nancy Seely.)

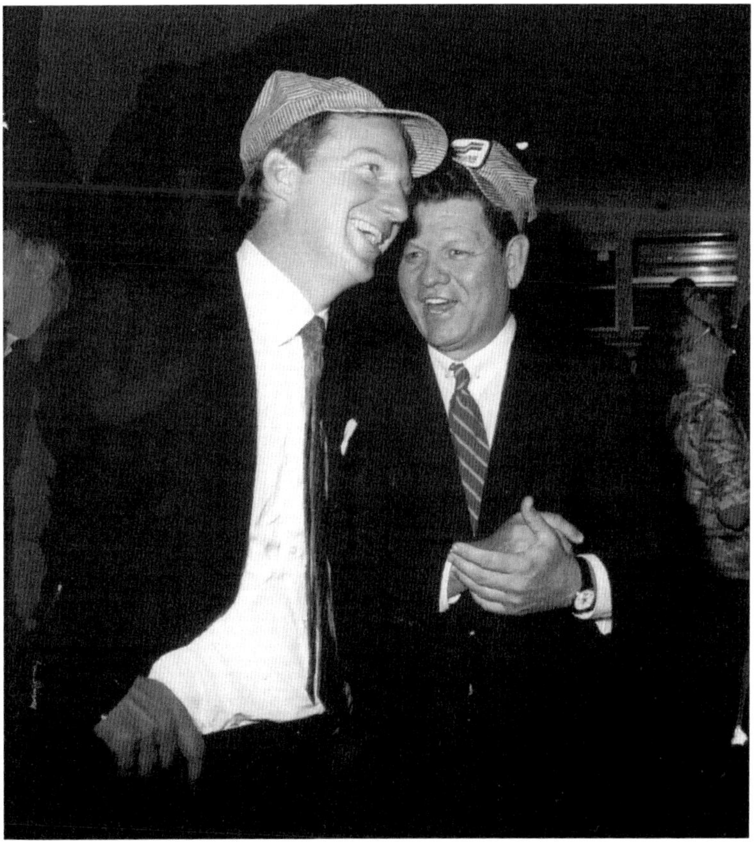

## Jake Godbold

Jacksonville native Jake Godbold grew up in a Northside housing project with a commitment to make his city better. He served on the Jacksonville City Council from the year before consolidation took effect until 1979, and was council president for seven of those years. He had planned to get out of politics and focus on his company, but, when the sitting mayor resigned to run for governor, Godbold was appointed to serve the last six months of the mayoral term. Excited over the progress he and his team accomplished, Godbold ran again, serving as mayor until 1987 and leaving his mark on the city he loves.

Mayor Godbold built an atmosphere that allowed a public-private partnership to thrive. Soon after he won the election, he met with his political opponents and convinced them that their mutual love for Jacksonville trumped any political differences. Under his tenure, Jacksonville, which he nicknamed the "Bold New City of the South," saw several brick-and-mortar projects revitalize the Downtown. He started the Jacksonville Jazz Festival and initiated construction of the Jacksonville Landing and the Southbank Riverwalk.

He was also passionate about bringing an NFL team to Jacksonville. With little notice, Godbold inspired thousands of residents to fill the city's football stadium in an effort to convince Baltimore Colts owner Bob Irsay to move his team to Jacksonville. Godbold and Irsay landed in a helicopter on the field to thousands of cheering fans, many of whom wore "Jacksonville Colts" tee shirts. The city did not get the team, but the people were falling in love with the idea, and they did eventually get their own franchise, the Jaguars.

The opening of Jacksonville's convention center in 1986, during Mayor Godbold's administration, was cause for great celebration. Here, one of the developers, Steve Wilson (right), enjoys the grand opening with Mayor Jake Godbold. (Courtesy of Jake Godbold.)

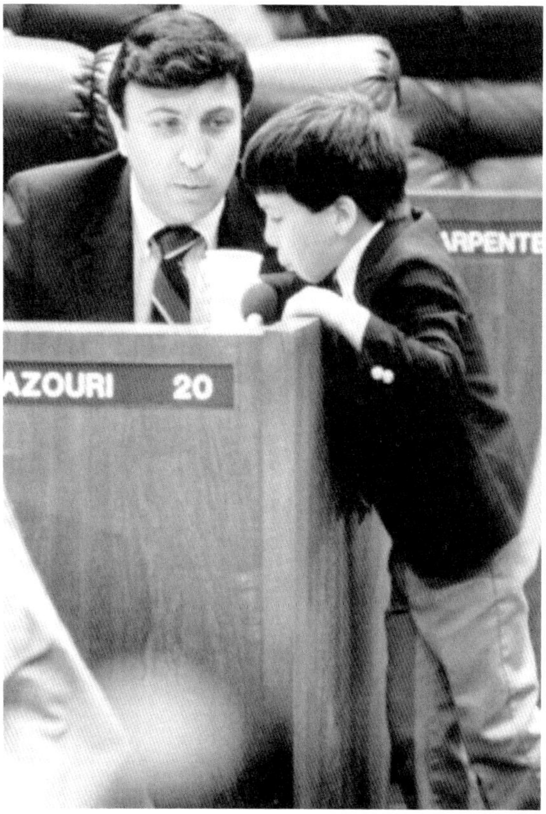


### Tommy Hazouri

Childhood friends say Tommy Hazouri wanted to be mayor of Jacksonville since he was in ninth grade. The Jacksonville native cannot remember that, but he does admit to an early start in politics, serving as class president and working his way up from there.

The youngest of four boys, Tommy was the only one interested in politics, inspired by the Camelot spirit of the Kennedy years. He wanted to spend his life making a difference for his community. After graduating from Jacksonville University with a degree in government, Tommy secured two key internships, one with Mayor Lou Ritter and the other with US congressman Charlie Bennett. He then worked for Florida representative Carl Ogden, the majority leader.

In 1974, Tommy was elected to the legislature as a state representative, a position he held for 12 years. In 1987, he was elected mayor of Jacksonville, and he spent the next four years working to fulfill campaign promises: getting rid of tolls, cleaning up the air and odors of Jacksonville, improving school infrastructure, tearing down the Blodgett housing project and relocating residents to better housing, keeping Maxwell House Coffee Downtown, and bringing in new businesses, including Merrill Lynch. As a one-term mayor, Tommy accomplished a great deal, and he gives two main reasons for his success. One, his campaign supporters created a mosaic of Jacksonville, giving him a broad base of support throughout the community. And two, after working in the legislature for 12 years, he was accustomed to getting results in 60-day increments. His team understood that and worked hard.

In 2004, he ran for the Duval County School Board, where he served two terms. He is grateful he has been able to keep the promises he made, which he could not have done without the support of his wife, a schoolteacher, and his son. In the 1986 photograph above, six-year-old Tommy Hazouri Jr. takes a sip from a drink at his dad's desk in the center aisle of the Florida House of Representatives, where the legislator had his son working as a page for the day. (Courtesy of State Archives of Florida, *Florida Memory*, www.floridamemory.com/items/show/20499.)

## Ed Austin

From helping shape the government structure for the newly consolidated City of Jacksonville as general counsel in the early 1970s to creating a renaissance for the city as its mayor in the 1990s, Ed Austin left his mark on what Jacksonville is today.

Before World War II, Ed earned his master's degree from Duke University and taught school. As a paratrooper during the war, he suffered a back injury that forced him out of the service in 1957. He the earned his juris doctorate from the University of Florida and began practicing law in Jacksonville. In 1963, the governor appointed him the first public defender for the Fourth Judicial Circuit Court, a position he held until he was elected state attorney in 1969. During that time, he earned a reputation as a fair man of great character. His second-in-command, John Delaney, said Ed's background as a coach and teacher helped him inspire his staff to make the right calls and work better.

Ed became mayor in 1991 and had the distinction of serving when the NFL awarded its 30th franchise to Jacksonville. Although he served only one term, his lasting legacy as mayor is the River City Renaissance, which generated true urban renewal and revamped the city's historic Downtown neighborhoods. The project breathed new life into the African American neighborhood of La Villa, once so vibrant it was known as the "Harlem of the South." Other outcomes of the River City Renaissance included transforming the old civic auditorium into a new center for the performing arts, renovating the Gator Bowl, building the Sulzbacher Center for the homeless, and redeveloping the Jacksonville Zoo and Gardens.

Ed Austin died in 2011 at the age of 84. He was predeceased by his wife of 39 years, Patricia.

Pictured at a 1978 media conference against casino gambling are, from left to right, Gov. Reubin Askew, Orlando state attorney Robert Eagan, Jefferson County sheriff James Scott, Jacksonville state attorney Ed Austin, and William Troelstrop of the Florida Department of Law Enforcement. (Courtesy of the State Archives of Florida, *Florida Memory*, www.floridamemory.com/items/show/134525.)

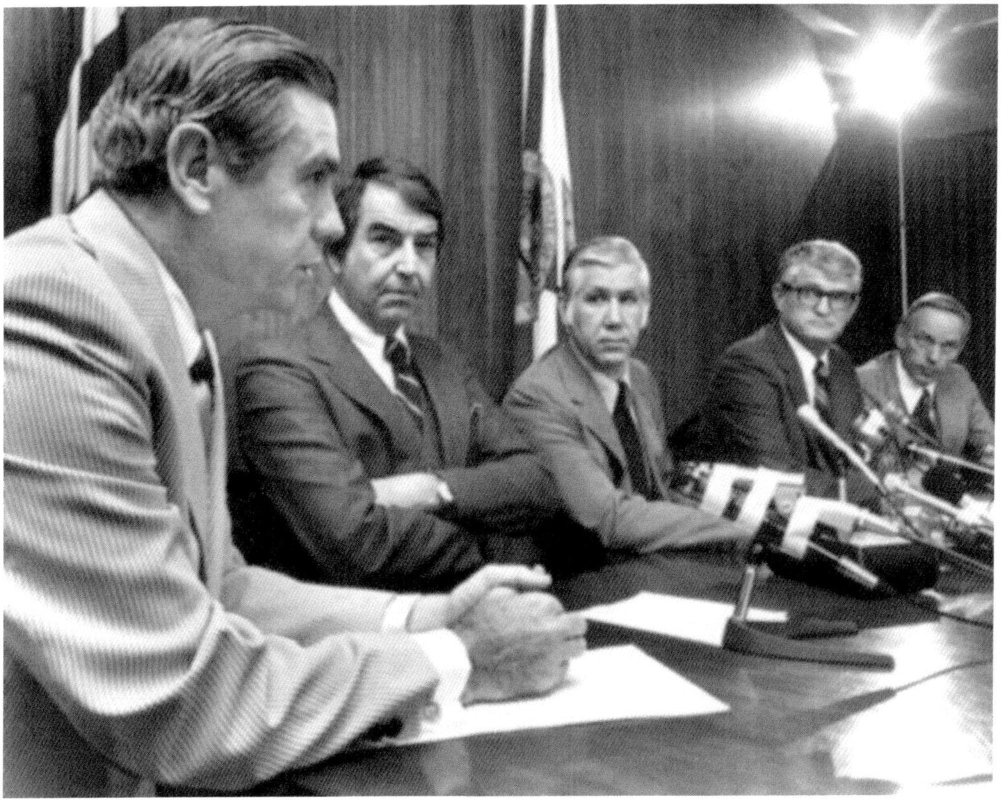

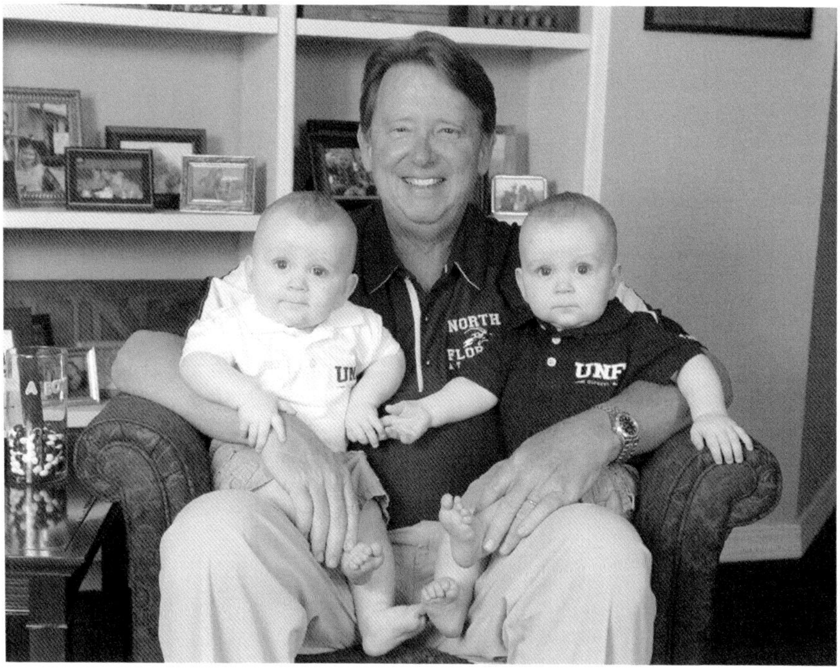

### History Lessons

Although he dreamed of becoming a history professor, John Delaney has spent his career making history. He opted for law school and developed an affinity for criminal law. Two days after graduating law school, he went to work for Ed Austin, the Jacksonville state attorney.

Austin was a "big thinking guy" who constantly sought to make the office better. When he asked John to take on special projects that ranked low on the totem pole, John wondered if he was working his way into a dead-end. But his efforts earned him the No. 2 position as the chief assistant state attorney, which he held until 1991, when Austin became mayor and appointed John first as general counsel and then as chief of staff.

Nearing 70, Austin decided one term was enough, and John decided to explore other options. Then four businessmen approached him about running for mayor, which he did, and he won, becoming the first Republican mayor since Reconstruction. He had learned to consistently seek ways to make things better, and he capitalized on those skills. He worked with the National Parks System to expand parks in Jacksonville, resulting in the largest urban park system in the United States, with 337 locations on more than 80,000 acres throughout the city. One of Jacksonville's most popular mayors, John ran for a second term unopposed, the only time that has ever happened in the city's history.

John convinced voters to approve a half-cent sales tax to finance $2.25 billion in improvements, while at the same reducing the property tax. The far-reaching Better Jacksonville Plan resulted in a new main library Downtown, a new Veterans Memorial Arena, new baseball grounds, infrastructure improvements, environmental preservation projects, economic development (including the Jacksonville Equestrian Center and additions to the zoo), and a new courthouse project, which eventually became wrought with cost problems under his successor.

In 2003, John was tapped as president of the University of North Florida, a state university with more than 16,000 students, 600 faculty, and more than 1,000 staff. The university has an annual economic impact of nearly $1 billion in Northeast Florida. As the university's chief fundraiser, John helped double the university's privately funded endowment.

John and his wife, Gena, have four children and twin grandsons, Jack and Owen Milford, shown here with their grandfather. (Photograph by Jennifer Grissom; courtesy of University of North Florida public relations.)

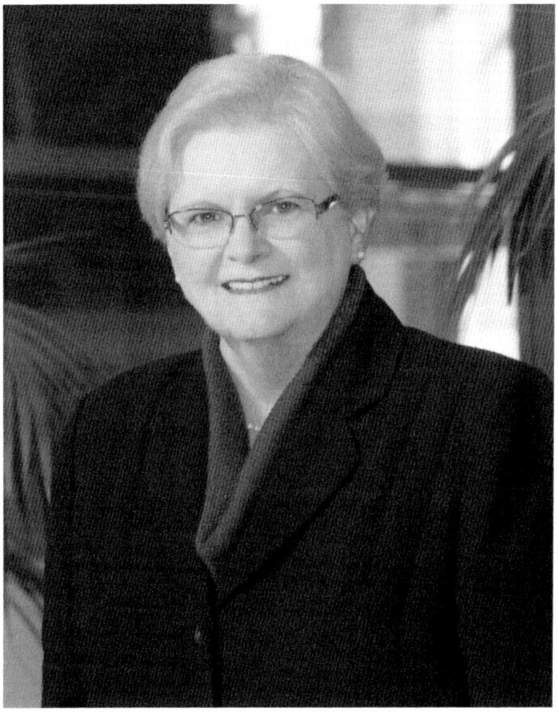

### Tommie Broach Darm

Tommie Broach Darm was teaching in New York when she recognized her gift for reaching students who "just don't get it." She returned home to Jacksonville, and, in 1973, started the Broach School, for students who fall through the cracks in traditional classrooms. Decades later, Tommie was ordained a minister and helped launch Highpoint Community Church, where she adopted some of the same techniques to help new Christians that she had used in reaching students. (Courtesy of Tommie Broach Darm.)

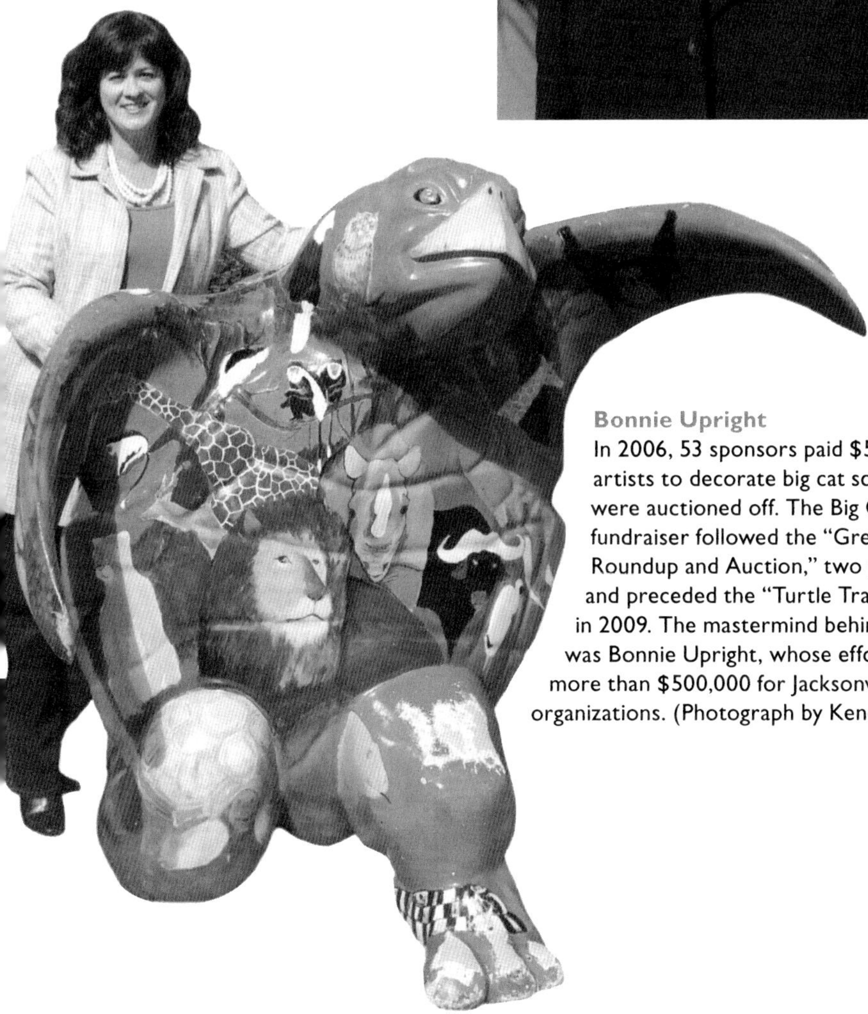

### Bonnie Upright

In 2006, 53 sponsors paid $5,000 apiece for artists to decorate big cat sculptures, which were auctioned off. The Big Cats for Kids fundraiser followed the "Great Sea Cow Roundup and Auction," two years before, and preceded the "Turtle Trails" fundraiser in 2009. The mastermind behind the events was Bonnie Upright, whose efforts raised more than $500,000 for Jacksonville's nonprofit organizations. (Photograph by Kendall Brunson.)

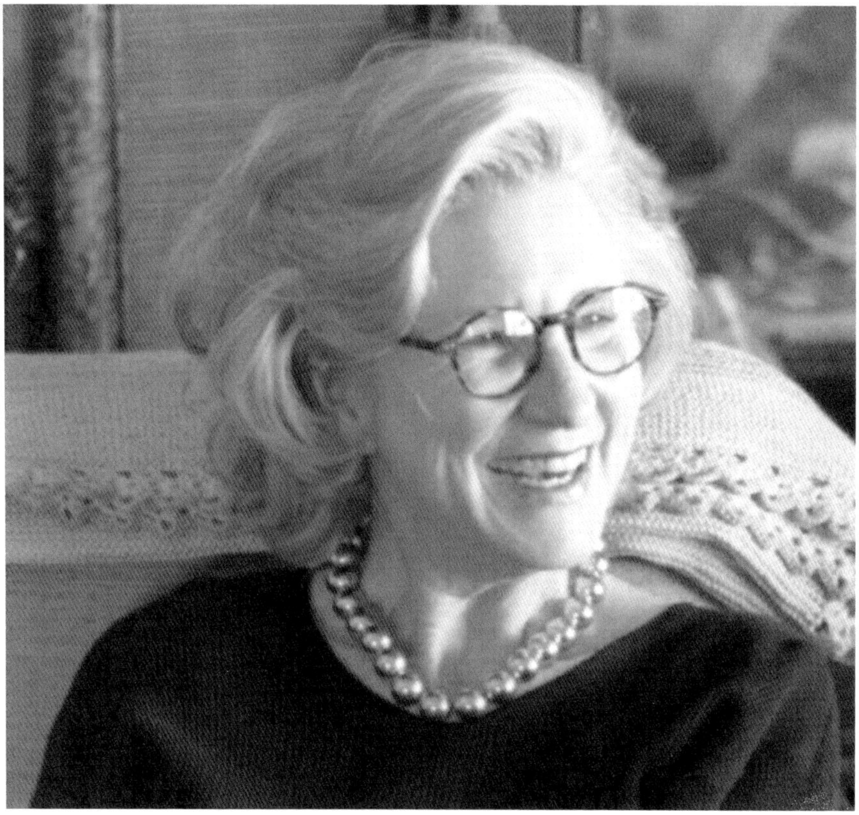

### Evelyn Hughes Nehl

Evelyn Hughes Nehl was the daughter of a Southern Baptist minister and lived a proper Southern life. She cherished her three children and was an active and accomplished member of community theater in Jacksonville.

When Evelyn lost her talented son, an accomplished artist and award-winning actor, to AIDS in the early 1990s, she felt very much alone. It was a time when few people in Jacksonville spoke openly about AIDS or HIV, often using code words that only those who knew would fully understand. Evelyn learned the code and discovered another grieving mother in her high-rise condominium building. Their shared pain united them.

When Evelyn's son was to receive a posthumous award for a critically acclaimed one-act play he wrote and performed, she traveled to California to accept it on his behalf. During that trip, she saw the NAMES Project AIDS Memorial Quilt displayed on the *Queen Mary*.

"It was such a stunning and moving experience that I decided then that it must come to Jacksonville," she wrote in a letter asking for the support of local patrons. More than 10,000 people visited the quilt when it came to Jacksonville in March 1992. The event raised $20,000 for direct services for people living with AIDS and, more importantly, tore down the wall of silence. People began to talk about the disease. During the event, doctors and other medical professionals had the opportunity to receive continuing medical education about AIDS and HIV.

Evelyn understood that when the love of a mother for her son opens doors, she can touch the hearts of thousands. Evelyn herself convinced Jacksonville to make sure that people living with HIV could have access to the care and support they need. She traveled to see the quilt on display in other cities, knowing full well the healing, encouragement, and comfort the display brings to others. (All courtesy of Robin Patton.)

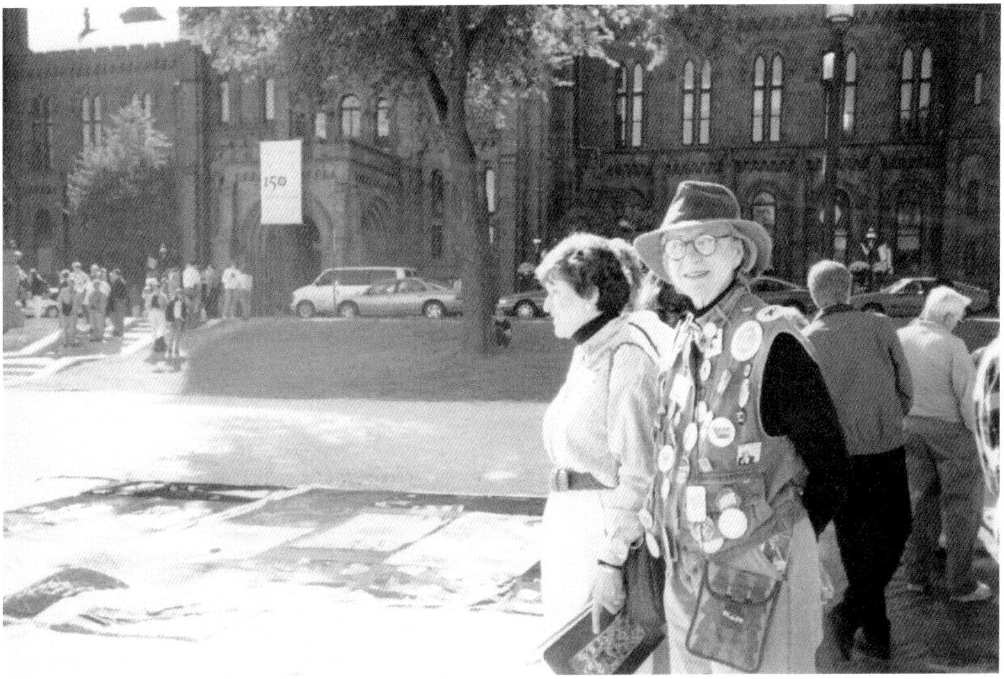

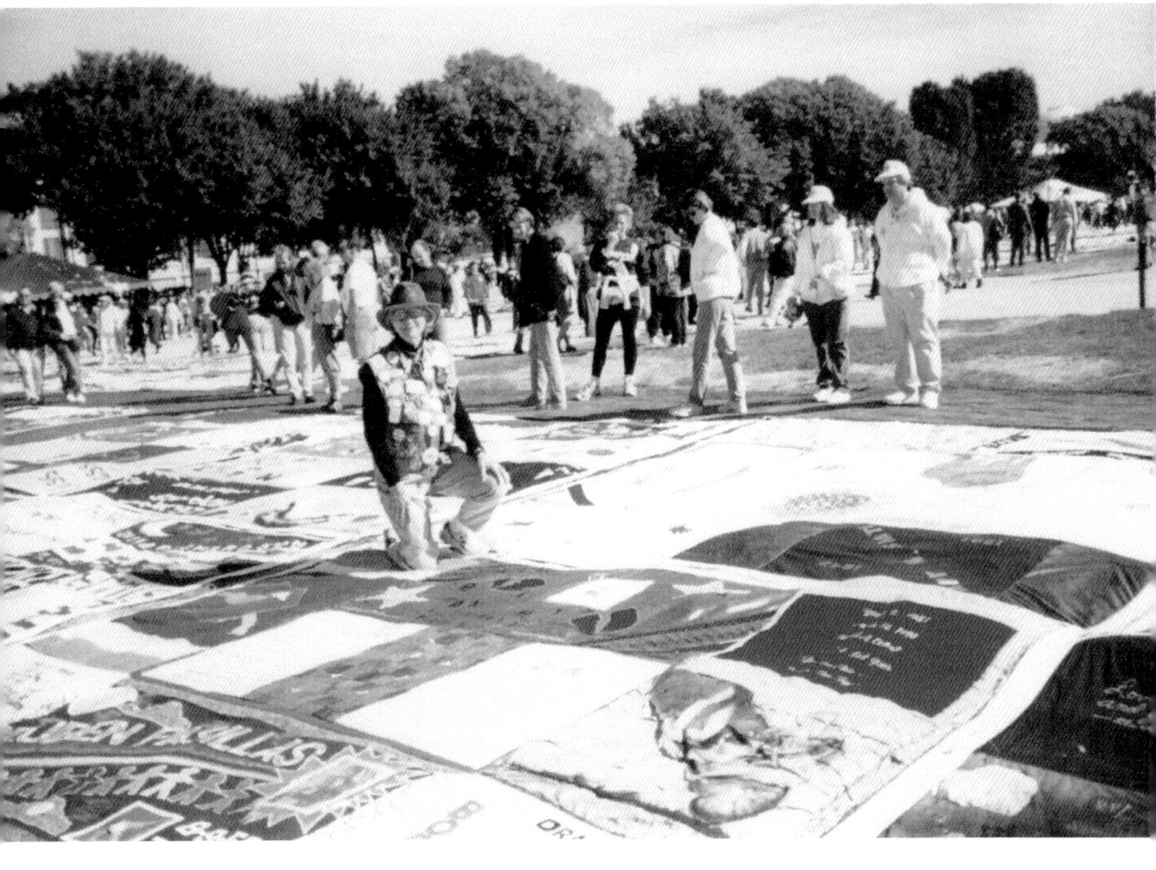

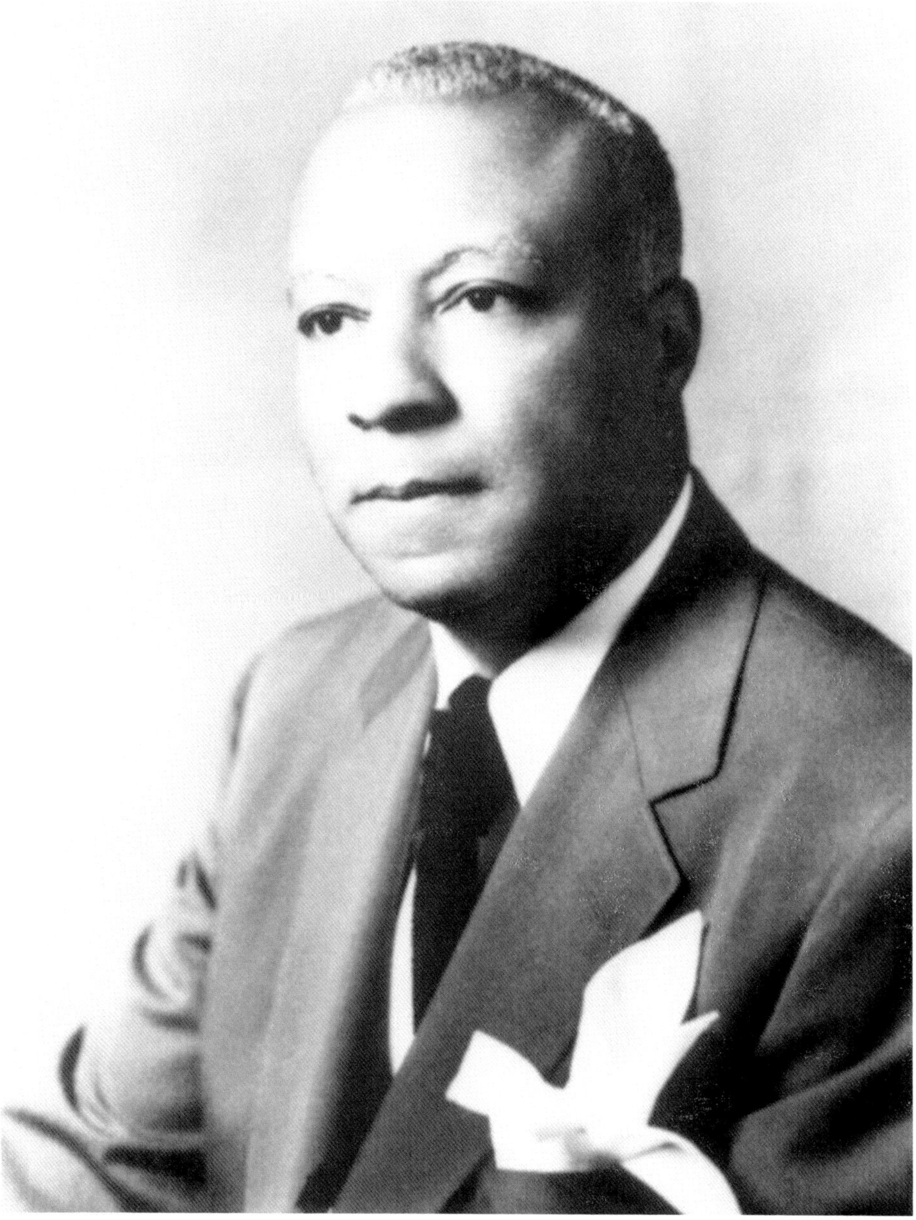

**A. Philip Randolph**

Asa Philip Randolph was born in Crescent City in 1889 but moved to Jacksonville at the age of two because his father, a minister, considered Jacksonville to be friendly towards African Americans. He went to Harlem to study acting at the City College of New York but changed majors to economics and politics to calm his parents' concern. After organizing a union of elevator operators in New York City in 1917, he organized the Brotherhood of Sleeping Car Porters (BSCP) for the employees of the Pullman Company in 1925. That union eventually won $2 million in pay increases for employees, a shorter workweek, and overtime pay. Philip was a lifelong civil rights advocate. In 1964, Pres. Lyndon B. Johnson presented him with the Presidential Medal of Freedom. (Courtesy of the State Archives of Florida, *Florida Memory*, www.floridamemory.com/items/show/33464.)

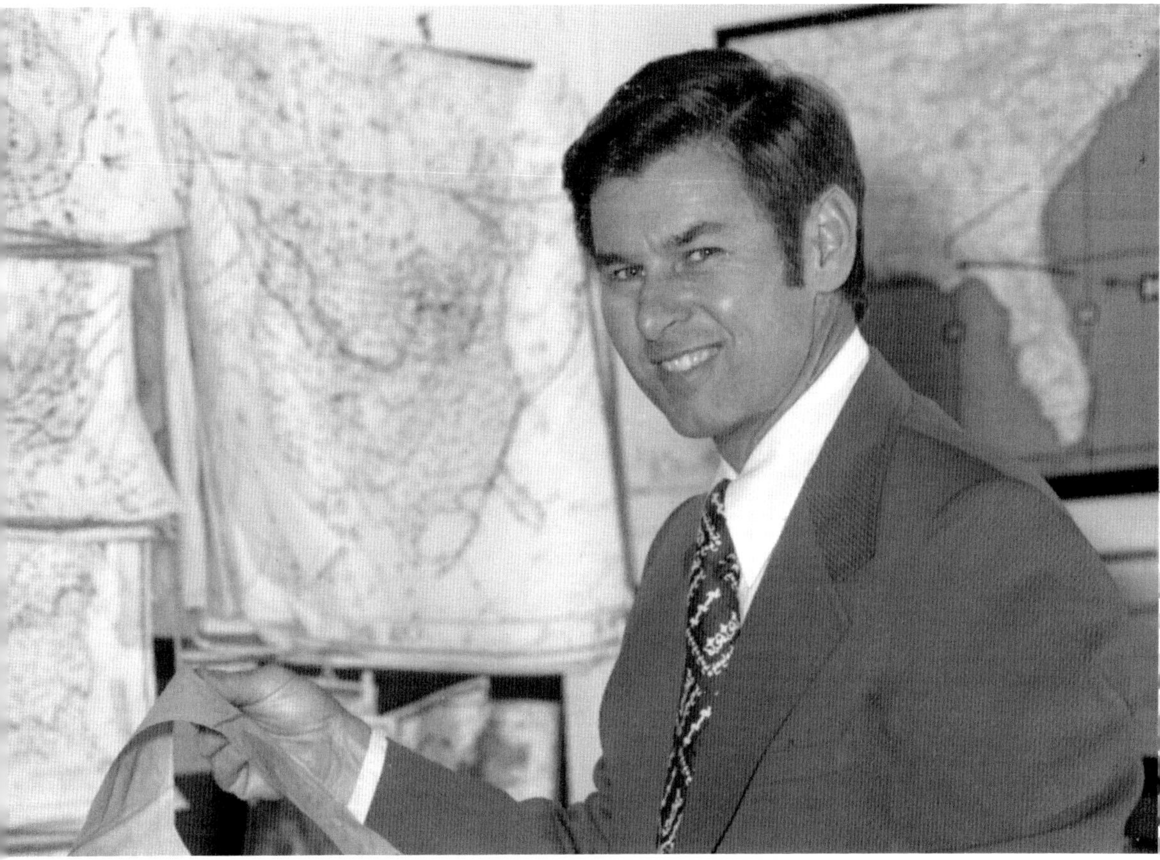

George Winterling
A familiar face to television viewers in Jacksonville for almost 50 years, semiretired meteorologist George Winterling pioneered broadcast meteorology. After graduating from Robert E. Lee High School, he served in the Air Force before returning to Jacksonville to attend Jacksonville Junior College (now Jacksonville University). He graduated from Florida State University with a degree in meteorology in 1957 and worked for the US Weather Bureau (now the National Weather Service) for five years.

In 1960, Hurricane Donna inflicted havoc from Florida to Canada, killing more than 350 people and causing nearly $1 billion worth of damage. The Category 5 storm convinced Winterling that the media needed knowledgeable people in weather emergencies. In 1962, Winterling created a paradigm shift in broadcasting when he suggested a big idea to Jacksonville's WJXT management: weather broadcasts by a meteorologist. Less than two years later, Winterling was the only weather forecaster to warn Jacksonville residents that Hurricane Dora would strike the First Coast.

Before the days of satellite, Winterling invented weather maps by painting clouds on film to portray weather systems throughout the country. In addition to being the first to predict rainfall, Winterling also created the "humiture" index to account for the combination of humidity and heat, which the National Weather Service later began using as the heat index.

A member of the American Meteorological Society since 1963, Winterling also taught meteorology as an adjunct professor at Jacksonville University from 1975 through 1994. He semiretired from WJXT in 2009. (Courtesy of WJXT Channel 4.)

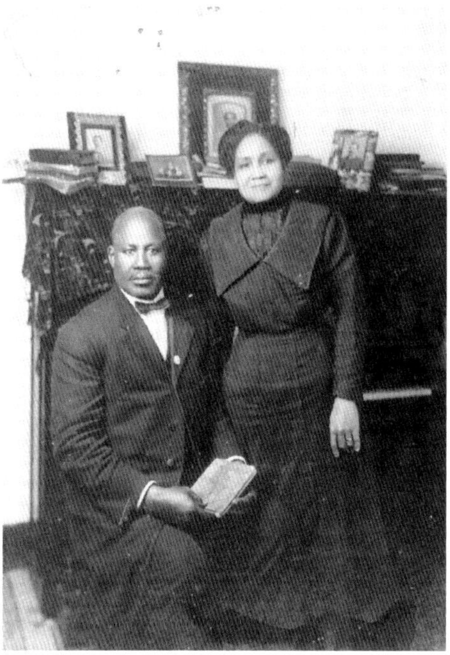

### Abraham Lincoln Lewis

Abraham Lincoln Lewis cofounded the Afro-American Life Insurance Company and was Florida's first black millionaire. Because of segregation, he established American Beach in 1933 as a beach resort for African Americans just north of Jacksonville. It played host to many famous celebrities through the 1950s, including Ray Charles, Zora Neal Hurston, and Cab Calloway. (Courtesy of the Eartha M.M. White Collection, Thomas G. Carpenter Library, University of North Florida, Jacksonville, Florida.)

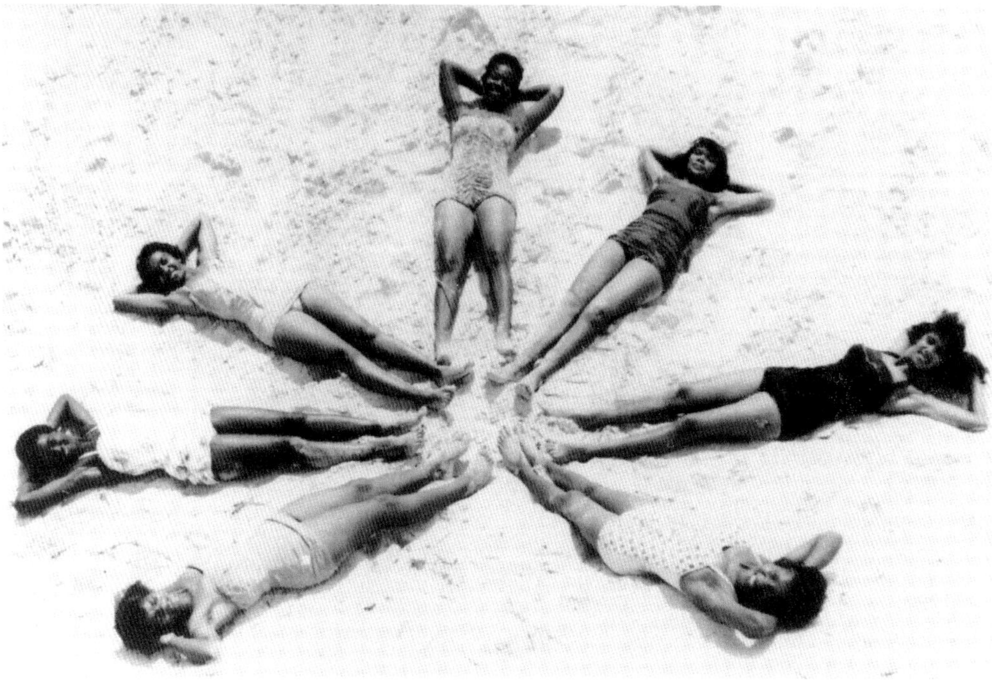

### Miss American Beach

From the 1930s through the 1950s, American Beach provided Northeast Florida's African American community a beach for relaxation and recreation. A special event of the American Beach community was its beauty pageant. This photograph is from the American Beach beauty pageant, Miss American Beach. (Courtesy of the Eartha M.M. White Collection, Thomas G. Carpenter Library, University of North Florida, Jacksonville, Florida.)

## MaVynee Betsch

Abraham Lincoln Lewis's great-granddaughter MaVynee Betsch is better known as "the Beach Lady." MaVynee was raised in the lap of luxury and graduated from Oberlin Conservatory of Music in Ohio before traveling through Europe studying voice and singing in opera houses. But Florida was home.

She returned to the First Coast to help preserve American Beach, her great-grandfather's legacy. The beach was hit hard in 1964 by Hurricane Dora, and, after segregation ended, the beach was no longer as popular.

MaVynee fought to preserve not only this history, but the environment as well. Her generous donations to causes important to her depleted her inheritance by the late 1970s. She raised public awareness of the beach's history, gave tours, and fought for the environment until her death in 2005. To this day, MaVynee is an environmental icon. (Photograph by Charles Woods; courtesy of Nowhere Productions.)

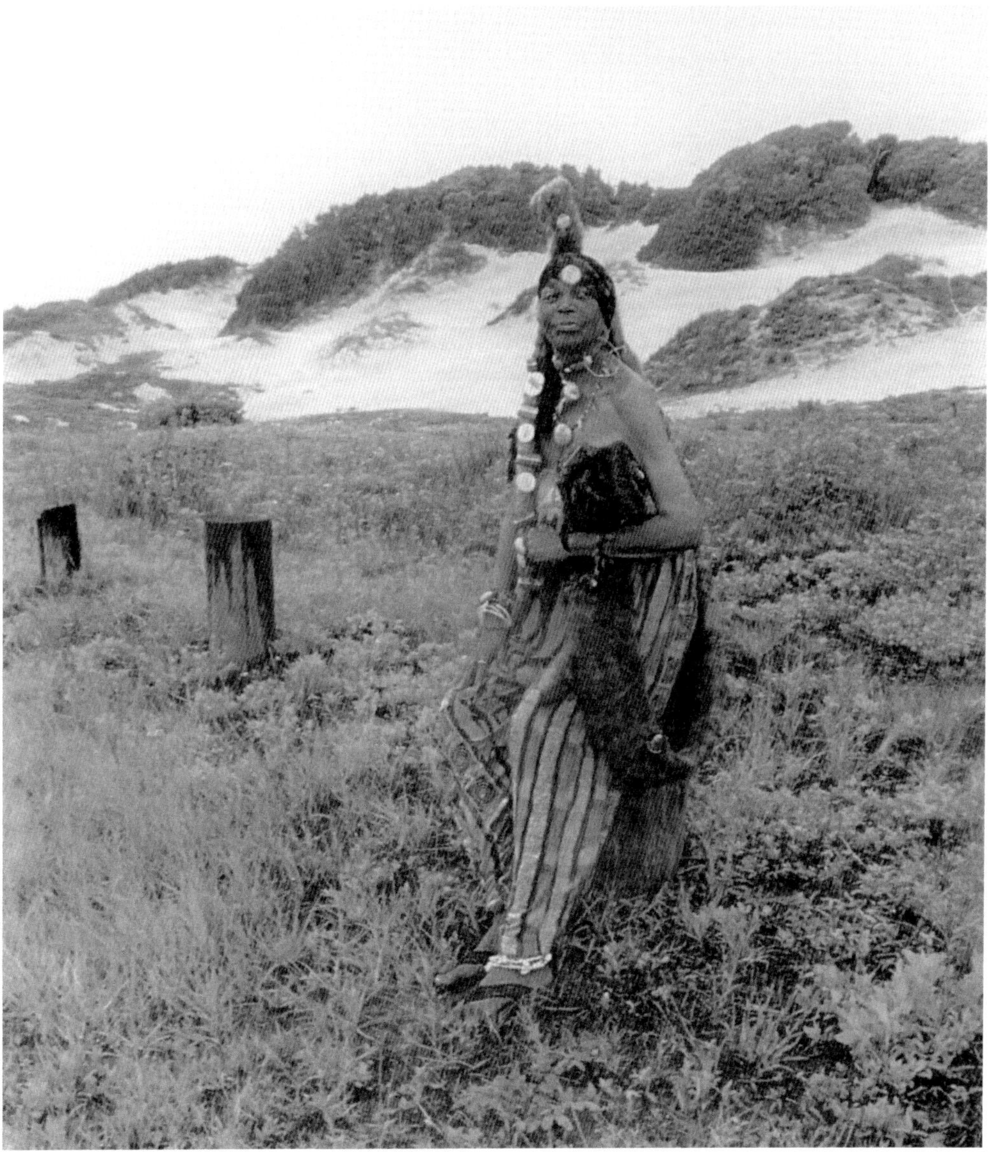

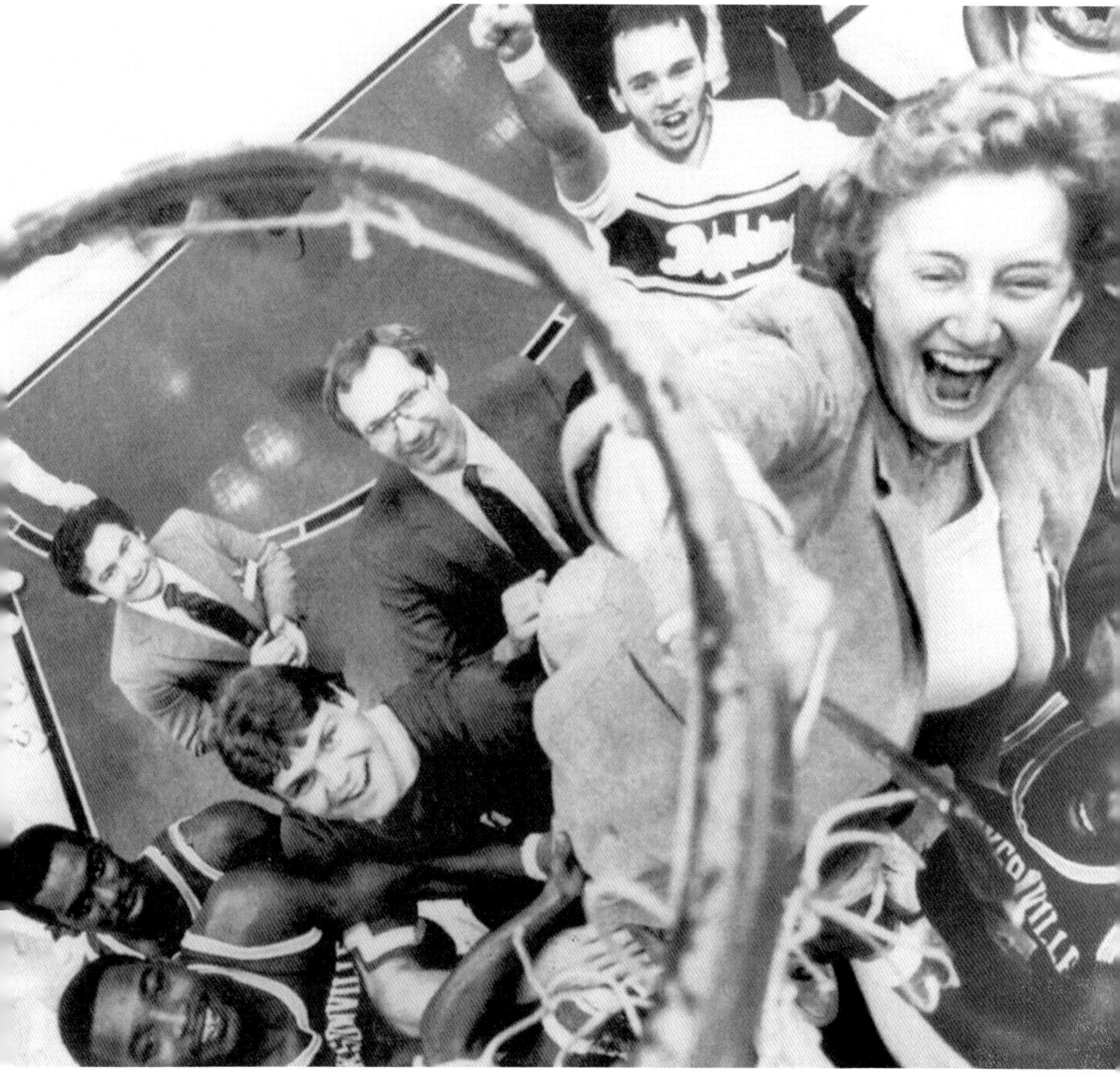

**Fran Kinne, Dolphins' Good Luck Charm**

The Jacksonville University Dolphins considered JU president Dr. Fran Kinne, who hugged them before every basketball game, their good luck charm. When weather delayed her plane for the Sun Belt Tournament in Birmingham, Alabama, in 1986, they did not get their hug until halftime, when they were down by one point. Post-hug, the Dolphins went on to win the game and then hoisted Fran to cut down the net. (Courtesy of Jacksonville University.)

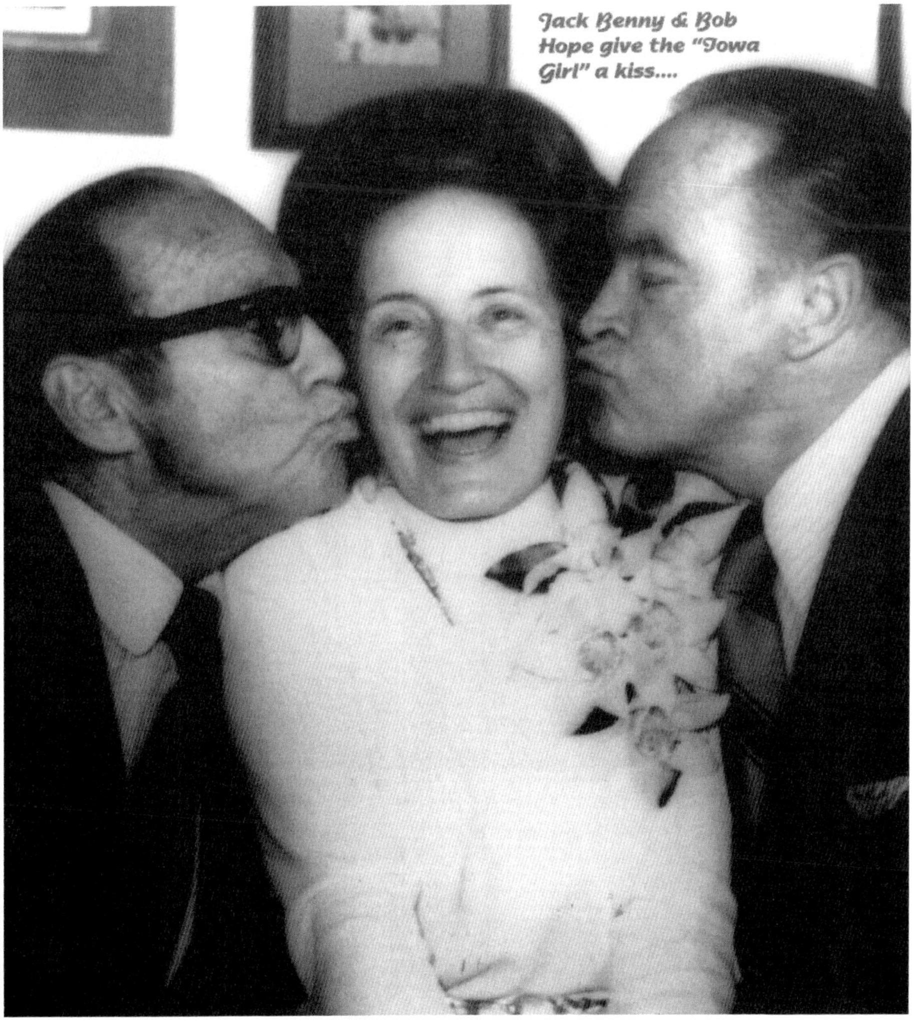


## Florida's First Female University President

When Jacksonville University hired Frances Kinne as an assistant humanities professor in 1958, no one expected the relationship to last well into the 21st century. But last it did.

An Iowa native, Fran brought not only her Midwestern work ethic, but also a wealth of influential relationships reaped from her marriage to Col. Harry Kinne and military life overseas. The first American to earn a doctorate in Germany after World War II, Fran earned doctorates in three disciplines. At JU, she soon founded the College of Fine Arts. She later became dean of the university, and, in 1979, she became the first woman to be named a university president in Florida.

Apparently unaware that Fran's brother was a four-letter athlete, sportswriters expressed fear that she would be the death of the Dolphins sports program. On the contrary, she hugged the basketball team before every game and became one of the most beloved university presidents of all time.

In her autobiography, *Iowa Girl: The President Wears a Skirt*, she recounts her friendships with Bob Hope, Charlton Heston, and Jack Benny, all of whom helped raise funds for the university. Fran became chancellor emeritus in 1994 and continues to support JU today. Fran Kinne continues to be sought after for teaching and public appearances. In April 2014, just weeks before her 97th birthday, Fran told an audience of 1,300 women at the Generation W conference, "You can excite, promote—you can do anything you want to do if you keep a positive attitude." (Courtesy of Jacksonville University.)

### The Preservationist

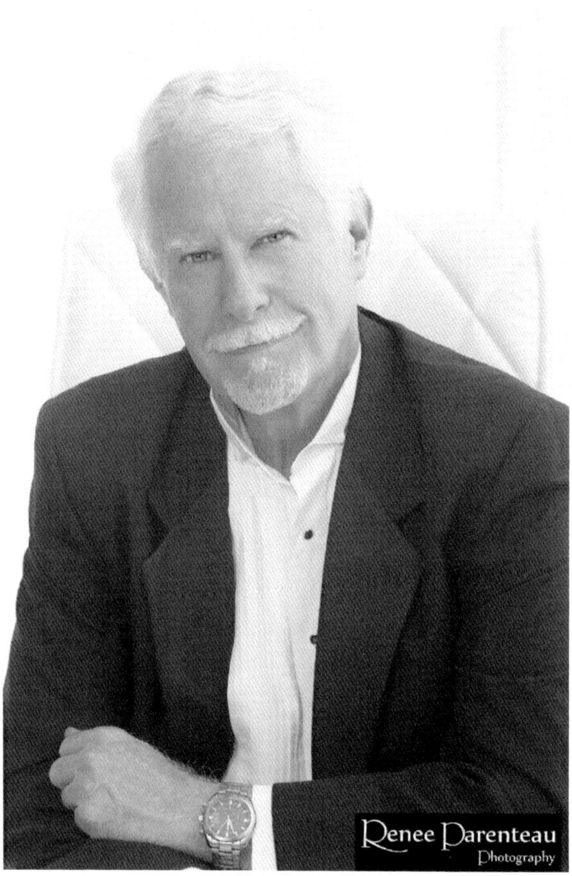


Wayne Wood grew up in South Florida and remembers spending summers on one of Jacksonville's most desired streets, known as "The Row," a series of beautiful homes lining Riverside Avenue. Unfortunately, only two of the 50 mansions remain today.

After graduating with his doctorate in optometry from the University of Houston in 1971, Wayne moved to the River City to join his uncle's practice. Living in the neighborhood he nostalgically remembered, he saw the homes in Riverside and Avondale being demolished or neglected. Wayne organized a citizen's meeting, and Riverside Avondale Preservation (RAP) was born. The organization has grown into one of the largest neighborhood preservation groups in the South.

Wayne notes that to make the neighborhood once again attractive to the community, he had to become their public relations advocate. His first book, *A Bicycle-Walking Tour of Riverside and Avondale*, was published in 1976. The book features one of the most beautiful homes on Riverside Avenue, a home that would later become Wayne's residence.

Wayne has since written books on several subjects, including the "Great Fire of 1901" and local artist Courtenay Hunt. He also wrote a book on Henry J. Klutho with architect Bob Broward. Over the course of 12 years, he wrote his most notable book, *Jacksonville's Architectural Heritage: Landmark for the Future*. After its release in 1989, the book sold out in 10 days, and it is now in its fourth printing.

About 20 years ago, while giving an optometry speech in Portland, Oregon, Wayne took the streetcar Downtown and saw the Saturday Market under a bridge; inspiration struck. When a patient of Wayne's mentioned he was designing plans for the new Fuller Warren Bridge, the vision for the Riverside Arts Market (RAM) became reality.

Five governors and four mayors later, RAM debuted under the Fuller Warren Bridge in 2009. On opening day in 2009, RAM drew more than 40,000 visitors. Wayne jokes, "I get an A for persistence." (Photograph by Renee Parenteau; courtesy of Wayne Wood.)

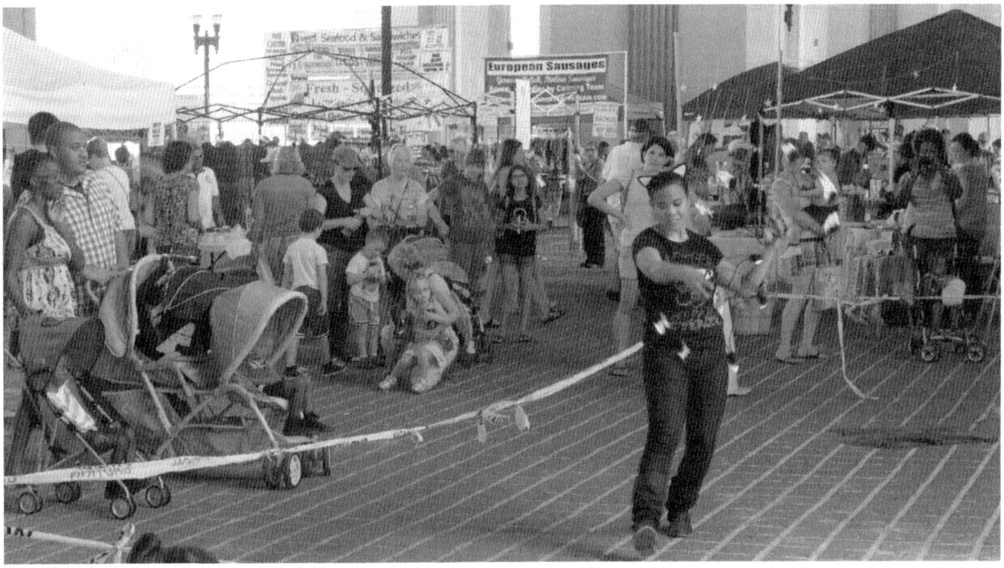


**Riverside Arts Market**
In a few short years, the Riverside Arts Market (RAM) has transformed into a Jacksonville institution. Locals flock under the Fuller Warren Bridge on Saturday mornings to buy groceries, watch live entertainment, and shop for clothes and handmade goodies. RAM creator Wayne Wood says he wanted it to be "a seven-ring circus." He also says RAM is the "best work of art I've ever created." Above, Wayne's idea for a seven-ring circus comes to fruition as a fire dancer entertains visitors. (Photograph by David Howard.)

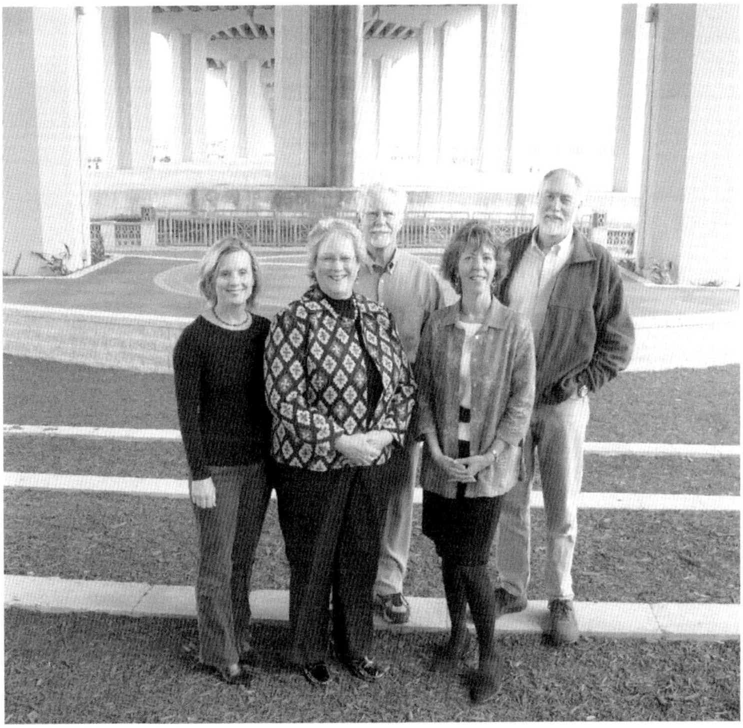

**RAMROD**
As Wayne's vision inched closer into a reality, he formed RAMROD (Riverside Arts Market Research Operations and Development) with Doug Coleman, Cindy Guy, Pamela Telis, and Teresa Fish (all pictured). Two weeks before the opening, the team brought on Tony Allegretti as market director. (Photograph by Kirk Chamberlain Studio; courtesy of Wayne Wood.)

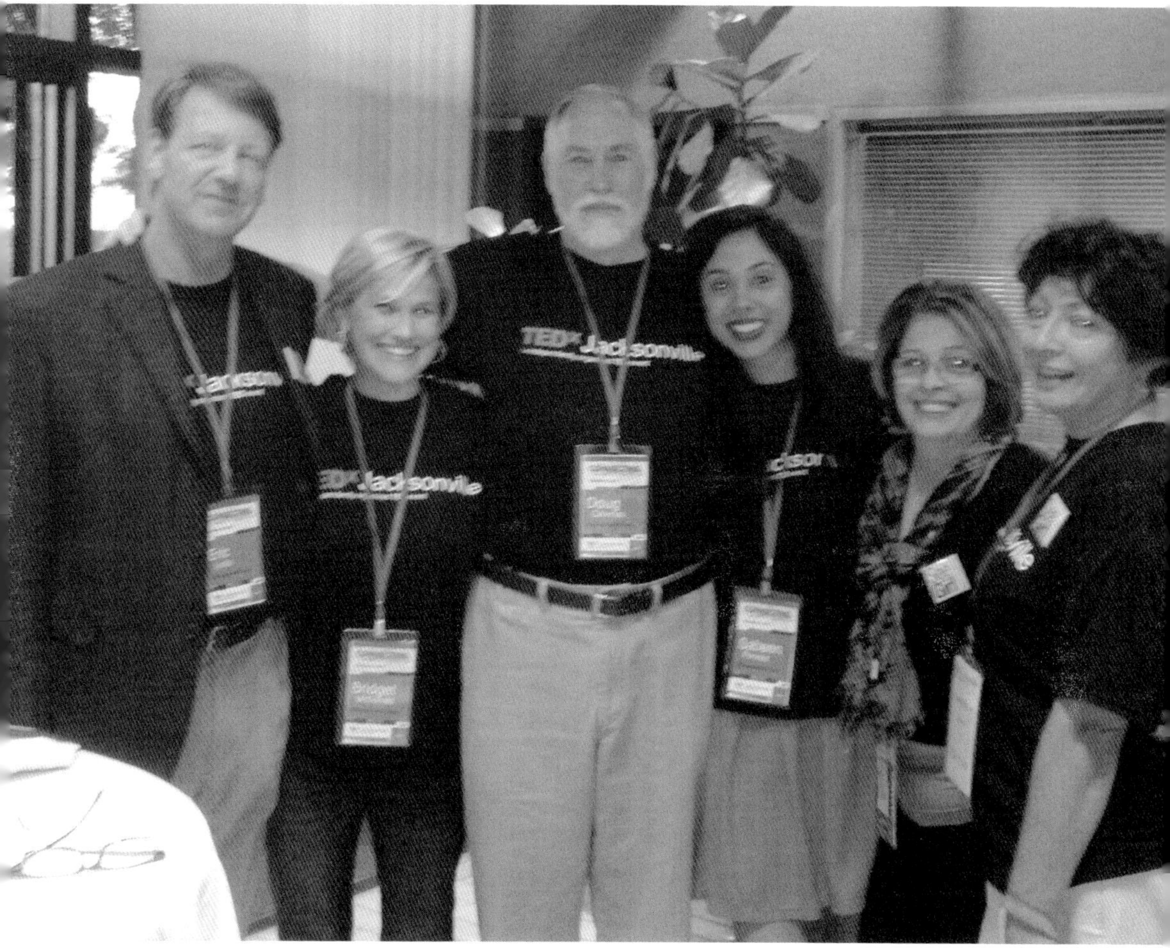


**Doug Coleman**

After Doug Coleman sold his business, Coleman Ski Tours, he felt that he owed his time to the city. For several decades, Doug had already been working to improve the River City. He has been on the board of Riverside Avondale Preservation (RAP), the North Florida Land Trust, and the Jacksonville Sister Cities Association. Doug was also a member of RAMROD, the team that brought Wayne Wood's vision for Riverside Arts Market (RAM) into fruition.

When he booked a trip to Muskegon, Michigan, in 2011 to attend ArtPrize and a TEDx event, Doug did not have high hopes. But that trip to small-town Muskegon energized and inspired Doug to bring similar events to Jacksonville. Although his idea for the Epoch Project, an arts-and-technology crowd-funding event, could not find enough financial backing, TEDxJacksonville has become a venue for positive change in the River City. Doug (center) is seen here at a TEDxJacksonville event. (Courtesy of Doug Coleman.)

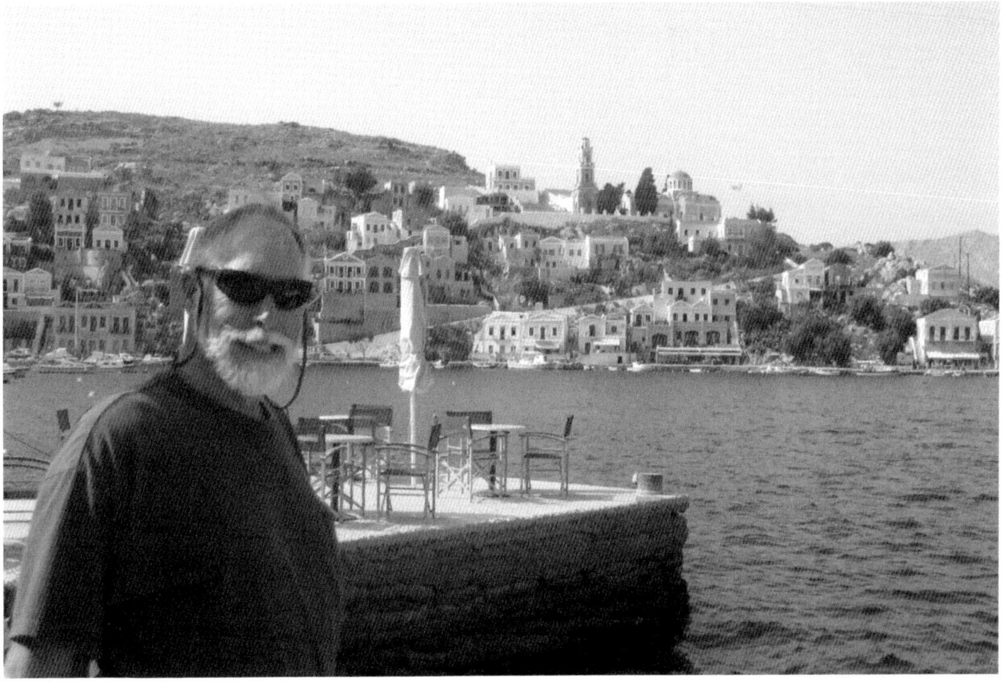

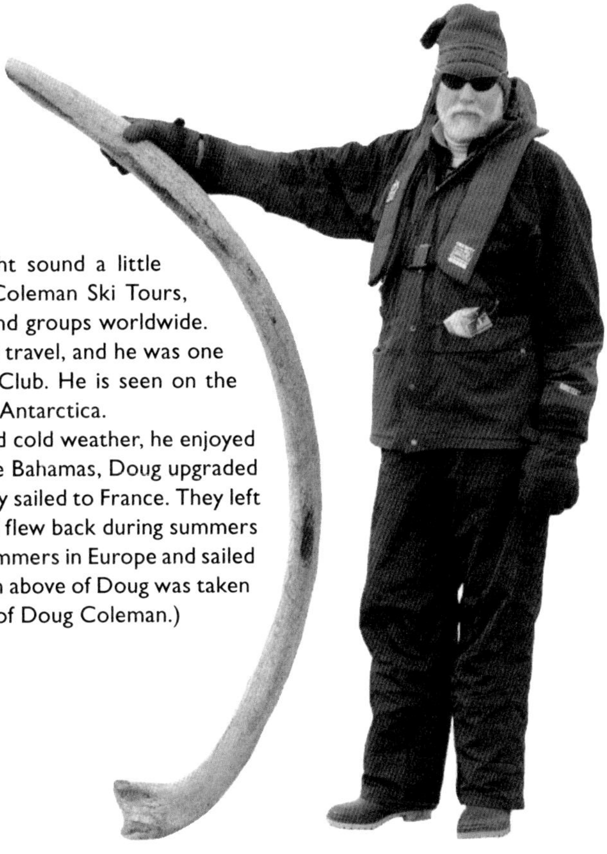

### The Adventurer

A ski tour company in the South might sound a little weird, but Doug Coleman's business, Coleman Ski Tours, organized trips for families, churches, and groups worldwide. Doug and his wife, Mary, love to ski and travel, and he was one of the founders of the Jacksonville Ski Club. He is seen on the right with a whale bone off the coast of Antarctica.

Although his business revolved around cold weather, he enjoyed all outdoor activities. After sailing to the Bahamas, Doug upgraded to a bigger boat and, in 1999, he and Mary sailed to France. They left their boat in Europe during the year and flew back during summers to sail. They spent more than a dozen summers in Europe and sailed to two dozen countries. The photograph above of Doug was taken on Simi Island, Greece. (Both courtesy of Doug Coleman.)

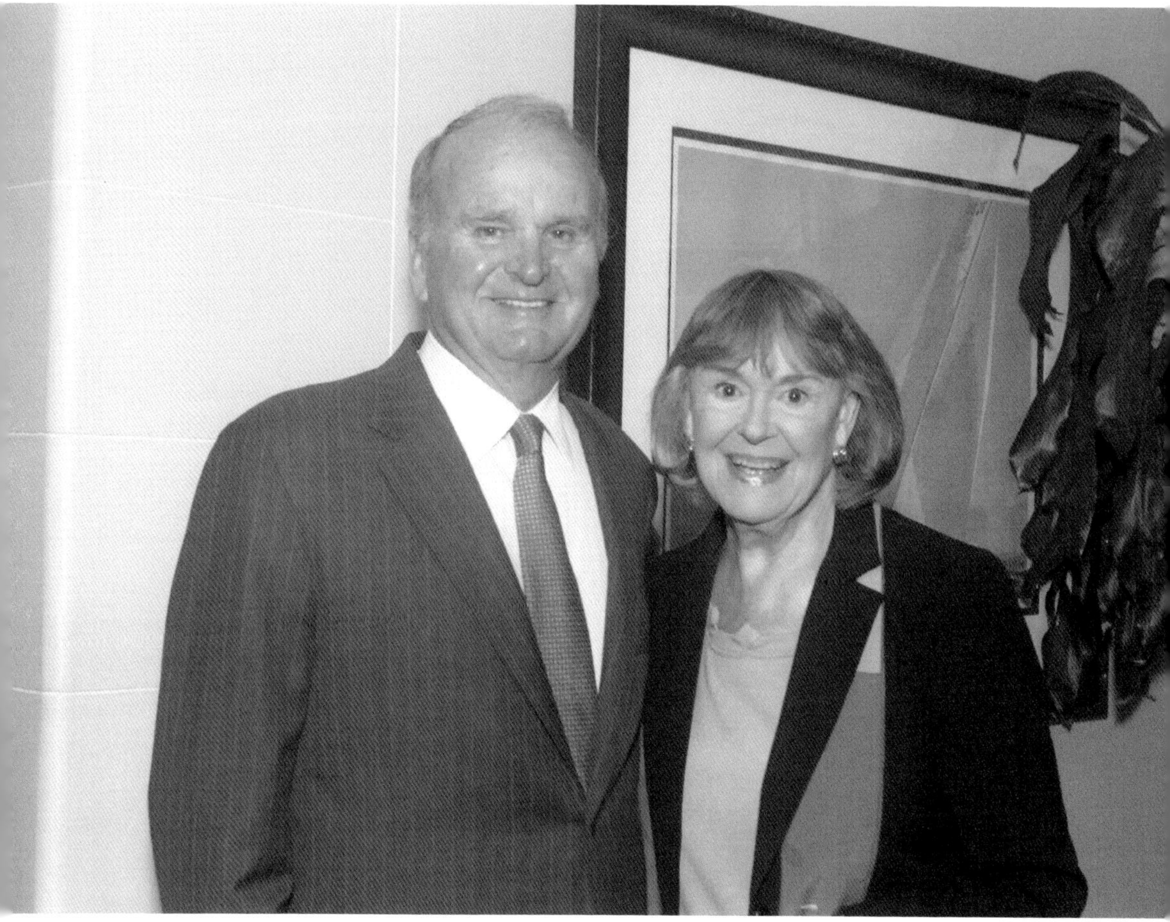

**The Philanthropist** (ABOVE AND OPPOSITE PAGE)
Delores Barr Weaver is not afraid to cause trouble, especially when it comes to issues that flame her passion. Delores and her husband, Wayne Weaver, moved to the First Coast in 1993, the same year they were awarded the Jaguars franchise. Before the team played its first game, Delores created the Jaguars Foundation and donated more than $140,000 to local charities.

In the *Chronicle of Philanthropy*, Nina Waters, president of the Delores Barr Weaver Policy Foundation, says Delores is "a pot stirrer and she has encouraged us to be bolder."

Delores convinced six television stations to simultaneously air *Straight Talk*, a safe-sex and pregnancy prevention show for teens. *Straight Talk* ran from 1995 to 2011. "Children having children is not a good thing," she says. She's especially passionate about protecting women and children. She began the Delores Barr Weaver Policy Center, a support system for girls in the juvenile justice system and foster care and girls who are at risk. Delores also donated $500,000, with another $500,000 in matching funds, to Protect Our Defenders, an organization helping women and men who are sexually assaulted in the military. Ever since the tragedy at Sandy Hook Elementary, she has been working to curb gun violence by partnering with the sheriff in a gun buyback program and advocating for gun registration.

Delores says that, other than her family, she is proudest of "being able to bring the Jaguars to Jacksonville." Even though the Weavers sold the team in 2011, they have remained in the city. They immediately felt at home on the First Coast and have made it a priority to invest in the community. After selling the team, Delores immediately donated $50 million to the Jacksonville Community Foundation. Without a doubt, Delores has transformed lives through her charitable giving.

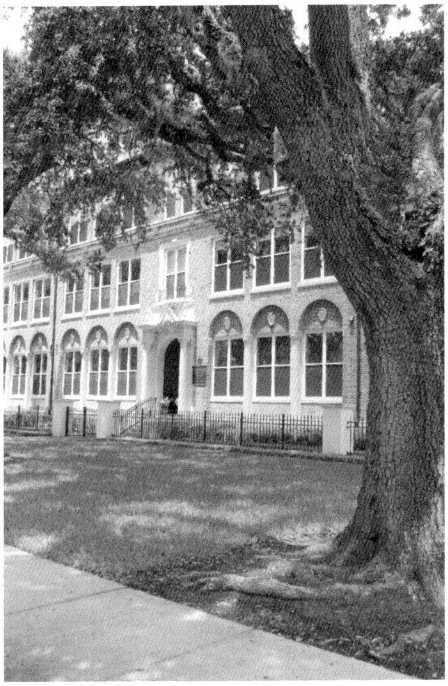

Delores has also made other transformations. After many long walks past an abandoned school building in Riverside, Delores kept saying to herself, "Someone should do something about it." As it turns out, she was that someone. The John Gorrie School has since been transformed into luxury condominiums, where Delores painstakingly chronicled the history of the school, leaving future generations and residents clues to the building's past.

Delores is a powerhouse, unafraid to tackle everything from local issues to actual mountains. In 1989, at her suggestion, she and Wayne climbed Mount Kilimanjaro. (School photograph by Kendall Brunson; others courtesy of Delores Weaver.)

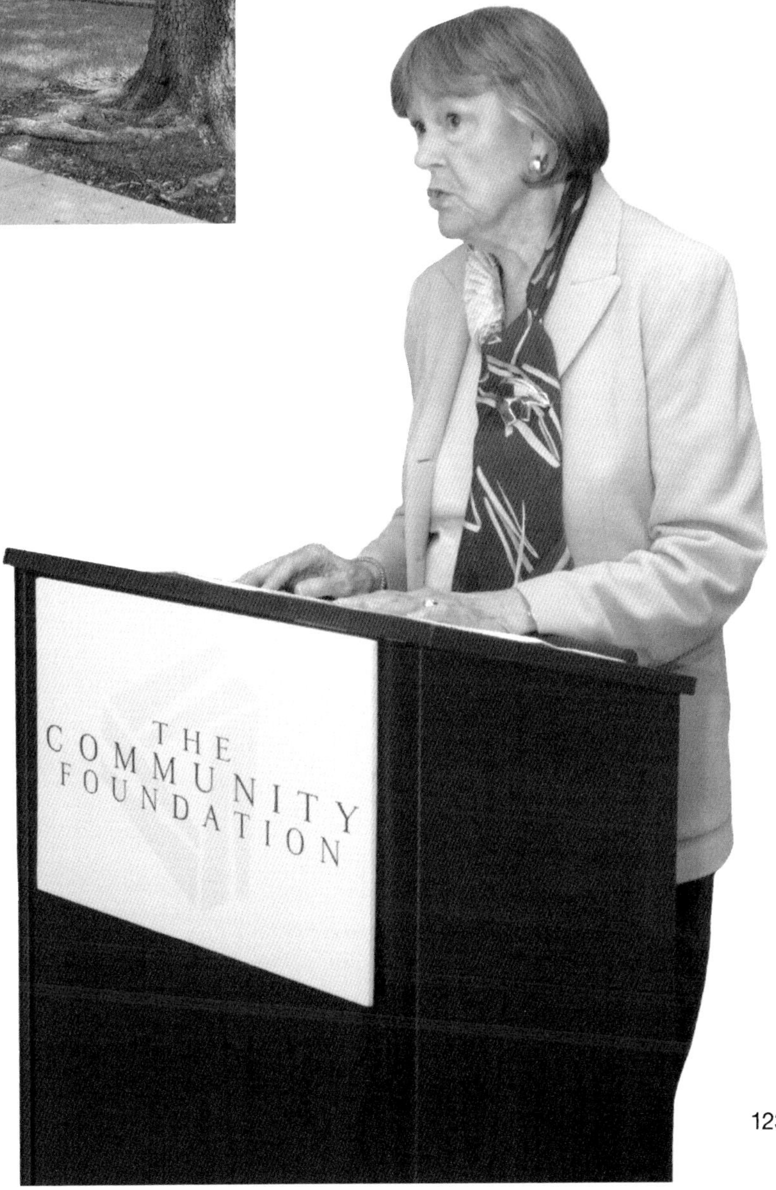

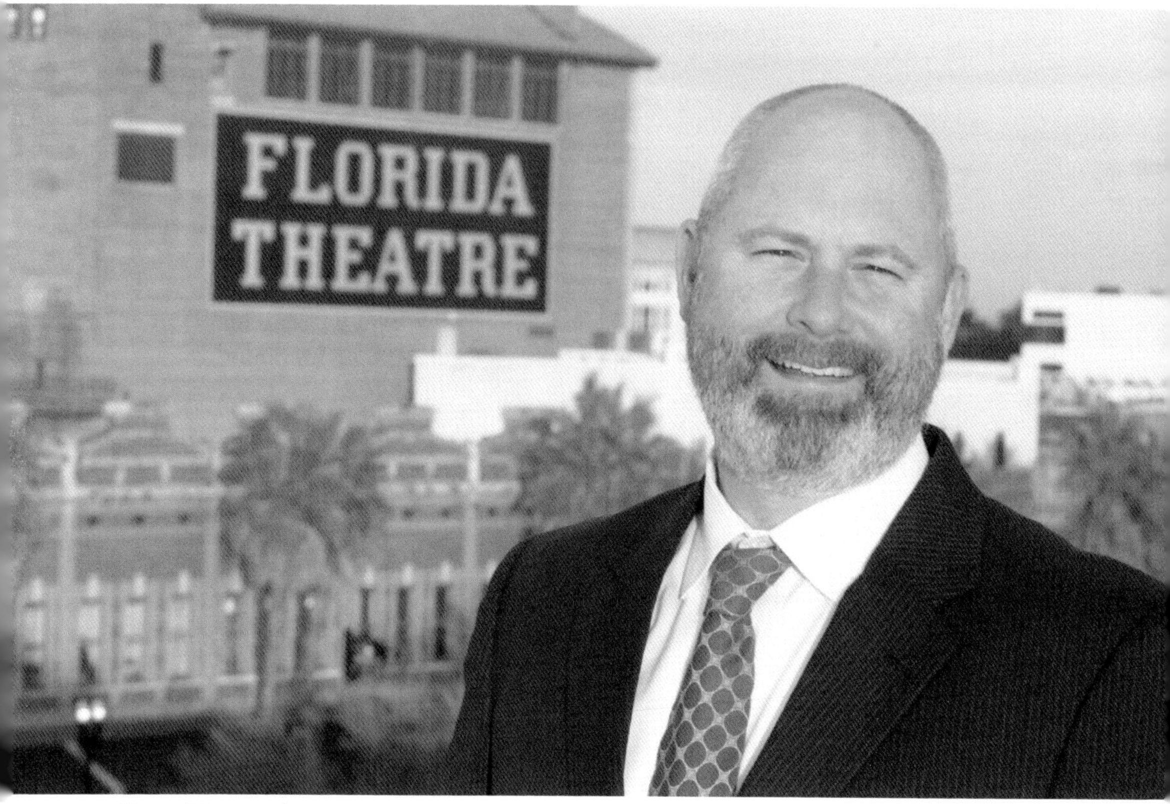


**Tony Allegretti**

It is difficult to think of another person who has had the same singular impact on Downtown development as Tony Allegretti.

When Tony moved from Daytona to Jacksonville for a job in the mid-1990s, he immediately fell in love with the River City. His involvement in the revitalization efforts of Downtown came after writing Theatre Jacksonville's newsletter, and, in 2000, he talked himself into a job as its marketing director. From there, he pitched and implemented the idea of 100 Windows of Art to the newly formed Downtown Vision, resulting in a virtual art show along city sidewalks.

In addition to restoring the 1951 Market Street lofts with a business partner and starting *Springfield Arts and Living* magazine, Tony also began a nonprofit called Art and Bills, a pop-up gallery that connected patrons with how they were supporting the artists.

Tony's largest, and lasting, imprint on Downtown is the First Wednesday Art Walk. After a trip to Seattle's First Thursday Art Walk, he brought the idea back to Jacksonville and developed it with Downtown Vision. Little did he know just how successful Art Walk would become. For the first event in 2003, Tony hoped 250 people would come, but it is estimated that more than 1,000 visitors flocked to Downtown. A decade later, it is a Jacksonville institution uniting artists with the community.

By far, Tony's most delicious projects are Burrito Gallery, which opened Downtown during Super Bowl week in 2005, and Uptown Market, in Springfield.

It is difficult to find a project in the urban core that Tony has not touched. Not only has he acted as director of the Riverside Arts Market (RAM), bringing free Wi-Fi and bike valets to the project, but he also created Community First Saturdays as director of Downtown engagement for the chamber of commerce.

Always looking forward, Tony is taking over as executive director of the cultural council for the First Coast. He loves how accessible the city is, and he wants to help others make meaningful contributions to Downtown. (Courtesy of Tony Allegretti.)

# BIBLIOGRAPHY


Bartely, Abel A. *Keeping the Faith: Race, Politics, and Social Development in Jacksonville, Florida, 1940–1970.* Westport, CT: Greenwood Press, 2000.

Broward, Robert C. *A Prairie School Masterpiece: The History of the St. James Building.* Jacksonville, FL: Jacksonville Historical Society, 1997.

Davis, Thomas Frederick. *History of Early Jacksonville.* Jacksonville, FL: The H. & W.B. Drew Company, 1911.

Kinne, Dr. Frances Bartlett. *Iowa Girl: The President Wears a Skirt.* Jacksonville, FL: Bailey Publishing & Communications, Inc., 2000.

Schafer, Daniel L. *Anna Kingsley.* Revised and Expanded Edition. St. Augustine, FL: St Augustine Historical Society, 1997.

Stowell, Daniel W., ed. *Balancing Evils Judiciously: The Proslavery Writings of Zephaniah Kingsley.* Gainesville, FL: University Press of Florida, 2000.

Ward, James Robertson. *Old Hickory's Town: An Illustrated History of Jacksonville.* Jacksonville, FL: Old Hickory Town, Inc., 1985.

Wood, Wayne. *A Bicycling Tour of Riverside & Avondale.* Jacksonville, FL: Riverside Avondale Preservation, Inc., 1976.

———. "Henry John Klutho: An Architect for a New Century." The Jacksonville Historical Society. www.jaxhistory.com

———. *Jacksonville's Architectural Heritage: Landmarks for the Future.* Gainesville, FL: University Press of Florida, 1996.

# INDEX

# INDEX